SARTRE'S ANTHROPOLOGY AS A HERMENEUTICS OF PRAXIS

Dedicated to Marjo,
Ronja
and Winnie

Sartre's Anthropology as a Hermeneutics of Praxis

KRISTIAN KLOCKARS
Department of Philosophy
University of Helsinki

Routledge
Taylor & Francis Group
LONDON AND NEW YORK

First published 1998 by Ashgate Publishing

Reissued 2018 by Routledge
2 Park Square, Milton Park, Abingdon, Oxon OX14 4RN
711 Third Avenue, New York, NY 10017, USA

Routledge is an imprint of the Taylor & Francis Group, an informa business

Publisher's Note
The publisher has gone to great lengths to ensure the quality of this reprint but points out that some imperfections in the original copies may be apparent.

A Library of Congress record exists under LC control number: 98073020

ISBN 13: 978-1-138-34654-3 (hbk)
ISBN 13: 978-1-138-34659-8 (pbk)
ISBN 13: 978-0-429-43723-6 (ebk)

Contents

Preface

This work deals with *the legacy of Sartre*. It's set up originates from the mid 1980's when I found myself explaining, to myself and others, that my interest in philosophy was mainly rooted in a concern with understanding human beings. This general orientation was, however, simultaneously narrowed down by my more specific interest in the philosophy of Sartre, and broadened by my steadfast experience that this concern with 'understanding' had to be linked with questions concerning the normative grounds of critical social theory. The theses that I here have put forward concerning the standpoint I call 'a hermeneutics of praxis' is intended to bring all these themes and interests together. It thus functions for me both as a way of 'going beyond Sartre by the means of Sartre' and as a preliminary formulation of a research project in philosophy and critical social theory.

The book is a revised version (some sections have been shortened, others extended) of my doctoral dissertation *On How to Understand Human Beings and Human Reality: Sartre's Anthropology as a Hermeneutics of Praxis* (University of Helsinki, 1997).

Several persons have made valuable, critical and encouraging comments on earlier versions of this book, or otherwise, knowingly or unknowingly, contributed to the formation of my perspective. I wish to express my deepest gratitude to them: the honourable and friendly opponent on the occasion of my dissertation Thomas Flynn (thanks also for the whisky and the long walk), Heikki Kannisto, my professor Ingmar Pörn, whose genuine will to understand, critical comments and open-mindedness have constantly encouraged me to go on, Marjo Ruismäki, whose love, friendship and therapeutic reflexivity are invaluable sources of happiness, Esa Saarinen, whose pressing encouragement has been a source of energy, my colleague Thomas Wallgren, whose pertinent diagnoses of the times almost puts one at the heart of the present, Dag Østerberg, Bernt Österman, whose "is it really quite certain?" constantly makes me rethink my grounds.

I also wish to thank Karl-Otto Apel for the Melbu-seminar on Rhetoric and Truth in 1988, Thomas Hackman for music, morality and politics, my parents Arla & Ola Klockars for constant support, Martin Kusch for a lecture course on hermeneutics, Ilkka Niiniluoto for giving me an opportunity to finish the dissertation, Kari Palonen and Hannu Sivenius, who both have commented on my interpretations of Sartre. In addition, I wish to thank all the students that, during the years, have participated in my courses at the Department of Philosophy. They have witnessed the gradual coming into existence of the views, interpretations and standpoints expressed and discussed in this work, and their presence have constantly encouraged and forced me to express myself more intelligibly. Furthermore, various badminton partners, such as Thomas Hackman, Calle Kindberg, Markus Kåhre and Bernt Österman have kept the ball in play during the writing of this book, forced me into corners and given me opportunities to smash. And last but not least: the elixir of life that originates from my daughters Ronja, who wanted me to play at being a lion and a cat, simultaneously, and little Winnie, louder and sweeter than the Pooh.

The Department of Philosophy, University of Helsinki, The Finnish Cultural Foundation and The Swedish Cultural Foundation have financially supported my research.

List of Abbreviations

Works of Sartre:

EH	*L'existentialisme est une humanisme*
EaH	*Existentialism and Humanism*
EN	*L'Être et le Néant:*
BN	*Being and Nothingness*
CM	*Cahiers pour une morale*
NE	*Notebooks for an Ethics*
CRD	*Critique de la Raison dialectique,* including QM, Tome I and CRD II.
QM	*Questions de méthode*
CRD II	*Critique de la Raison dialectique*, tome II
SM	*Search for a Method.*
CDR	*Critique of Dialectical Reason*, vol. 1
CDR II	*Critique of Dialectical Reason,* vol. 2
IF or IF 1, 2, 3	*L'Idiot de la famille,* tomes I-III
FI 1, 2, 3, 4, 5	*The Family Idiot*, vols. 1-5

1 Introduction

Outline of a Perspective

This work investigates the philosophy of Jean-Paul Sartre from the point of view of the question *how we are to understand human beings and human reality*. It focuses on the *project of an anthropology* set up by Sartre in his second major philosophical work *Critique de la Raison dialectique* (1960, hereafter abbreviated CRD). Within the perspective of this anthropology I mainly focus on the question of *the intelligibility of human praxis*, or *how we are to understand what we ourselves do*.

The primary purpose of my investigation is not, however, purely interpretative, but to investigate Sartre from the point of view of an interest *to assess his contribution in a contemporary perspective*. In order to do this, I reconstructively interpret the standpoint of Sartre as *a hermeneutics of praxis*. By 'a hermeneutics of praxis' I generally mean a standpoint on the possibilities, limits and extent of philosophical thought, and a conception of man, that are hermeneutical in character (in a broad sense), and which takes 'praxis' or 'human action in a social context' as its paradigm (see below in this chapter).

My investigation is not intended to claim that Sartre, who is not a self-declared hermeneutician, actually should be included within the class of 'full-blown' hermeneutical philosophers, such as Martin Heidegger, Hans-Georg Gadamer, Paul Ricouer and Gianni Vattimo. Such an attempt would be futile, and could not succeed without doing considerable violence to the original material. For instance, such an interpretation is decisively prevented by the lack of at least one crucial hermeneutical theme in Sartre: a thorough treatment of the question of the consequences of historicity for the status, validity and hopes of philosophical thought. Sartre remains a thinker that vacillates between metaphysical and postmetaphysical thinking.

My use of 'a hermeneutics of praxis' is intended to communicate mainly three claims and questions. (1) *There are* many strongly *hermeneutical traits in Sartre's later anthropology*. Sartre's attempt to reconcile existentialism with Marxism drives him towards a standpoint that comes close to hermeneutics, although it is also different in important respects to those of, for example, Heidegger, Gadamer and Rorty. (2) I pose the question whether the idea of a hermeneutics of praxis could be seen as a *possible solution to the internal tensions of Sartre's conception*, and thus whether it would be a good way of thinking 'with Sartre beyond Sartre'. As I see it, in CRD Sartre is leaning towards a hermeneutical kind of solution, although he does not, in important aspects, take the full step out. A question is then whether it is possible to develop this conception in the direction of a more coherently hermeneutical standpoint, or whether for example the co-presence of a philosophy of praxis with hermeneutics remains an indissoluble tension. A 'hermeneutisation' of the later Sartre would have the benefits to enable one to emphasise the more fruitful and original parts of his social and historical thinking, while pushing, for example, the Utopian Marxist traits which today appear considerable dated, to the background. (3) I raise the issue whether a hermeneutics of praxis, as a standpoint inspired by Sartre, can constitute a *living challenge to contemporary thought*.

In this sense, my investigation is intended to be more *systematic* than *historical* in character. The combination of a broad formulation of thematic orientation (to understand human beings and human reality) with a more specific interpretative stance (a hermeneutics of praxis) is intended to communicate my intention to investigate *what kind of answer* Sartre's anthropology gives to the question how we are to understand human beings and human reality.

The complete work of CRD consists of two volumes in the original French, and three in the English translation. The first volume includes the important prefatory essay *Questions de méthode* (QM), which has been published in English as a separate work (*Search for a Method*, SM). Sartre never completed the second volume. The unfinished manuscript, edited by Arlette Elkaïm-Sartre, was published posthumously in 1985 (CRD II).

Although I set up the perspective of CRD as main framework, the investigation is not limited to the scope of CRD alone. The ideas presented in that work are both a continuation, a modification and, in my opinion, a substantial improvement of the existential ontology developed by Sartre in his earlier work, the existentialist magnum opus *L'être et le néant* (EN). This implies that many central ideas of EN are integrated (although often in a modified manner) into the anthropology of CRD. Consequently I shall include many issues of EN within my interpretation of CRD.

Furthermore, the ideas expressed in CRD as such leaves one in a state of unease. The work is both unfinished in itself and unclear concerning its relation to certain other philosophical themes developed by Sartre, notably the *psychology of the person* and *ethics*. In the years following the publication of CRD Sartre returned to the problem of morality, almost wholly neglected in that work. In my investigation I shall include an account of Sartre's views on ethics (see Chapter 9). In his existential biography on Gustave Flaubert, *L'Idiot de la famille* (IF), again, Sartre returns to the question how one is to understand an individual. This work throws considerable light on how Sartre's *idea of a method* actually is to be understood, amongst other things, and I shall consequently include it within Sartre's anthropology. In summary then, the full scope of Sartre's anthropology, as presented in CRD, must not be limited to what is found in that work alone.

CRD was Sartre's second major philosophical work. Many things are at stake in it: the legacy of existentialism, the problems of Marxism, the question of a unified foundation for the human sciences, rationality, etc. From the point of view of my investigation, the main thing is that Sartre presents it as an attempt to lay *the foundations for an anthropology*. It is not, however, altogether clear what Sartre actually means by 'anthropology': philosophical anthropology, a unified science of man or, since IF is described as "... the sequel to *Search for a Method*" (FI 1, p. ix (1)), the writing of existential biography? I argue that the scope of Sartre's anthropology cannot be limited to any of these perspectives as such, but that it constitutes a multidimensional research orientation. I shall differentiate between five main dimensions.

Although CRD clearly is philosophical in nature, the idea of anthropology expressed there cannot be limited to the idea of a *philosophical anthropology* in the sense of *a general theory of human nature*. As is well known, Sartre rejects the idea that human beings would share a universal nature, and therefore a theory of human nature cannot form the answer to the question how one is to understand human beings and human reality. However, this does not mean that Sartre would reject all forms of *universalisation* concerning human being. In the place of a theory of human nature Sartre develops an existential-phenomenological *ontology of existence*, or alternatively a *theory of the intelligibility of the human condition*. Since such an ontology, in so far as it is concerned with the human mode of existence as a whole, may be claimed to inherit the task of a philosophical anthropology, I shall call it a *modified kind of philosophical anthropology* (1).

The investigation in CRD is most concretely set up as a critical investigation of *rationality* (2). This investigation, again, is primarily oriented towards the development of a unified anthropological *method* (3). But the scope of Sartre's work is not limited to these theoretical-philosophical tasks: in its extension in essays and works like IF, the anthropology also encompasses concretely carrying out a *empirical-interpretative* investigtions of real human beings (e.g. the biography of a person), real social events and practices (e.g. colonialism, the role of the intellectual) (4). Sartre's anthropology also characteristically incorporates a *normative dimension* (5). This includes both a concerns to embrace the tasks of a *critical social theory* (e.g. Marxism) and to develop an *ethics*. These together constitute the *five major dimensions of Sartre's anthropology*. An important aim of my investigation is to clarify what these consist of, and to make intelligible their co-presence in the singularity of a project.

At stake in such a clarification of what Sartre means by 'anthropology' is more than just a question how to label one's research. Since 'human being' is one of the principal orientations of Sartre's philosophy, the question is directly linked to the very foundations of Sartrean thought. In addition, a clarification of this issue touches on very general issues concerning the self-understanding of philosophy, and is therefore destined to reach beyond being just an interpretation of Sartre.

I thus pose the question of the self-understanding of Sartre's anthropology with an interest to examine the status, relevance and limits of such a project in a contemporary perspective. I am of the opinion that the challenges raised by Sartre have not yet been sufficiently met. This does not mean that I would agree with Sartre, not even on his major points, nor that I posit a Sartrean anthropology as the solution to the contemporary problems in philosophy. My claims are more limited than that. For example, Sartre's project today clearly appears dated. The interesting thing is to ask why and in what sense it is dated, and what, perhaps, deserves to be saved.

An attempt to assess Sartre's contribution in a contemporary perspective is a very complex task, indeed. This is not only due to the fact that Sartre's production is so vast. In addition, the issues discussed by Sartre span over almost the whole field of philosophy (from ontology to ethics) and reach into many central domains of human life (from personal existence to politics). I neither hope nor have the intention to present a final assessment aiming to 'settle the issue of Sartre' (which would violate my conception of philosophy), nor does my work cover all of the issues discussed by Sartre. Furthermore, my investigation is not based on some kind of a 'total overview' of the contemporary scene (which would be impossible).

The question of the contemporary relevance of Sartre's position can naturally not be limited to the question of the relation between Sartre and hermeneutics. Although some, such as Gianni Vattimo (1997), indeed describe hermeneutics as *the* mood of the times, there are clearly other orientations and themes that claim and deserve equal weight in this context:

critical social theory, postmodernism, etc. In order to discuss the issues triggered by these, I have picked out a certain thematic constellation intended to orient my investigation as a whole. Thus, I would like my investigation to be read as concerned particularly with the following four themes:

(1) how are we to understand and interpret our own and other's actions and undertakings? (the intelligibility of praxis),
(2) how are the aims and impact of studies of human beings and human reality to be understood? (the discursive self-understanding of the human and social sciences),
(3) how is one to assess the social reality and times in which one lives? (the critique and diagnosis of society and 'the present'),
(4) what is rationality? (the problem of rationality).

These may be said to express the thematic orientation that guides the systematic of my investigation. I shall not, however, study these issues in a direct way, but mainly restrict myself to discussing them in relation to Sartre. I shall end this part with a brief overview of how I see their interrelations.

The question how we are to understand human action is self-evidently linked to the self-understanding of the human and social sciences (1-2). The human and social sciences study (amongst other things) *the domain of human behaviour and action*. In addition, the research of these scientific disciplines itself constitutes a human undertaking: *research is a particular kind of praxis*, which (directly or indirectly) participates in culture. Furthermore, the question of the intelligibility of what we do is not reducible to a problem of the sciences alone: it has obvious relevance for the issues of everyday life.

On the contemporary scene, several currents (including Sartre) agree with the position that the human and social sciences are participatory in nature: hermeneutics, critical social theory, feminism, post-structuralism and postmodernism, Rorty's neo-pragmatism, etc. (cf. Habermas 1978, Rorty 1980, Hollinger (ed.) 1985, Dews 1987. These naturally have different conception on how the relation between an intellectual enterprise (discursive praxis) and everyday (individual and social) praxis is to be understood. This raises the problem of the *discursive self-understanding* of the human and social sciences.

The idea of a critical social theory, in a particularly pregnant way, manifests the problem of the relation between the 'scientific' task of understanding and the normative dimensions of intellectual participation (2-3). Critical social theory, in its own self-understanding, embodies a normative-critical, or, as Habermas says (1978a, pp. 308-11), critical-emancipatory interest. This raises at least two issues. First, what are the *normative foundations of social critique and diagnosis*? Second, since critical social theory is also a kind of 'scientific' enterprise, based on the demand to develop a well-grounded understanding of the reality studied, it is not only founded on normative issues. This raises the problem of the *relation between understanding and critique* (1-3).

The problem of rationality, again, is common both to the search for knowledge and understanding (1-4), and to the normative foundation of critique (3-4). 'Reason' or 'rationality' encompasses both questions of the foundation of knowledge (theoretical reason), and questions of the normative justification of actions and critical evaluations (practical and moral reason). One may thus argue that *understanding* and *critique* are *united in the problem of rationality*. But such a thesis cannot, especially today, neglect the fact that this connection is often vigorously criticised, in particular through in the so-called *discourse on modernity and postmodernity*. Thus, many (self-declared or alleged) postmodernists question the very *value and status of reason*, in relation both to the ethical imperative to understand and to the idea of a well-grounded critique.

As a summary of this introduction then, the motives that orient my investigation are characteristically twin-headed. On the one hand, they are rooted in my experiential encounter with the philosophy of Sartre. This I take to consist of mainly four, partly conflicting, elements: (i) a certain experience of affinity between Sartre's ideas and my own views, (ii) an initial, but not interrogated, perception that a Sartrean kind of anthropology contains elements that are still relevant today, (iii) a simultaneous observation that there are aspects of Sartre's philosophy that today appear dated and surpassed, and (iv) that Sartre is no longer read as a philosopher of primary relevance. Today, the substance of Sartre's philosophy seldom reaches beyond the limited, although quite large, group of Sartrologues. As a hermeneutical aspect of my own investigation I thus recognise the need to find out what I am to make of such a conflictual experience. On the other hand, my investigation is rooted in an interest to explore certain exciting, but unsettled, issues within contemporary thought. But due to the presence of the first kind of motivation, I found it more natural to tackle these issues by clarifying my conception of Sartre.

Thus, in opposition to the kind of venturesome impression my use of such grandiose themes as 'understanding human beings', 'knowing what one is doing?' and 'discursive self-understanding' may raise, the actual aims and hopes of my investigation are much more limited in scope. I do not search for any definitive answers to these questions: I do neither believe in nor strive for a level of total elucidation on such issues. What I do presuppose, however, is that a philosophical investigation of a limited material may contribute to understanding what is involved and at stake in such broadly conceived issues. By asking questions of a general nature philosophy makes a contribution, but this is necessarily realised in a situation where the investigator himself cannot be fully aware of the content, scope and impact of what he or she is doing.

These observations were intended to place my investigation of Sartre's anthropology within the perspective and scope I would like to see it. For when I raise the question 'what is Sartre's anthropology?', I am not only interested in its empirical content, nor only in Sartre's own self-understanding, but in the question what meaning and status such a project may possibly have from a contemporary point of view. What is done? What are the presuppositions? Where does it lead us?

On Sartre and the Sartre-Reception

I have thus decided to read Sartre's conception both *itself as a kind of* hermeneutics and *from the point of view of* contemporary hermeneutics. By 'hermeneutics' I thus mean both a *tradition* and a certain *thematic orientation*. My interpretation of Sartre will then have a reconstructive intent[1]: to re-build Sartre's conception partly by means of themes that are not explicitly found in Sartre.

By 'hermeneutics' I shall primarily mean a certain three-fold thematic orientation. First, hermeneutics is concerned with *the understanding and interpretation of human reality.* Second, hermeneutics is a philosophical standpoint based on *an ontology of human being-in-the-world.* This latter demarcation implies that I by 'hermeneutics' primarily mean what may be called the Heidegger-Gadamer line of hermeneutics. This orientation is closely related to Sartre's philosophy through their common historical link with phenomenology. Third, hermeneutics is a philosophical standpoint that supports *a thesis of historicity* and the idea of *reflexive, internal investigation.*

I do not restrict the domain of hermeneutics to the classical domain of the interpretation of texts, text-like objects or, as Gadamer says, to the investigation of "... the linguistic constitution of the world" (1976a, p. 13).

The main reason for this is that, while the philosophical standpoint in CRD has much in common with the hermeneutical turn of phenomenology in Heidegger and Gadamer, Sartre does not take language or linguisticality, but *praxis* as his paradigm. This will also imply that I shall explore the possible tensions between *a hermeneutics of language* and *a hermeneutics of praxis*. By 'a hermeneutics of praxis' I shall thus generally mean:

(1) a conception which takes the domain of human praxis as the main object in interpretative study,
(2) a conception based on the thesis that praxis forms the paradigmatic key for an ontology of human being-in-the-world, and
(3) a conception according to which a paradigm of praxis implies historicity and the reflexivity of philosophical investigation.

There are mainly three *interpretative motives* for my choice to use this rather technical phrase to characterise Sartre's standpoint. First, it is intended to turn the attention (both of 'experts' and 'laymen') away from the, in my opinion, problematic label of 'existentialism', and towards the view that the standpoint Sartre develops in CRD is closely related to the hermeneutical turn of phenomenology. My choice is thus intended to be both critical in relation to certain other interpretations of Sartre, and informative in relation to how I think CRD is to be read. Second, it is intended to communicate that Sartre in CRD actually is deeply concerned exactly with the problems of understanding, interpretation and historicity, and that his conception encompasses a perspective on human beings and their praxes as beings-in-the-world, or a conception which, as Sartre says, emphasises their "... bonds of interiority ..." (CDR, 52 (167)) with the world. Sartre's conception is thus both similar to and different from Heidegger's and Gadamer's, and thereby constitutes a challenge. Third, the relations between Sartre and hermeneutics have not, in my opinion, been sufficiently explored. As István Fehér observes in his recent article "Sartre and Hermeneutics" (1994), it is both important and relevant to open up such a field of comparison. Although Fehér's claim that "... we owe the first significant valorisation ... of this sort of relevance ... to ... Richard Rorty" (1994, p. 65) is not altogether justified[2], I agree with him that the hermeneutical dimensions of Sartre's philosophy have not been sufficiently studied.

As I said above, I shall focus on the problem of *the intelligibility of human praxis*. I argue that this theme is both *fundamental* and *limited* to Sartre's anthropology. It is fundamental in the sense that Sartre claims that humans are beings of action, and that the reality in which we live — including personal and family life, culture, society and history — is primarily to be understood on the basis of what we do. It is limited in the sense that Sartre does not claim that such an action-perspective would exhaust the intelligibility of the human.

A major, but often neglected, dimension of Sartre's philosophy is his view that consciousness, projects and actions must be understood on the basis of their *internal relations with the world*. This idea I take as one of my starting points. Sartre is often described as and/or accused of being a *dualist*.[3] As evidence is most often used the ontological contraposition of being-for-itself (consciousness) and being-in-itself (thing-like being) in EN. It is certainly true that Sartre upholds a qualitative distinction between consciousness and things, but one often neglects that EN is explicitly set up as an attempt to overcome the Cartesian dualism between subject and object, consciousness and body (BN, pp. xxi-xxiv, 3f, 305, 617-25). The main argumentative means used by Sartre to achieve this end is the idea of an internal bond between consciousness and world, consciousness and body, freedom and situation, action and situation, etc. I shall thus strongly emphasise, what Dag Østerberg (1993, p. 9) calls, the *situationist* dimension of Sartre's standpoint.

The question to what extent Sartre in fact succeeds in his anti-dualist attempt is another story. As Sonia Kruks (1990, pp. 53-56) observes, in EN Sartre vacillates between a clear-cut rejection of dualism, and other formulations that seem to reintroduce dualism. In my opinion, a major reason for this vacillation is that there are mainly two things at stake in EN. On the one hand, Sartre tries to overcome dualism. On the other hand, Sartre anyway takes his main task to be to defend the view that human beings are free and responsible for who they are and what they do, despite the pressing demands of the circumstances (BN, pp. 33-45, 511-31, 553-6, see also EaH pp. 28-31). The rhetorical force of this second thesis often overshadows the first, although it is not intended as a rejection of it. In my opinion, this vacillation is more clearly removed by Sartre in CRD, and this is one reason why I consider CRD an improvement in relation to EN.

In order not to misconstrue the actual scope of Sartre's anthropology as a hermeneutics, it is important to emphasise that it is more directly set up with the goals of a *critical social theory* in mind. As I mentioned above, hermeneutics and critical social theory share the assumption that anthropological research is participatory in character. Critical social theory, however, differs from hermeneutics by interpreting this participatory dimension to imply the task explicitly to engage in the normative foundations of critique and diagnosis. It is thus obvious that I do not, as sometimes has been the case, regard the orientations of hermeneutics and critical social theory as antagonistic (see Apel et al. 1971). On the contrary, I shall explore the connections and unresolved tensions between the quest for understanding and normative aims. I shall thus understand Sartre's *hermeneutics of praxis as central both* to his *critical social theory* and his *ethics*.

I have chosen to approach Sartre from the point of view of his second major philosophical work, or CRD, and not the first, or EN. Today, it is still more common to take EN as starting point, and to read Sartre 'chronologically', that is, to interpret CRD as a modification of and addition to EN. Furthermore, since my investigation is not restricted to be 'an interpretation of CRD', and since I have chosen a theme that is generally seen as central to the early and not the later Sartre, my choice may appear controversial.

I differentiate mainly three motives for my choice of the perspective of CRD as main framework. First, *the themes* I want to investigate are actually treated explicitly by Sartre *mainly in CRD* (and related works), and mostly implicitly in EN. It is in CRD where Sartre sets up the project of an anthropology, where he seriously engages in the problem of interpretation, where he investigates the intelligibility of praxis and where he takes on the self-understanding of a critical social theory. I find it more natural to approach these issues in a straightforward fashion as they are discussed in CRD.

Second, I consider the standpoint of CRD to be an *improvement* in relation to EN. The conception of man in CRD, the discourse on knowledge, the decision to treat the problem of rationality, the theories of praxis, social formations and social conflicts, in my opinion constitute a substantial improvement in relation to the earlier position. I shall not, however, scrutinise this thesis in any detail, but restrict myself to occasionally commenting on the relations between the earlier and the later position. In relation to the debate about the continuity and/or discontinuity between these works, I shall not take up a definite position, but restrict myself to pointing out certain, important differences between them, while not neglecting their obvious and well-established continuity.[4]

Third, although there is a continuos flow of studies of CRD, and many scholars continue to emphasise its importance, CRD is still largely *unknown* and *neglected* in contemporary philosophy. One may identify many reasons for this: CRD makes up, what Sartre himself calls, a "... mountain of notes ..." (CDR, p. 821 (13)), and it is notoriously difficult to overview, it is unfinished and it appears to be more Marxist (that is, 'out') than existentialist.

As I mentioned above, my choice to study Sartre from the point of view of CRD does not mean that I shall neglect other works. Besides EN, IF and other relevant works published by Sartre during his lifetime, I use the large amount of posthumously published manuscripts. The most important ones are: the notebooks for an ethics written immediately after EN, *Cahiers pour une morale* (1983, CM), Sartre's commentary on Heidegger's conception of truth in *Vérité et Existence* (1989, English translation1992), the second volume of CRD (CRD II, 1985, English translation 1991) and the manuscripts for a second ethics in the middle of the 1960:s (see Chapter 9). These throw considerable new light on the overall conception and changes of Sartre's philosophy, and they have already triggered a large amount of commentary.

My investigation is thus, to a certain extent, set up as a countermove in relation to what I experience as common tendencies in the reception of Sartre. I shall sift out four such tendencies. My classification is not intended to exhaust the reception of Sartre, and in order to counterbalance possible one-sidedness I shall also mention works whose approach is closer to my own.

First, Sartre is read as an *existentialist philosopher whose main work is EN*.[5] Works that fall within this class often move around the well-known themes of Sartrean existentialism: consciousness, being-for-itself, transcendence, freedom, anguish, bad faith, authenticity, etc. In studies of these issues, CRD is still often treated only in passing, if at all. A main reason for such neglect is the (obvious and correct) association of Sartre with existentialism (which makes his philosophy relevant) and the (also justified) identification of CRD with Marxism (which makes it out of date). In contrast to this I shall understand my investigation as neither about the fate and legacy of existentialism, nor about the dialectic, nor the legacy Marxism. I find it important to investigate Sartre's philosophy independently of the heavy historical burden of such currents and concepts.

Second, Sartre is read as *'a man of his times'*. The philosophy is then interpreted in the light of Sartre's engagement in the issues of his times. To simplify slightly, the impact and relevance of Sartre's personal life on his philosophy is sometimes treated as equally important as what Sartre actually writes. There is nothing wrong as such with such an idea-historical approach. On the contrary, it is closely related to the hermeneutical kind of position I take up in my work. I nevertheless maintain that such an approach risks to overshadow what Sartre in fact writes, especially in his philosophical works.[6]

A large part of the contemporary feminist reception of Sartre unfortunately characteristically combines these two 'limitations'.[7] A main reason is that the feminists are not primarily interested in Sartre as such, but in the impact and relevance of Sartre's thought on Simone de Beauvoir; what is at stake is a re-assessment of de Beauvoir's *Le Deuxième Sexe* (1953). The critical reading of Sartre in Michèle Le Dœuff is thus mainly concerned with the overt masculinity of Sartre's conception of human being in EN, mainly as expressed through the notions of being-for-itself and transcendence. This issue falls outside the scope of my investigation, and I shall not discuss it in any detail, but I maintain, along with Sonia Kruks (another contributor to the feminist discourse on Sartre) that "... the reduction of existentialism to early Sartreanism ... is a gross distortion" (1990, p. 9, see also pp. 83-91 and 104-12).

Third, Sartre is not read at all as a thinker of contemporary relevance, but mentioned only in passing, if at all. As examples, consult the writings of Habermas, contemporary interpretations of hermeneutics, Foucault, Derrida, Charles Taylor, etc.[8] An argument of my investigation is thus to show if, and in what sense, this constitutes a neglect of a potentially still relevant and important position.

Fourth, few contemporary Sartre-studies — interesting and important as they may be — realises substantial contact with contemporary currents and debates.[9] In short, they are interpretations of Sartre but neither attempts to assess Sartre in a contemporary perspective nor to develop Sartre's insights on the basis of current debates. In case Sartre's philosophy is compared with other's, it is most often in relation to the ones Sartre himself read: Hegel, Marx, Husserl, Heidegger, de Beauvoir, Merleau-Ponty, etc.

Let me add a few contributions that come closer to my own interest to read Sartre in a contemporary perspective, and which has been a spark of inspiration for me. André Gorz makes use of Sartre's notions and ideas in his studies of the present social and political field (1968, 1991). Thomas R. Flynn, in several articles (1976, 1992) and in the books *Sartre and Marxist Existentialism* (1984) and *Sartre, Foucault and Historical Reason* (1997), discusses issues that either are not typically Sartrean (epistemology), not as such found in Sartre (the problem of collective responsibility), or on which Sartre's discourse is characteristically unfinished (philosophy of history). Steve Hendley, again, in his book *Reason and Relativism: A Sartrean Investigation* (1992), focuses on Sartre's standpoint on rationality in CRD, and discusses it in relation to Foucault, Habermas, Lyotard, Feyerabend and Rorty.

Outline of the Work

I thus set up an investigation of Sartre's anthropology that focuses on a certain theme: the intelligibility of praxis as a Sartrean key to the question how we are to understand human beings and human reality. I claim both that this theme is central to Sartre's philosophical concerns, and that it has not yet been sufficiently studied and assessed. But although I claim centrality to this theme, I do not claim that it is the main theme and concern of Sartre's philosophy as a whole. I readily acknowledge that one might justifiably choose some other themes as central to Sartre: freedom, ontology, the problem of morality, etc.

The fact that I focus on themes like understanding, knowledge and the self-understanding of the human and social sciences means — at least in the light of the rather well-established rumour that existentialism is critical of knowledge and science — that my investigation, to a certain extent, goes against the current. I shall emphasise the strong presence of knowledge-oriented themes in Sartre, of such untypical issues as epistemology, the problem of rationality and philosophy of science. On the other hand, although my study in this sense re-situates Sartre within a more classically academic sphere, I shall be careful not to reduce away the non-academic concerns with existential issues that steers much of Sartre's work. Sartre commits himself to dealing with issues of everyday life and the historical present, and his outlook is characteristically not oriented towards science and academic philosophy. However, although this is the case, it is still the fact that Sartre's philosophical writings are 'heavy reading', and do not easily open themselves to persons outside the sphere of higher education. In my opinion, this was not sufficiently reconsidered by Sartre.

In Chapter 2 I comment on the perspective of my work as centred on the problem of understanding, and discuss the relation between Sartre and contemporary issues, such as the discourse on modernity and post-modernity. In Chapter 3 I give an introductory outline of the five dimensions of Sartre's project of anthropology mentioned above. Chapter 4 deals with hermeneutics, mainly as Gadamer expresses it.

In Chapter 5 I do basically two things: I present Sartre's conception of human being (modified philosophical anthropology) and characterise Sartre's philosophical standpoint, with a special interest to its hermeneutical traits. This chapter thus both picks up certain themes discussed in Chapters 3 and 4, and anticipates certain other themes to be discussed mainly in Chapters 6 and 8.

In Chapter 6 I give an outline of CRD as seen as a critical investigation of reason. It thereby links up with my first account of the debate on rationality in Chapter 2. In chapter 7 I discuss Sartre's concept of praxis, its nature as action, materiality and sociality, and connect it to an account of the general framework of Sartre's social theory. This chapter continues my reflections on Sartre's hermeneutical standpoint, and deepens my treatment of Sartre's conception of human being in chapter 5. The concept of praxis is also central for Sartre's conception of rationality (Chapter 6), his epistemology (Chapter 8) and for the normative issues discussed in Chapter 9.

In Chapter 8 I discuss the epistemological issues involved in Sartre's conception of the intelligibility of praxis, taken as the Sartrean key to the problem how we are to understand human beings and human reality. From the point of view of my attempt to illuminate and assess Sartre's hermeneutics of praxis seen as a concern with understanding, this chapter might be seen as a kind of point of culmination. But this does not make the following chapter (9) any less important. In that I investigate the normative dimensions of Sartre's anthropology: his views on ethics and critical social theory. The chapter adds an important new perspective on all the problems that I have discussed in the previous chapters, and it resituates my concern with the problem of understanding discussed in Chapter 2. In the conclusion (Chapter 10) I summarise my views on Sartre's anthropology and conclude my assessment of it.

Notes

1 Habermas defines reconstruction as "... taking a theory apart and putting it back together in a new form in order to attain more fully the goal which it has set for itself" (1979a, p. 95). My attempt at a reconstruction is not that much intended to pursue the original goals of Sartre, but to read it with certain other and more contemporary interests in mind.

2 Before Rorty especially Manfred Frank (1977, 1980) have pointed out hermeneutical dimensions of Sartre's work. Frank is however mainly interested in the hermeneutics at play in Sartre's biographical interpretation of Flaubert, and less concerned with the hermeneutical traits of Sartre's philosophy as such. See also Maler 1986.

3 The characterisation of Sartre as a dualist is most often found in works which treats Sartre's philosophy only occasionally, or which are critical of it. See for example Stevenson 1974, p. 82, Butler 1990, p. 12 and 129, Le Dœuff 1991, pp. 55-100. For a discussion of the anti-dualist stance of Sartre, see for example Aronson 1980 pp. 93-103, Dreyfus and Hoffman 1981 pp. 229-45, Flynn 1984, pp. 3-4, Cooper 1990, pp. 57-94 and Howells (ed.) 1992, pp. 326-42.

4 For a brief overview of this debate, see for example Flynn 1984, p. xii. Since

the mid 1980's, the posthumous publication of Sartre's notes and manuscripts — especially CRD II and Sartre's notes on ethics (1992a and other writings, see Chapter 9) — continue to throw new light both on Sartre's philosophy as a whole and on the relation between EN and CRD. This means that the 'well-established continuity' may have to be reconsidered. I shall not, however, discuss this matter.

5 Examples of such limitation (which may be well justified from the point of view of the particular interests of the researcher) can be found in Morris 1976, Saarinen 1983, Detmer 1986, and Gadamer 1988. I do not, however, regard these as 'bad' works.

6 This issue concerning the relation between history of ideas and philosophy arises in many interpretations of Sartre. I do not want to pick out any particular work as representative, but restrict myself to mentioning some of the many works that explicitly study this relation: Burnier 1966, Aronson 1980, Colombel 1986-7, Hayman 1986, Cohen-Solal 1987, Davies 1987, Boschetti 1988 and *Les Temps Modernes's* special number on Sartre (1990, nos 531-533, esp. vol. II).

7 See for example Butler 1990 and Le Dœuff 1991, esp. the second notebook. I do not claim that the kind of critique against Sartre levelled by Le Dœuff is completely without justification. That is too complex an issue for me to take a standpoint on here.

8 In the case of Habermas, consult the name index and respective pages in some of his major works (1978, 1987a, 1987b, 1992). In relation to hermeneutics, neither the volume Hermeneutics and *Modern Philosophy* (Wachterhauser (ed.) 1986) nor the existentialist-deconstructivist interpretation of hermeneutics in Caputo's *Radical Hermeneutics* (1987) contain any more than passing references to Sartre. Rorty (1980) is an exception. Foucault comments, mainly indirectly, on Sartre in 1970, pp. 312-43, 1972, pp. 9-15 and in various interviews (1988a, pp. 20-22, 32 and 44, 1989a, pp. 40-44. Derrida denounces "... the anthropologistic reading ..." of phenomenology in Sartre as "... a mistake" (1982a, pp. 114-17). Taylor, again, in *Sources of the Self*, a book that touches on a very Sartrean theme, does not mention Sartre (1989).

9 Consult for example the different collections of articles on Sartre that has been published during the last decades: Silverman and Elliston (eds.) 1980, Jameson (ed.) 1985a, König (hg.) 1988, Les Temps Modernes 1990, nos 531-533, Aronson and van der Hoven (eds.) 1991 and Howells (ed.) 1992. One finds exceptions to my characterisation in these, but they are clearly in minority.

2 Sartre and Contemporary Thought: Understanding vs. Totalisation

The Search for a Comprehensive Understanding

Before I engage in the actual content and arguments of Sartre's anthropology, I find it important to outline one point of view from which I deal with the question of contemporary relevance. Initially there are many self-evident candidates for such a task: poststucturalism (esp. Foucault and Derrida), critical social theory (esp. Foucault and Habermas), hermeneutics (esp. Gadamer, Ricoeur and Rorty), postmodernism (esp. Gorz, Lyotard, Jameson and Rorty), etc. However, instead of focusing on these currents of contemporary thought as such, I shall pick out a theme that appears to be particularly suitable for my aims (although it is naturally not the only possible one): the polarity between *understanding* and *totalisation* internal to the question *how to understand human beings and human reality*. By reading Sartre from the point of view of this theme, one enters a problem field that is highly relevant in all the different currents mentioned.

I think one legitimately can claim that Sartre's project of anthropology aims to provide guidelines for the task to reach *a comprehensive understanding of human beings* and their *historical reality*. Sartre's project, expressed in this way as a concern with *knowledge*, initially recognises two conditions, which a conception of *truth* (in the human context) must fulfil: *historicity* and *totalisation*:

> ... if there is to be any such thing as a Truth in anthropology, it must be *in becoming* and it must be a *totalisation* (CDR, p. 822 (14)).

By 'a truth in becoming' Sartre means that the concrete truths of human beings are always tied to the historical circumstances. By 'totalisation', again, Sartre means an account that, in the ideal case, enables one to integrate all relevant facts into a comprehensive and covering historical narrative, without reducing away the multidimensionality of concrete reality, or relapsing into relativism. Thus, Sartre claims the need for "... a *monism* of interpretation" (CDR, 15 (135)) that preserves the uniqueness of historical events and individual actions.

Sartre thus proposes the ideal of a *comprehensive understanding of concrete reality*, and *totalisation* as a central notion of this ideal. In contrast, a strong current in contemporary thought after Sartre — from Michel Foucault to postmodernism and Edward Said — is deeply *suspicious* towards the very *idea of a totalising understanding*. In *L'Archéologie du savoir* Foucault (in an indirect critique of Sartre) thus rejects the idea of "... a total description [that] draws all phenomena around a single centre — a principle, a meaning, a spirit, a world-view, an overall shape..." for containing false hopes, and proposes to replace this with "... a general history..." that focuses on discontinuities, transformations, thresholds and differences, and which rather "... would deploy the space of dispersion" than totalise (1972, p. 10). Lyotard, again, proposes nothing less than *war* against the idea of totalisation: "We have paid a high enough price for the nostalgia of the whole and the one ... The answer is: Let us wage a war on totality; let us be witnesses to the unpresentable; let us activate the difference and save the honour of the name" (1984a, pp. 81-82).

The sharp polarisation characteristic of the philosophical high tide (the 1980's) of the *discourse on modernity and postmodernity* has today given place to a more moderate mood. A good example is Edward Said. In *Culture and Imperialism* he describes himself as "... temperamentally and philosophically opposed to vast system-building or totalistic theories of human history", but still claims to be interested in an "understanding of the whole ... [concerned with] the character, interpretation, and direction or tendency of cultural experience" (1993, p. 4 and 13). That is, Said seems to assert the importance of an understanding of the whole different than the "... totalising attitude towards the subject matter" (CDR, p. 16 (136)) Sartre searches for.

However, a study of Sartre's conception shows that he is actually much closer to these critics than what may be expected. For example, Sartre constantly emphasis the need to respect the heterogeneity and multidimensionality of concrete human reality, and the refusal to reduce the concrete to abstract categories:

> ... if one totalises too quickly, if one transforms — without evidence — signification into intention, and result into an objective deliberately aimed at, then the real is lost ... The dialectical method ... refuses to reduce; it follows the reverse procedure. It surpasses by conserving, but the terms of the surpassed contradiction cannot account for either the transcending itself or the subse-

> quent synthesis; on the contrary, it is the synthesis which clarifies them and which enables us to understand them (SM, pp. 45 and 151 (58, 114)).

On the basis of these observations, at least the following two questions seems to need an answer: 'what is the relation between the idea and ideal of a comprehensive understanding and that of totalisation?' and 'what is actually at stake in the critique of totalisation?' In the following I shall briefly illuminate the relation between Sartre's project and the contemporary scene concerning these matters, beginning with a discussion of the concept of *understanding*.

Dimensions of the Concept of Understanding

The concept of understanding has gradually come to occupy a central place in contemporary thought (cf. Bernstein 1983 and Franklin 1995). At the beginning of the 20th-century it was raised to the foreground as central to *the human and social sciences* especially by Wilhelm Dilthey and Max Weber. Dilthey argued in favour of a methodological distinction between the explanatory, universalising and objectivating perspective of the natural sciences, and a concern with the understanding of the historically unique characteristic of the human sciences (1976a, pp. 170-77). Dilthey also claimed affinity between this view and the tradition of *hermeneutics*, or textual interpretation (1976c, pp. 247-48). Since then a perspective centred on understanding has quite generally been labelled *a hermeneutical perspective*. Thus, although Weber both rejects Dilthey's claim that understanding is opposed to explanation and refrains from using the term hermeneutics (1947, pp. 88-98), Weber is today commonly recognised as a hermeneutical thinker. Especially through the contributions of Heidegger and Gadamer, the theme of understanding was raised from the more limited realm of the human and social sciences to a theme of primary *philosophical* importance. Also within the analytical tradition the concept of understanding has been raised to the foreground, although a bit later than in the Continental tradition (see also Chapter 4).

By 'understanding' I shall mean roughly 'to experientially grasp something as intelligible to thought in a comprehensive manner'. I thus raise '*comprehensive*' as the core meaning of 'understanding'. By 'comprehensive', again, I mean the kind of unifying properties, which fall under such concepts as 'unified', 'holistic', 'synthetic' or, less ambitiously, 'contextual' or 'relational'. On the basis of this account, to understand means to grasp something as related to something else, a context, theoretical model, world-view, action, etc. The use of five different concepts to explain what is meant by 'comprehensive' is intended to communicate that I do not take any initial standpoint on how tightly integrated the different phenomena treated must be in order for understanding to have been achieved.

I also want to retain that two-dimensionality of the concept of understanding, which is common in hermeneutics. That is, by 'understanding' one may mean either a *spontaneous experience* of something as intelligible (understanding as ontological feature of human existence), or *an intellectual project* to make something intelligible (the strive for better understanding). The latter is often referred to as the task of *interpretation* as the method whereby a deeper and more correct understanding is reached.

This general characterisation gives only a first indication of what is meant by 'understanding'. In the following, I shall broaden my account by indicating the discursive field of phenomena, themes and other concepts within which I place my own discourse.

The word 'understanding' typically carries quite many, more or less, different meanings and connotations. Understanding is a multidimensional concept, and in philosophy it is relevant in many of it's central thematic domains: epistemology, philosophy of science, ethics, social and political philosophy, etc. I shall discuss three such ('intensional') meanings of 'understanding': (1) understanding as a *knowledge-type* concept, (2) understanding as a *meaning* oriented concept and (3) understanding as a *normative* concept. In addition, I shall discuss four concepts, which may be claimed ('extensionally') to stand in contrast or opposition to 'understanding': (4) *knowledge*, (5) *critique*, and (6) *praxis* and (7) *rationality*. As is obvious, the latter series is closely related to the first, and I shall not treat them as radically separate issues.

As a *knowledge-type concept* understanding most often plays the role to emphasise a *broader*, *holistic*, *humanely* centred and *experiential* kind of knowing. It is then contrasted with the analytical, fragmenting and universalising kind of knowledge that dominates the modern conception of science. Mainly two reasons motivate this distinction. First, within the human sciences one has been observed that universalisation and analyticity are perhaps not the most fitting scientific ideals for a study of the complexities and particularities of historical reality. An important thing with historical reality is that it is in every case unique. Consequently, the task of the human and social sciences is not primarily to discover general laws of history, but to make the particular and unique intelligible.

Second, according, for example, to the phenomenological and existentialist critique of knowledge, the scientific concept of knowledge is unable to account for the experience of meaning (presupposed by the sciences), and the existential dimensions of knowing. As Husserl observes in *Die Krisis der europäischen Wissenschaften,* exactly due to the ideal of universalisation "in our vital need ... this idea of science has nothing to say to us. It excludes in principle the questions which man ... finds the most burning: questions of the meaning or meaninglessness of the whole of this human existence" (1970, p. 6). Thus, as a knowledge-type concept, 'understanding' can be raised both in opposition to a narrow analysis of 'knowledge', and as another type of knowledge (1, 4).

The concept of understanding may also be used in a way that stands in opposition to any kind of concept of knowledge (cf. Berenson 1981, pp. 11-14). Thus, whereas all knowledge-type concepts must be seen as inherently connected to 'claims to truth' and to the opposition between truth and falsity, 'understanding' need not inherently concern truth, but the domain of *meaning* so important in human life (2, 4). To understand a linguistic expression does not necessarily imply a knowledge of the truth or falsity of what is said, but an experiential grasp that an expression makes sense in a certain context (language as system, communicative situation, etc.).[1]

The concept of understanding is often used in (explicitly or implicitly) *normative* and *moral* context (3). Take for example the everyday phrase 'having an understanding for someone'. This connotes a connection to the normative dimension of moral acceptance, although it certainly does not semantically imply 'acceptance'. To say that I have an understanding for what A did does not imply that I accept his conduct, but it does connote that I am genuinely prepared to consider whether or not what A did is acceptable from the point of view of A's own presuppositions, and that I may even be prepared to accept these. That is, in this context 'understanding' is opposed to 'outright rejection' as a matter of principle, moral or other.

Certain philosophical treatments of the concept of understanding also emphasise this normative dimension. Thus, Wittgenstein claims that 'to understand means to know how to go on' (1952, pp. 59-61), or that understanding involves a kind of practical knowledge or normative know how, and Gadamer declares that "... to understand means primarily for two people to understand each other. Understanding is primarily agreement or harmony with another person" (1975, p. 158), or that understanding involves intersubjective recognition and (normative) agreement.

On the other hand, understanding is sometimes seen as opposed to such things as *critique* and *praxis* (5, 6). If we limit ourselves 'just to understand', we may be charged both of refraining from genuine critical assessment and of avoiding the question of the practical consequences of such assessment. Richard J. Bernstein, it seems to me, attempts to draw the consequences of this objection in his interpretation of Gadamer. According to Bernstein, Gadamer's view that hermeneutics is inherently tied to the ethical dimension of practical wisdom (Aristotelian *phronesis*) indicates the task to step beyond mere hermeneutics (understanding), and engage in the practical realisation of Gadamer's dialogical ideal: "They lead us — with a deepened understanding of human finitude — to the genuinely practical task of concretely realising in our historical situation what he has so nobly defended as being central to our humanity" (1985, p. 290). The connection of this with Marx' famous 11th thesis on Feuerbach is obvious: "the philosophers have only *interpreted* the world, in various ways, the point is to *change* it" (1986, p. 23). Bernstein, however, insists that we can no longer share Marx' revolutionary self-confidence (1983, p. 231). Anyway, this opposition between understanding and critique/praxis implies that the task to understand may be considered as *too limited*, and that it may even be ethically and politically opposed to that of critique and practically changing the world.

In relation to the concept(s) of *reason* or *rationality*, again, understanding may also be seen either as in conformity or in opposition (7). If one by 'understanding' means another kind of knowledge, or if it is seen as closely related to practical wisdom, understanding may be claimed to constitute an *alternative conception of rationality*, different from the scientific-rational one. On the other hand, in ethical and political discourse 'rationality' is often placed on the opposite side to 'understanding'. Thus, Maurice Merleau-Ponty distinguishes in *Les Aventures de la dialectique*, (on the basis of Alain) between "... *a politics of reason* which ... ties all the problems together, orients itself on a future ... where all the problems are solved ... postulates a new beginning through an overthrow of existing relationships" and "... *a politics of understanding*, which ... takes man as he is, at work in an obscure world, resolving problems one at a time..." (1973, pp. 3-4, my italics)[2]. That is, in an ethical and political context, 'understanding' is sometimes used in order to oppose to the rational, cold and calculative use of the intellect, and in order to defend a respect for the individualities of situations and persons. This opposition is today perhaps most clearly manifested in the debate between *liberals and communitarians* (see for example Mulhall and Swift 1992), and in the discourse on *modernity and postmodernity*.

This exploration of the different meanings and dimensions of 'understanding' indicates, at least, that it may pull one in many different directions depending on which meaning one chooses. This multidimensionality also implies that any attempt to define 'understanding' in some more specific sense would most certainly looses some of these dimensions on the way. My choice to focus on 'understanding' is thus intended *to open a certain discursive field*, which connects and interrelates the above discussed dimensions and areas, rather than to separate them analytically. I shall thus be concerned with how issues of knowledge and epistemic rationality are connected to issues of everyday human existence, ethics and the rationality of praxis.

Understanding, Reason and Totalisation in Contemporary Thought

Described in this way, a discourse centred on the ideal of understanding transcends the dimension of knowledge: the concept of understanding is variously related to issues of knowledge, ethics and politics, the problem of rationality, etc. The multidimensional and unspecified nature of the concept is probably one reason why Sartre chooses his standpoint in CRD as one centred on a perspective of understanding (or comprehension and intelligibility). Sartre obviously took his friend Merleau-Ponty's challenge seriously, and tried to meet it by attempting to combine a focus on understanding with a conception of rationality. Unfortunately, however, Sartre never managed to work out this thematic field in a manner that even would have satisfied him. His final analysis of reason is missing due to CRD being unfinished. The task to reconstruct it is thus left to the interpreter.

The most concrete background to Sartre's project is *not* the *purely philosophical* task to connect epistemic with ethical issues. Instead, the set up is rooted in a certain *diagnosis of the times* that, at least initially, follows the Hegelian-Marxist tradition of social thought: the intelligibility of individual persons and social events are internally related to social conditions and history (cf. Flynn 1992, pp. 215-20 and 1997, pp. 19-22). Understanding ourselves requires understanding our times. Thus, according to Sartre "the link of our investigation is none other than the fundamental identity between an individual life and human history (or, from the methodological point of view, the 'reciprocity of their perspectives')" (CDR, p. 70 (184)).

Furthermore, Sartre claims that a "... 'philosophical crisis' is the particular expression of a social crisis" (SM, p. 7 (22)). He diagnoses his own times exactly in terms of such a socio-philosophical crisis. The philosophical dimension of this crisis is manifested mainly in the two dominating currents of *positivism* — or analytical reason — and *Marxism* (after Marx)

— or the dogmatic use of the ideal of totalisations. According to Sartre, both of these currents are guilty of two misconceptions concerning the intelligibility of the human: they raise the scientific ideals of *universalisation* and *analyticity* as central (see for example SM, p. 25-9). As alternatives Sartre raises *totalisation* and a *synthetic* or dialectical *conception of rationality*.

According to Sartre's diagnosis, universalising schemes that are based on abstract, conceptual relations does not enable thought to make concrete human reality intelligible. They replace the depth of the concrete with abstract schemes such as the covering law-model: "... the constitutive schema of [the physicist's hypothesis] *is universalising, not totalising*. It determines a relation, a function, and not a concrete totality" (SM p. 25 (32), my italics). Marxism was originally such an attempt to preserve the totality, but Sartre's critique of contemporary Marxism is particularly harsh regarding their success on this matter:

> Marxist formalism is a project of elimination. The method is identical with Terror in its inflexible refusal to *differentiate*; its goal is total assimilation at the least possible effort. The aim is not to integrate what is different as such, while preserving for it a relative autonomy, but rather to suppress it ... The totalling investigation has given way to a Scholasticism of the totality. The heuristic principle — 'to search for the whole in its parts' — has become the terrorist practice of 'liquidating the particularity' ... Marxism ought to study real men in depth, not dissolve them in a bath of sulphuric acid (SM, pp. 48, 28 and 43-44 (48, 35 and 45)).

The ideal of analyticity — or dividing the studied object into its constituent parts — is thus also directly opposed to Sartre's ideal of searching for a *synthetic but interpretative* account of concrete reality.

The social crisis, again, is manifested by the fact that "one of the most striking characteristics of our time is that *history is made without self-awareness*" (SM, 29 (35), my italics). There is *a crisis in the understanding of what we do*. This crisis is social in nature, since the understanding of what one does is an important feature of the reproduction and reconstruction of social reality: it participates in the self-definition and self-formation of the movement of history. The question of the understanding of what we do is directly connected to how human beings (in co-operation) can influence and steer their own historical environment, and thereby to how we can avoid alienation, or that our contemporary history becomes something completely different than what we intend with it. Sartre thus strongly affirms the connection between the practical task of *well-informed action* and the epistemic-theoretical task of *understanding*.

Sartre's solution, then, is a certain combination of *existentialism*, with its focus on the individual and unique and *Marxist social thinking*:

> Existentialism refuses to abandon the real life to the unthinkable chances of birth for the sake of contemplating a universality limited to reflecting indefinitely upon itself. It intends ... to find mediations which allow the individual concrete — the particular life, the real and dated conflict, the person — to emerge from the background of the *general* contradiction of productive forces and relations of production ... it wants to reintroduce the unsurpassable singularity of the human adventure", and to develop "... a veritable *comprehensive knowing* which will rediscover man in the social world and which will follow him in his praxis — or, if you prefer, in the project which throws him toward the social possibles in terms of a defined situation (SM, pp. 57, 176 and 181).

I shall return to the details of this conception in the subsequent chapters. I shall end this chapter with an outline of a certain problem field opened up by contemporary thought.

This two-fold nature of Sartre's project — the ideal of totalisation on the one hand, and the imperative of a non-reductionist understanding on the other — raises the issue how Sartre's solution fares in relation to the contemporary intellectual currents concerned with the understanding of the present. The dominating currents of today seem to have settled their scores with Sartre by giving a negative answer to this question: for both the moderns and the postmoderns *Sartre is out*. Are we to accept this assessment? I'd like to answer with a moderate 'No!' by claiming that *contemporary thought has not yet really met the challenges of Sartre's standpoint*. However, I also claim that if Sartre's standpoint is to count as relevant today, it needs to be reconstructed and developed.

In the case one by 'understanding' means the kind of comprehensive or totalising intellectual grasp I outlined above, a problem of understanding might arise either (i) if one is not able to totalise the domain in question or (ii) if the very idea of a totalising understanding is challenged and criticised. In the perspective of the *discourse on modernity and postmodernity*[3], the important thing is that Sartre sets himself to defend and not challenge the idea of a totalising perspective.

One of the typical traits of postmodernism is the imperative to replace all kinds of totalising meta-narratives, as Lyotard says, with a type of understanding that is suspicious of the existential and political consequences of such totalising models. In *La Condition postmoderne* Lyotard thus describes the condition of the epochal change to postmodernity as a new disbelief and suspiciousness towards grand and all-encompassing metanarratives, which typically has oriented life in modernity (1984, pp. xxiii-xxv). The postmodern experience of the world, and of us, does no longer embrace a belief that the aim to understand us and orient our practices should be realised by the means of all-encompassing narratives such as *progress*, a *unified scientific world-view* or world-changing *political ideologies* of the Marxist type. Lyotard finds it important to replace such metanarratives with smaller and more specific narratives, which are more sensitive to the complexities of concrete reality.

One dominating theme in the debate on modernity and postmodernity is *language* and *discourse*. Of course, the philosophical discourse on language (and the so-called linguistic turn) is characteristic of 20th-century thought at large, and it can in no way be limited to the time-diagnostic discourse on modernity and postmodernity. During the last decades, however, philosophers such as Foucault, Lyotard, Habermas and Rorty have engaged in the problems of language, discourse and communication as issues inherently connected to the understanding of the times in which we live.

For example Rorty, in *Philosophy and the Mirror of Nature* — partly inspired by existentialism and hermeneutics, Sartre and Gadamer — took up a strongly polemical position. He propagates for a view according to which the classical epistemological task of philosophy has to be reviewed within the framework of the *edifying* task of discourse. Rorty proposes to set "... epistemologically centred philosophy ... aside" and establish philosophy as an "... activity [which] is ... edifying without being constructive ... [and] *supposed* to be abnormal [in a Kuhnian sense], to take us out of our old selves by the power of strangeness, to aid us in becoming new beings" (Rorty 1980, p. 357 and 360). In this sense, Rorty understands the task of philosophy in relation to it's times as an endless participation in the "... conversation of mankind" (Rorty 1980, p. 389).

Foucault, again, studied the role of social and discursive practices in science. By 'a discursive formation' Foucault generally means 'a set of types of claims that, at a certain period, is accepted as justified modes of discourse' (see Foucault 1972, pp. 21-78 and 178-98 and Dreyfus and Rabinow 1982, pp. 44-125). A discursive formation is thus characteristically connected to the ideas of unity and totalisation. The important thing for Foucault, however, is (i) that totalising discourse also encompasses social practices of exclusion, whereby certain kinds of discourse are condemned as unjustified or irrational, and (ii) that this connection between totalisation and exclusion is inherently connected to social relations of power (1979, pp. 25-31 and 1978, pp. 1-13 and 135-59, see also Dreyfus and Rabinow 1982, pp. 126-207). Thus, according to Foucault, all attempts at a totalising understanding of human beings and human reality, regardless of whether they are objectivistic or hermeneutical, are inherently connected to the social practice of steering, disciplining and controlling human beings. That is, the idea, so dear to Sartre, that a new and better model of totalisation may have a critical-emancipatory impact is criticised by Foucault as seriously missing its goal.

In the light of these observations, it is no surprise that these thinkers are characteristically suspicious towards the importance of a theory of *rationality*. As Foucault says in "The Subject and Power":

> ... since Kant, the role of philosophy has been to prevent reason from going beyond the limits of what is given in experience; but from the same moment ... the role of philosophy is also to keep watch over the excessive powers of political rationality. Which is a rather high expectation ... The relationship between rationalisation and excesses of political power is evident. And we should not need to wait for bureaucracy or concentration camps to recognise the existence of such relations. But the problem is what to do with such an evident fact? ... Shall we try reason? To my mind, nothing would be more sterile ... I think that the word rationalisation is dangerous. What we have to do is analyse specific rationalities rather than always invoke the progress of rationalisation in general (Foucault 1982, p. 210).

If philosophy is to keep some kind of emancipatory interest, the task even to engage in the development of a new conception of rationality is dubious. One ought rather to confine oneself to *the analysis and critique of existing and specific forms of rationality*, without any totalising aim in view.

In summary, then, the combination of the two themes of an emphasis on the crucial role of the particular and of discursive practices, and the suspicion towards problematising in terms of rationality, embodies a challenge to Sartre's views on a totalising model of rationality. The main claim is, it seems to me, that all attempts at totalisation must necessarily loose the multidimensionality of the reality studied, and that all such perspectives are connected to social practices of exclusion and steering. A totalising perspective cannot therefore fulfil the intention to have an emancipatory function, quite the contrary it might become repressive.

These conceptions, although quite widespread, have naturally not been appreciated overall. The clearest example of opposition is found in Habermas. In opposition to the claims of the postmodernists, and more in line with Sartre, Habermas defends the view that philosophy should, in fact, exactly be concerned with the problem of rationality:

> Philosophical thought originates in reflection on the reasons embodied in cognition, speech and action; and reason remains its basic theme ... philosophy in its post-metaphysical, post-Hegelian currents is converging toward the point of a theory of rationality ... (Habermas 1984, p. 1-2).

Habermas, furthermore, strongly argues against the possibility and value of the postmodernist rejection of the theme of rationality:

> The radical [in a negative sense] critique of reason exacts a high price for taking leave of modernity. In the first place, these discourses can and want to give no account of their own position ... At the same time, they resist any return to forms of religious thought, whether dogmatic or heretical. So an incongruity arises between these 'theories', which raise validity claims only to renounce them, and the kind of institutionalisation they undergo within the business of science (Habermas 1987b, p. 336).

Habermas thus interprets the position of a radical critique of reason as a performative self-contradiction. A discourse that rejects all appeals to rationality is unable to give any kind of grounds for its inferences and views, since the appeal to grounds exactly conveys a belief in rationality.

Habermas's theory of communicative rationality is such an attempt to develop a theory of rationality, by situating reason in discourse and communication (1992b, pp. 44-48 and 1992c, pp. 139-46). By this move Habermas believes he can preserve the Hegelian-Marxist and existentialist idea to ground rationality in everyday life (interpersonal communication and social action), satisfy the demands of a historisized, post-metaphysical thinking in which "all attempts at discovering ultimate foundations, in which the intentions of First Philosophy live on, have broken down" (Habermas 1984, p. 2) (by means of a formal and procedural concept of rationality) and preserve, what he calls, the unity of reason without reducing away the diversity of its voices.

Thus, Sartre's ideal to combine a perspective centred on the understanding of concrete reality, in all its depth, with a synthetic or totalising conception of rationality is both outrightly rejected and loosely supported by the currents of contemporary thought. The passage quoted from Said indictaes that this problem has again been raised to the focal point. This also indicates that the challenge of Sartre has perhaps not really been met yet. With this perspective in mind, I set off on my journey through Sartre's anthropology.

Notes

1 In the analytical tradition 'meaning' is often been defined in terms of the conditions under which something can be assumed to be true, and in this sense 'meaning' may be seen as inherently connected to 'truth' (cf. for example Dummett 1993). I shall not, however, go into this issue. My distinctions are mainly oriented towards bringing forward different issues that are triggered by the use of the concept of understanding.

2 It is not Merleau-Ponty's intention to choose any of these options (as Alain chooses a politics of understanding), but to point out the necessity of choosing both. In this sense Merleau-Ponty, in a work that is critical of Sartre's liaison with the French Communist Party in 1952, in fact points towards the kind of solution that Sartre tries to realise in CRD.

3 To get an overview of this debate, see for example Habermas 1987b, Wallgren 1988, Harvey 1989 and Docherty (ed.) 1993.

3 The Project of Anthropology

Anthropology and Existentialism

In the Preface to CRD Sartre — in a rather breathtaking manner — identifies the fundamental theme of the work to be to answer the question "... whether there is any such thing as a *Truth of Man*?" (CDR, p. 822 (14), my italics). In a more concrete fashion the project is characterised as aiming at the constitution of an *anthropology*:

> My intention is to raise one single question: do we today have the means to constitute a structural and historical anthropology? (CDR, p. 822 (14)).

Even for a reader only provisionally familiar with the works of Sartre, these declarations hardly comes as a surprise. Sartre's existentialism, it is often said, is mainly concerned with 'man'; its anthropological stance is a well-known fact. As Sartre himself describes it:

> I consider man to be the domain of philosophy, that is to say that all other problems can only be understood in relation to man ... Everything in the world that concerns philosophy is the world in which man is, and necessarily the world in which man stands in relation to how man is in the world (Sartre 1972a, p. 83 (my translation)).

The anthropological stance of Sartre's philosophy is thus easily recognisable. More difficult is to say exactly what it boils down to. For one thing, by '*anthropology*' one may mean several different things: an empirical discipline that studies different human cultures (cultural anthropology), a general heading for the sciences of man, a biological theory of the nature of Homo Sapiens, philosophical anthropology, etc. (cf. Pappé 1967 and Marquard 1971). Since Sartre is a philosopher, and the investigation of CRD is clearly philosophical in nature, one may expect he in fact means *philosophical anthropology*. By '*philosophical anthropology*', again, is generally meant an investigation of *the general essence of human nature*. Historically this discipline is connected both to the quest for *a unified foundation for the sciences of man* (the 'classical' tradition of Vico, Hume, Mill and Dilthey) and to the rise of *philosophies of life and existence* (the existentialist tradition of Kierkegaard, Nietzsche, Jaspers, etc.).

The kind of standpoint introduced for example by Heidegger and Sartre, however, is suspicious towards the possibilities of a theory of human nature. In *Sein und Zeit* Heidegger criticises contemporary anthropology for being based on an insufficient ontology, and claims that no further progress can be made within anthropology without thorough ontological investigation (1962, pp. 48-52). Heidegger's fundamental ontology is not oriented towards a conception of human nature, but deal with the more general question of being. But not even Heidegger altogether dismisses the value and possibilities of a philosophical anthropology; he only claims that ontology must provides its foundation (1962, p. 17).

In his early works, such as *Esquisse d'une théorie des émotions* (1962, pp. 15 and 24-25) and EN, Sartre initially follows Heidegger on this point. In EN Sartre explicitly distinguishes phenomenological ontology from the aims of anthropology: "... our present investigation *does not aim at constituting an anthropology*" (BN, p. 282 (329), my italics), and he also posits the general question of being as fundamental (p. xliii). In Sartre, however, this latter declaration remains rather hollow. He indeed discusses different meanings of the concept of being, and recognises the need for a unified conception, but the actual investigation in EN is confined to the level of 'a phenomenology of human being-in-the-world'. Heidegger considered this step as only the first in a general ontology. Sartre soon dropped his interest in the general question of being, and gradually settles for what may be called *a study of the human condition, its ontology and principles of intelligibility*.

In the immediate time following the publication of EN and the Second World War, Sartre begins to engage more directly in the problems of anthropology. In the introductory essay to the first edition of the journal *Les Temps Modernes* (October 1945), he declares that "we would like our journal to contribute in a modest way to the elaboration of a synthetic anthropology" (1988b, p. 261). This anthropology was intended to study contemporary events and literary works with the intention to "... sort out the conception of man that inspires each one of the conflicting theses, and will give its opinion in conformity with the conception it maintains" (p. 255). Thus, a two-fold task is outlined: to develop *a correct conception of man* (on the basis of the philosophy of EN) and *to engage writing in a critique of contemporary life* on the basis of this conception.

In the 'high tide' of existentialism (after the war and until the beginning of the 1950's), Sartre's interest in dealing with these issues philosophically was mainly expressed in the form of a *critique of the idea of a human nature* and in the *task to develop an ethics.* Especially in polemical essays, such as *L'existentialisme est une humanisme* (EH) and *Réflexions sur la Question Juive* (both 1946), Sartre is keen to emphasise that there is no such thing as a human nature. In the place of a conception of man based on a 'nature' Sartre posits an outline of 'the human condition':

> ... we do not believe in 'human nature' ... For us, man is defined first of all as a being 'in a situation'. That means that he forms a synthetic whole with his situation — biological, economic, political, cultural, etc. He cannot be distinguished from his situation, for it forms and decides his possibilities; but inversely, it is he who gives it meaning by making his choices within and by it ... What men have in common is not a 'nature' but a *condition*, that is, an ensemble of limits and restrictions: the inevitability of death, the necessity of working for a living, of living in a world already inhabited by other men (1948, pp. 59-60, my italics).

For Sartre, a 'nature' seems to imply a static orientation independent of the circumstances, such as 'being good or bad', 'being steered by universal unconscious drifts', etc. The concept of a condition, in contrast, emphasises our dependence on concrete situations, our possibilities to do things differently and to change ourselves and the circumstances, that is *freedom*.

This claim clearly has an ethical dimension. Sartre criticises conceptions that posit the existence of a universal human nature because they objectify what fundamentally is a dynamic and free project. At his most polemical extreme, Sartre thus declares that "man is nothing else but that which he makes of himself" and that this "... places the entire responsibility for his existence squarely on his own shoulders" (EaH pp. 28-29). He also describes existentialism as "... a doctrine that renders human life possible" (p. 24).

Although Sartre's early philosophy is thus clearly centred on human being and the human condition, it is; in fact, not until CRD that he raises the idea of an anthropology to the absolute focus of his concerns. In CRD, however, Sartre's attitude to existentialism has changed. This has the consequence that those who tend primarily to recognise Sartre as an existentialist, the encounter with CRD is a rather puzzling experience. In the first place, he now identifies his standpoint with that of *Marxism*: he claims that Marxism "... remains ... the philosophy of our time. We cannot go beyond it because we have not gone beyond the circumstances which engendered it" (SM, p. 21 (30)) and relegates existentialism rather bluntly as "... an *ideology*" (SM, p. 8 (22)).

In the second place, in QM Sartre actually initially uses 'anthropology' as a general heading for the *sciences of man* (e.g. psychology, sociology, history, etc.), and not as a philosophical discipline. In a second step, again, he characterises his own contribution as a study of *their foundation*. In a third step, this task is identified with the rather 'academically dry' idea to develop a *unified methodology for the sciences of man* (SM, p. 35, 168-76). This re-orientation may surprise, especially if one is accustomed to regard existentialism as anti-science in its ground tone (see Warnock 1969, p. xvii). Why this sudden concern with science? Why did not Sartre press forward on with his fruitful idea of an existentialist ethics, but turned to 'a problem of method'?

I do not think one should get too much stuck on these polemical declarations. A closer examination of Sartre's position reveals that his view on the ideological nature of existentialism does not mean that it should be dismissed, quite the contrary. Thus, by 'ideology' Sartre does not mean 'untrue' or 'only a political doctrine', but a position that is *still true to some extent*, but *only partially* so (SM, pp. 14-34). This has the consequence that he in fact describes his own (slightly modified) existentialism as "... the foundation of all inquiry", as a conception that takes "... on the human dimension (that is, the existential project) as the foundation of anthropological Knowledge" (SM, p. 181 (132)). But since this foundation is still only a part of the whole truth, Sartre also imagines a future when it will be ".... absorbed, surpassed and conserved by the totalising movement of philosophy" (ibid.).

In addition, Sartre critique of contemporary Marxism is actually very harsh. He reproaches the Marxists for having "... played the positivists game" (CDR, p. 23 (142)): they have come to believe that their ideas and doctrines are "... concrete truths ... clear, precise and univocal, [that they] *already* constitute a *knowledge*" (SM, p. 35 (40)). According to Sartre, the ideas expressed by Marx and developed by his followers must be considered "... only as guiding principles, as indications of jobs to be done, as problems ... as regulative ideas". Thus, "... everything remains to be done; we must find the method and constitute the science" (ibid.).

Concerning the ethical dimension, in CRD Sartre seems to have dropped it altogether. In 1948 he gave up his attempt to develop an existentialist ethics, and CRD was a kind of project that replaced the idea of an ethics. Thus, Sartre later described this as a period when "... moralism began to yield to a realism ... a political realism ... that ... blocked out all ideas of morality" (1978d, p. 78). This would imply that CRD is political in nature, but that it does not constitute an ethics. However, this separation of ethics and politics did not satisfy Sartre for long (1978d, pp. 78-81) and in the years after CRD he returned to ethics. But he still did not regard ethics as independent of politics. Thus, in the manuscript to the *Rome Lecture* of 1964 (see Chapter 9) Sartre rather pompously declares that "... the historical moment has come for socialism to rediscover its ethical structure, or rather, to unveil it" (quoted by Bowman and Stone 1991a, p. 111). He also posits the task to create "an ethics of history", which would realise "the identification of history with the dramatic development of morality" (quoted by Anderson 1993, p. 128).

The Set Up of an Anthropology in *Questions de mèthode*

The question then remains: What does Sartre actually mean by 'anthropology'? As I said in the Introduction, at stake in the clarification of this issue is much more than just a question how to label Sartre's writings. Since 'human being' is one of the principal orientations of Sartre's philosophy, it is directly linked to the very foundations of his thinking, and bound to engage questions of fundamental philosophical importance.

In QM Sartre diagnoses contemporary intellectual life by the means of two negative observations. First, the sciences of man (including Marxism) misconstrue the human condition by a objectivistic model of science. They have lost their fundamental task to non-dogmatically *interpret* the unique features and particularities of concrete human reality, and become explanatory sciences mainly interested in discovering universal laws. Second, different scientific disciplines work within their own delimited sectors of human reality, use their own methods, and lack a common foundation. In CRD Sartre sets himself the task to develop such a foundation, that would co-ordinate and integrate the different methods used and become "... a rational anthropology" (SM, p. 169n (125n)).

Sartre repeats his view that there is no universal human nature which could function as the ultimate foundation for anthropology:

> This task of integration would be easy if one could bring to light some sort of *human essence*; that is a fixed collection of determinations in terms of which one could assign a definite place to the object studied. But the majority of anthropologists agree that the diversity of groups — considered from the synchronic point of view — and the diachronic evolution of societies forbid us to found anthropology upon a conceptual knowledge (SM, p. 169 (125)).

But Sartre does not accept the option of cultural relativism either. That is, although cultures and societies differ from each other in important aspects,

> ... conversely, a real communication and in certain situations a reciprocal comprehension are established or can be established between existents thus distinct (SM, p. 170 (125)).

These theses — no common nature, but the possibility of communication and the reciprocity of understanding — point towards mainly two tasks. First, one may search for guidelines by means of which cultural gaps can be bridged, although never fully removed. The idea of a *method* captures this idea of a series of mediating, interpretative procedures that may guide us, both in moving from cultural differences to a level of generality (conditions), and from generality (theory) to empirical study of the specific.

Second, if it is true that a real communication is possible between human cultures, their differences are not absolute. As Hendley observes, this implies the existence of *transhistorical* and *transcultural* conditions (p. 187-203, Sartre does not use these notions). By 'transhistorical' and 'transcultural' I mean features of the human condition that cut across the differences between cultures and historical periods, but which do not form ahistorical essences. If this thesis is interpreted hermeneutically (see Chapter 4), it could be taken to imply conditions common to historicity and culturality as such: language, social practices, institutions, etc. Commonness in conditions may result in essential differences between the concrete life of cultures: conditions are factors that may be lived and manifested differently in each culture. Sartre uses several notions that imply such transhistoricity: praxis, the practico-inert, mediated reciprocity, seriality, conflict. The presence of such notions perhaps justifies Hartmann's characterisation of the standpoint of CRD as *transcendental* (1966, pp. 8-25, 52-57, 69-70, 178-83, and 1988, pp. 358-59).

A large portion of the contemporary debate on objectivism and relativism concerns the actual status of such transhistorical and transcultural notions. Thus, one may ask whether or not they can be theoretically clarified. If one, for example, at the far end of one's account finds the social practices, does this lead one to consider a theory of social practice (as Sartre does), or does one settle with empirical-interpretative descriptions of different kinds of practices? Perhaps it would be possible to recast the polemics between Rorty, Foucault and Lyotard, on the one hand, and Gadamer, Habermas and Sartre, on the other hand as a debate about the status of such transhistorical categories (see Hendley 1991, pp. 187-203).

Sartre's mostly only implicitly expressed, standpoint that there are transcultural and transhistorical human conditions leads him to posit the possibility of what I call a *modified kind of philosophical anthropology*. The denial of a human nature is positively expressed in the form of the development of an ontology or theory of intelligibility of the human condition, posited on a level of universality. I shall discuss it in more detail in Chapter 5.

This ontology functions as the unified foundation of Sartre's "... *regressive-progressive* and *analytic-synthetic* method" (SM, 148 (112), my italics).[1] This idea of a method combining regressive analysis with synthetic and progressive interpretation is intended to capture the demands of an anthropology that is both *structural* and *historical*. By 'regressive analysis' Sartre means an interpretative study of the socio-historical circumstances that make up the background and conditions of, for example, an individual's life, an action, social events and the historical process (SM, pp. 133-46 and 148). The investigation moves regressively, or back- or downwards, and analytically, or by the means of differentiation's, from the concreteness of a particular experience, action or event, to the general features that forms their condition of intelligibility. By 'progressive synthesis', Sartre means an interpretative study that conceives of reality as temporal (SM, pp. 146-8). According to Sartre, such an interpretation is intended to *reconstruct*, or even *reinvent*, (presumably in a narrative form) the very movement whereby men shape and reshape themselves and the world in which they live. It thus moves progressively along the very movement that it attempts to reconstruct. It synthesises the significations found in the regressive analysis as they are concretely bound together in an individual solution, action or incarnated in the historical process.

Sartre's method is, importantly, set up on the basis of a *thesis of historicity*: "... if there is to be any such thing as a Truth in anthropology, it must be *in becoming* and it must be a *totalisation*" (CDR, p. 822 (14)). That is, the method should not be understood as a rigid, a priori scheme to be directly applied to the studied reality, nor should it be compared with the universalism of the natural sciences. Instead it should be seen as an interpretative and hermeneutical kinds of method, whose main objective is to make historical reality intelligible in its uniqueness and individuality. This method is characteristically open-ended and heuristic: it must be constantly open to the particularities of the object and *learn* from reality (SM, p. 133). For example, in IF Sartre declares that the "... method is *created* through the very work itself in obedience to the requirements of its object" (FI 1, p. x).

In this way, Sartre's conception of method (perhaps surprisingly) combines a theoretical perspective (or a notional approach, see Chapter 5) with the demands of empirism:

> the more easily [our inquirer] has at his disposal a philosophy, a point of view, a theoretical basis of interpretation and totalisation, the more he will force himself to approach these ends in a spirit of absolute empirism; he will allow them to develop, to release by themselves their immediate meaning, for he will have the intention of *learning*, not *rediscovering*. It is in this free development that we find the conditions and the first outline of the object's *situation* in relation to the social whole and its totalisation inside the historical process (SM, 165 (123)).

This co-presence of theoretical guidelines with the spirit of empirism is an inheritor of the phenomenological and hermeneutical demand to stick with things themselves; theory can only base itself on the internal perspective of the observer and participator, and it is confined to illuminating this experience. By this Sartre's conception of method is actually quite far away from the one criticised by Gadamer (see Chapter 4).

A Critical Investigation of Reason and its Normative Commitments

The scope of Sartre's anthropology cannot be limited to these two dimensions of an *ontology of the human condition* and a *method*. First, in CRD Sartre proposes as the main theme of his work *a critical investigation of reason*. Second, Sartre's identification of his anthropology with Marxism communicates an acceptance of *the normative intents of a critical social theory*. By this Sartre's project goes beyond the ontological and epistemological set up described above, and steps across the border to a discourse on normative foundations and the problem of morality.

In the common preface to CRD and QM Sartre retrospectively comments on the relation between these works: "... [in QM] I have tried to reveal the inner conflicts of philosophical anthropology, and at some points — in my chosen field of methodology — I have outlined provisional solutions to the problems" (CDR, p. 822 (14)). But he now recognises that a major shortcoming of this project, as it was outlined in QM, is the lack of foundation for the advanced theses: as long as the method appears "... merely as one option among others [and] we shall have achieved nothing, and our conclusions will remain conjectural" (CDR, p. 15 (135)). Sartre is not satisfied with the conjectural nature of his claims. Thus, in the main body of text of CRD he engages in the task to investigate their foundations and validity, even of proving their correctness.

Sartre declares that the investigation will have to settle "... whether the positivist Reason of the natural Sciences is the same as the Reason which is to be found in the development of anthropology, or whether the knowledge and comprehension of man by man involves not only special methods but also *a new form of Reason*" (CDR, pp. 822-23 (14-5), my italics). Sartre opts for the idea to develop a new conception of reason. According to Sartre, this conception of reason must be dialectical in nature: the dialectic, besides its affinity with the Marxist tradition, is the only concept that integrates the two demands of historicity and processual thinking. But it is not Sartre's aim simply to defend a ready-made conception, but to establish his own conception of dialectical reason. Thus, he defines his task as *a critique of dialectical reason*, in the Kantian sense of a 'critique':

> Our approach will therefore be critical in that it will be an attempt to determine the validity and the limits of dialectical Reason, and this will mean identifying both the oppositions and the connections between this Reason and positivist, analytical Reason (CDR, p. 823 (14)).

The project to develop a method proposed in QM has thus been transformed into a critical investigation of human rationality. This has the consequence that a limitation of the scope of Sartre's project either to a philosophical anthropology or to a method would be is misleading.

This transition to the problem of rationality constitutes a kind of *thematic rupture*, in relation both to QM and to the earlier phases of Sartre's philosophy. Whereas CRD on many other issues is a continuation of Sartre's earlier thematic concern, the idea to pose the problem of rationality is unique to CRD and it complies a move to a higher level of reflection. By the latter I mean that the problem of rationality is more fundamental than the issues dealt with by a phenomenological ontology (as expressed in EN) in the sense that it concerns the validity also of ontological statements. In addition, reason is also a theme that connects ontology to ethical issues. The problem of rationality includes both theoretical and practical reason, and it thus concerns the relation between ontology, epistemology and ethics.

The claim that an investigation of reason is situated on a higher level of reflection does not necessarily imply that it would be more abstract. According to Sartre's conception, dialectical reason is the reason embodied in our concrete engagements and not some a priori principles of thought. Thus, dialectical rationality is primarily the rationality inherent in human *praxis*. Sartre's investigation of reason is turned into an investigation of *the intelligibility of praxis*. This investigation includes a (structural and regressive) investigation of *the sociality of praxis* and a (synthetic and progressive) investigation of the intelligibility *of history*. These dimensions constitute the kernel domain of Sartre's investigation of reason.

A work that suggests itself as a forerunner to Sartre's Kantian critique of reason in history is Dilthey's critique of historical reason (1976b).[2] Dilthey investigated how knowledge of the cultural or historical world (Geistigen Welt) is possible, from the point of view of the standpoint that this world is constructed and shaped by individual subjects themselves (Dilthey 1976b, p. 207). He understood his project as an extension of Kant's critique of theoretical reason to the domain of history. A main difference between Dilthey and Sartre, however, is that Sartre's critique encompasses more than the question of our knowledge of the historical world. Dialectical reason is the rationality inherent in human action and history as such, and it is not to be confined only to the problem of knowledge in the historical sciences.

Reason is a *normative* concept. This normativity characteristically has two dimensions: the normativity involved in questions of *epistemological validity*, and the normativity involved in questions concerning the *justification or critique of action*. Sartre defines reason as a certain relation of correspondence between *praxis* and the *understanding* of praxis. This correspondence must, in my opinion, be seen as going in both directions: the correspondence between what we do and our understanding of it (epistemological normativity), and that between our interpretations of the world, our plans and the question of the justifiability of our choices of actions (practical, ethical and political normativity).

Although Sartre is not particularly explicit on this matter, one can claim that one of his primary intentions is to connect the *epistemological task of reaching understanding* with the *ethical-normative task* to investigate the *conditions of making history*. In QM Sartre thus outlines his standpoint on the relevance of a study of the intelligibility of history in the following manner:

> ... History, which is the proper work of *all* activity and of *all* men, appears to men as a foreign force exactly insofar as they do not recognise the meaning of their enterprise (even when locally successful) in the total, objective result ... the plurality of *the meanings* of History can be discovered and posited for itself only upon the ground of a future totalisation — in terms of the future totalisation and in contradiction with it. It is our theoretical and practical duty to bring this totalisation closer every day. All is still obscure, and yet everything is in full light. To tackle the theoretical aspect, we have the instruments; we can establish the method. Our historical task, at the heart of this polyvalent world, is to bring closer the moment when History will have *only one meaning*, when it will tend to be dissolved in the concrete men who will make it in

common (SM, 89-90 (75-76)).

This passage is an apt expression of what primarily brings *a Sartrean existentialism that focuses on human action in situation* and *Marxism* in contact: in the present circumstances, the results of our practical efforts are alienated, and only a social change oriented towards making possible a history made in common can remove alienation. The latter, highly Utopian, perspective is common to Marx and Sartre.

Sartre identifies the Marxism he is ready to accept primarily as a certain *conception of history* and a certain *normative-political framework on the ideal society*. In CRD the focus is on the former: the task of philosophy (and science) is to investigate *the historical conditions of possibility of the realisation of our projects*. In CRD Sartre largely identifies Marxism with the standpoint he calls *historical materialism*. According to Sartre, this standpoint — indicated and outlined by Marx, further developed by the Marxists — furnishes "... the only valid interpretation of human History" (CDR, p. 39 (157)). As its basic thesis Sartre picks out a passage in Marx that strongly resonates with his own existentialism:

> Men make their own history, but they do not make it just as they please; they do not make it under circumstances chosen by themselves, but under given circumstances directly encountered and inherited from the past (Marx 1978, p. 9, see SM, p. 30).

Sartre's alliance with Marxism is of course not simply a consequence of his philosophical thinking as such, but has strong political undertones.[3] A study of it could adopt at least two different attitudes: to study the Marxism of Sartre as such, or to treat his Marxism mainly as another name for a discourse concerning the normative foundations of critical social theory. I shall adopt the latter strategy. Today Marxism can no longer be claimed to represent the mood of the times, nor does the kind of Utopian perspective Sartre seems to identify with have much to give. Quite the contrary, I consider the kind of political Utopianism that bases itself on images of ideal societies that appears to be *wholly* different in kind than our own a first step towards a dangerous 'the end justifies the means'-thinking. Today, perhaps more than ever, critical social theory needs to focus more on critical-normative issues, rather than Utopian one. In this sense I think Lyotard's warning (see Chapter 2) should be taken seriously.

As I shall show in Chapter 9, Sartre's critical social theory appears highly insufficient at least if one bases one's interpretation on CRD only. Sartre's renewed interest in question of *ethics*, or in normative foundations, are thus of uttermost importance for a study of his critical social theory, and for his anthropology at large.

L'Idiot de la famille: a Possible and Actual Outcome of Sartre's Anthropology

I have traced the orientations and turns involved in Sartre's anthropology up until CRD, and interpreted CRD as a turn to the fundamental problem of rationality. The actual scope of Sartre's investigation in CRD, however, is much more limited than what my account so far indicates, especially in relation to the totality of the project of an anthropology as I characterise it. One cannot in fact regard CRD simply as a *new and wider framework* replacing that of EN: what Sartre actually discusses in CRD must equally well be regarded as *adding* something to the framework of EN, and as *filling a certain gap* in the overall conception.

CRD as such encompasses mainly two projects: the tasks to develop *a theory of social formations* (volume 1) and the to investigate *the intelligibility of history* (the projected volume 2). The theory of social formations is a study of the *materiality and sociality of praxis*, including a *theory of human relations as mediated reciprocities* and a typology of *social formations*: series, groups and institutions. The investigation of history is basically an study of the intelligibility of *conflict* and a discussion of the problem of *the unity of history*. As I mentioned, the manuscript to volume 2 breaks off long before it has reached its goal. Furthermore, Sartre also describes CRD as a study of the *foundation for sociological and historical knowledge* (CDR, pp. 66 and 69). Thus, in relation to the full scope of the anthropology as I characterise it, CRD is obviously an investigation of only a part of it. Dimensions that are left out of CRD, but which still are crucial to Sartre's standpoint are, for example, the 'psychological', the ethical and the existential-biographical. In this section I shall discuss the latter, and leave the former two to Chapters 5 and 9, respectively.

The task *actually to perform empirical-interpretative investigation* is an essential element of Sartre's anthropology. Thus, Sartre describes his biography on Flaubert, *L'Idiot de la famille*, as "... the sequel to *Questions de méthode*" and as an attempt to answer the question "what can we today know about a man?" (FI 1, ix, see also Sartre 1978b, p. 111). It thus clearly belongs within the scope of Sartre's anthropology. But why does Sartre describe it as the sequel to QM, and not to CRD as such?

IF is a biography of a person. It interprets Flaubert in the light of the circumstances in which he lived, and it interprets the circumstances in the light of how they were lived by Flaubert. Sartre sees this biography as both an *application* and *test* of his method (FI 1, p. x and Sartre 1978b). It is also a developed version of the idea of an existential psychoanalysis introduced by Sartre in EN (see Chapter 5). However, as a continuation and fulfilment of CRD, it actually re-situates the position of the theory of social formations and the concern with history. In the light of IF, the main body of text of CRD clearly manifests only a part, but not the whole of the method to understand a human being.

IF progresses narratively along a series of shifts between regressive and progressive interpretations.[4] One may describe it as spiralling towards 'the truth of Flaubert'. It sets off from an attempt to understand the presence of a certain kind of passive constitution in Flaubert, acquired in early childhood. In order to do this, Sartre interprets the relations between Gustave and his family (Part One: Constitution. Volume 1 in the English translation). In the second part (Part Two: Personalisation. Volumes 2 and 3) Sartre deciphers how the young Flaubert actually lived his acquired abilities and skills, and his situations, by studying how he, through his actions and undertakings, both unconsciously (non-reflectively) and consciously, constructs a certain personality.

In the third part Sartre interprets Flaubert's mental and physical breakdown at the age of 23 (Part Three: Elbehnon, or the last spiral. Volume 4, see Chapter 8). This had the factual consequences that Flaubert's career as lawyer ended, and his ambitions to become a writer were realised. Sartre interprets the breakdown, and Flaubert's consequent neurosis, as a kind of solution to the dilemmas of his personality, a solution carried out on a psychosomatic level. As Hazel E. Barnes writes, this event "... decisively fixed the meaning of his life ... and [it] did not essentially change thereafter" (Barnes 1981, p. 11). I shall discuss it in Chapter 8.

The fourth part is an attempt to situate and assess Flaubert, his personality and decisions, his neurosis and his conception of literature, on the basis of his relation to the times in which he lived (Part Four: Objective and Subjective Neurosis. Volume 5, see Chapter 9). Sartre interprets the literary demands of the age, both inherited and assessed by Flaubert himself, and the period in French history called 'the Second Empire' (1852-71). He raises a time-diagnostic issue concerning the relation between the subjective neurosis of Flaubert and the objective neurosis of the times. IF was intended to end with an interpretation of Flaubert's most well known literary work, *Madame Bovary*, but due to failing eyesight, Sartre was unable to complete it (1978a, p. 3 and 19-20). The issues discussed in CRD are relevant to the interpretation mainly in this last volume. IF involves much more of the ideas developed by Sartre in his early works than what may be expected on the basis of CRD.

I shall treat IF as both one *possible outcome* of a Sartrean anthropology among others, and as *the factual outcome* of it as realised by Sartre himself. Thus, one may distinguish between the discursive self-understanding of a Sartrean anthropology in general, and the actual way it was understood and concretely expressed by Sartre himself. Then one may, for example, ask whether IF mainly is a particular outcome of Sartre's personal interests, or if Sartre's actually sees the whole project as culminating in writing biographies? That is, if the question of intelligibility in the end should be seen as an *existential issue* concerning individuals and their place and possibilities in a larger historical context.

I neither think Sartre would have endorsed this latter interpretation, nor that the value of Sartre's method is reducible to the biographical dimension. Sartre's conception of method as centred on a theory of the intelligibility of praxis is a paradigm that stretches out both to issues of ethics and to the interpretation and diagnosis of social events. From the point of view of my interests, these other possible dimensions are more important than the biographical. It still remains true that Sartre in fact chose to write a biography on Flaubert and not to study, for example, contemporary society.[5]

Five Dimensions of an Anthropology

In summary then, one may distinguish between at least five dimensions, which together characterises the discursive self-understanding of Sartre's project of an anthropology:

(1) it investigates the structures of human existence or the human condition (ontology or a modified philosophical anthropology),
(2) it investigates the foundations and methodology of the sciences of man (anthropology as a covering name for the sciences of man),
(3) it is an inquiry concerning rationality (the question of the truth of man understood as a problem of rationality),
(4) it sets up the empirical task to interpret concrete human beings, their relations to their times and social events (anthropology as biographical or historiographical).
(5) it encompasses the normative task of diagnosing human beings, socie-

ties and the times (anthropology as critical social theory).

An answer to the question what Sartre means by anthropology must then not constitute a choice of any particular of the above mentioned five dimensions, but would consist in an attempt to reconcile the five dimensions into a conception that integrates them all.

In this investigation I shall perform such an integration by the means of focusing on a certain theme: the question of *the intelligibility of praxis*. In a hermeneutic fashion, Sartre conceives of this problem, not as a problem of facts, but as a *problem of meaning*. Sartre insists that the meaning of what we do is neither reducible to the intentions of the agents, nor to the context of action as such, but to a certain synthetic relation between them: meaning constitutes a relation between (1) the material, social and historical reality (achieved real meanings), (2) individual and concrete movements (project-meanings as foundation of the real), (3) which are conditioned by, moves beyond and are inscribed in material, social and historical reality (given, surpassed and created real meanings). A Sartrean anthropology may thus be described as oriented towards the deciphering of the *real meaning* of what we do.

In order to avoid misunderstanding, I emphasise that this interpretative choice neither precludes nor criticises an approach to Sartre that takes some other theme, for example morality or existential issues, as central. My choice is made with the intention to trace a certain thematic line in Sartrean thought, and it is not set up as the only correct or possible kind of approach.

In the light of this choice, the question how to assess Sartre's anthropology in a contemporary perspective turns into how one is to situate and assess the co-presence in a single project of all five dimensions mentioned, and their respective relation to the problem of the intelligibility of praxis. Such an attempt at assessment should, in my opinion, investigate at least two issues. First, the particular way in which Sartre himself understands the scope and limits of his project. Second the general features of such an orientation, independently of how Sartre himself understood them. In my investigation, I regard the second of these as the most central, although it can hardly be discussed without the first.

Notes

1 These terms are neither original to CRD, nor Sartre's own innovations. Both in *Esquisse d'une théorie des émotions* (1962, p. 93f) and the chapter on existential psychoanalysis in EN (BN, p. 460), Sartre elaborates with the idea of

a method of regression and progression. In QM, again, Sartre refers to the sociologist Henri Lefebvre as a major source of inspiration (SM, p. 51n). Furthermore, the idea of a method of regressive analysis and synthetic progression has a long history: it is, for example, already found in Kant's *Prolegomena* (1953, p. 31).

2 It is an unsettled issue whether and to what extent Sartre had studied Dilthey. It is quite evident that he had some knowledge of his ideas, at least through Aron's books on the philosophy of history and on German sociology (1961, see also 1975, pp. ix-24). Biographers such as Hayman (1986) and Cohen-Solal (1987) do not mention Sartre's relation to Dilthey. Goldthorpe (1992, pp. 149-50), on the other hand, is quite convinced that Sartre had studied him.

3 Since the end of the Second World War Sartre was constantly in debate with the Marxists. Through the years Sartre's self-understanding changed, from an initial harsh critique (1955a)), through a short-term co-operation with the French Communist Party from 1952 to 1956 (Sartre 1964 and 1969), to the again more critical attempt in CRD to reconcile existentialism and Marxism. In his later years Sartre distanciated himself even further from the Marxists (see especially Sartre 1974b and 1983).

4 For an illuminating exposition of Sartre's work on Flaubert, see Barnes 1981.

5 One might of course claim that CRD does just that. But my point is that Sartre chose to put his method to test, not in a study of contemporary society, but in an existential biography.

4 On Hermeneutics

Three Lines of Modern Philosophical Hermeneutics

In this work I investigate Sartre's anthropology both itself *as a kind of* hermeneutics and *in the perspective of* hermeneutics. By this I shall mean:

(1) that I interpret the *philosophical standpoint* of Sartre as a kind of hermeneutics (a concern with the ontology and intelligibility of human being-in-the-world),
(2) that the thematic orientation of Sartre's project is closely related to hermeneutics (understanding and interpretation), and
(3) that I shall attempt to reciprocally assess certain aspects of the relation between Sartre and hermeneutics (e.g. language vs. praxis, the issue of transhistorical conditions).

Sartre did not himself, except in passing, describe his philosophy as hermeneutical.[1] He was obviously familiar with the idea of hermeneutics through his reading of Heidegger. This could imply that his choice not to use the term means that he self-consciously chose not to adopt Heidegger's position on this point. One could thus claim that my interpretation drags a label and tradition on a standpoint that explicitly did not understand itself in terms of it. It thus stands in need of clarification and justification. I have given some of my reasons for this choice in Chapter 1. In this chapter I shall focus on the issue of hermeneutics itself, and return in Chapter 5 to an exposition of the hermeneutical traits in Sartre's work.

My interpretation is actually neither new nor that controversial, although the term 'hermeneutical' itself is rarely used in connection with Sartre. In QM Sartre claims that "to grasp the meaning of any human conduct, it is necessary to have at our disposal what German psychiatrists and historians have called 'comprehension'" (SM, p. 152-53 (115)), and by this he self-consciously aligns himself with the German tradition of hermeneutical thinking. Raymond Aron, again, characterises Sartre's position in CRD as "... a Marxism of understanding..." (Aron 1975, p. 5), that is, a hermeneutical Marxism. In addition, as I mentioned in Chapter 1, Manfred Frank, Rorty and Fehér have already explored hermeneutical aspects of

Sartre's thought.

What is meant by hermeneutics — its domain, problems and aims — is today a matter of divergent opinions. Hermeneutics has become one of the major intellectual currents of the age. Gianni Vattimo goes so far as to describe it as *the* mood of the times. As a consequence hermeneutics has, in Wachterhauser's words, become a "... catchword ... [that] has taken on a life of its own" and which nowadays seems to lack a univocal meaning (1986a, p. 5).

From being originally confined to the interpretation of texts (literary and biblical) and jurisprudence, hermeneutics was, especially through the contributions of Dilthey and Weber, raised to the foreground within *the human and social sciences.* Dilthey and Weber engaged in whether these need a different epistemology and methodology than the natural sciences. Hermeneutics, or the methodology of *Verstehen*, was proposed as such. In this century, especially through Heidegger's *Sein und Zeit* (1927) and Gadamer's *Wahrheit und Methode* (1960), hermeneutics was transformed into a major concern for *philosophy* in general. Heidegger and Gadamer argue that the problem of understanding cannot not limited to a concern for the sciences, since it is central to the human mode of being as such. Since the 1970's the debate has spread from its original geographical centre on the European continent to the Anglo-American analytical tradition, and today also the contributions of, for example, Charles Taylor (1971), Georg Henrik von Wright (1971), Donald Davidson (1984), Hubert L. Dreyfus (1980), Richard Rorty (1980) and Richard Bernstein (1983) can be claimed to be concerned with the issues of hermeneutics.

I shall not attempt a full overview of what is at stake in this debate, an overview that would somehow capture the interests and concerns of all these thinkers. Instead I shall make an initial classification of certain discursive lines within the contemporary debate on hermeneutics, and then give an outline of Gadamer's conception.

(1) The *epistemological-methodological* line of hermeneutics. According to this interpretation, hermeneutics is primarily concerned with the problem of knowledge and the methodology of the human and social sciences. Thus, Dilthey understood hermeneutics as "... the methodology of the interpretation of written records" (1976c, p. 249) and that "... hermeneutics [must be related] to the epistemological task of showing the possibility of historical knowledge and finding the means for acquiring it" (1976b, p. 229). It was initially these themes that were taken up by the analytical discourse on hermeneutics in the 1970's.[2] Since Sartre's anthropology has a strong methodological stance, it is obviously related to

this line.

From this one often distinguishes (2) the *ontological* or *philosophical* line of hermeneutics — or, what I shall call, the *Heidegger-Gadamer line*. Gadamer describes his contribution as a generalisation of the problem of hermeneutics (1975, pp. 225-45). Ontological hermeneutics generalises the problem of the conditions of understanding, from an epistemological issue to an issue concerning the mode of being of human existence as such. Thus, Heidegger describes his analytic of human existence as a hermeneutic (1962, p. 38 and 53), and Gadamer characterises hermeneutics as basically an ontology of our belongingness to the world (1975).

In relation to the epistemological-methodological line, Gadamer encourages us to turn our attention away from the specific problem of method in the human sciences, and towards the more fundamental problem of "... what the human sciences truly are" (Gadamer 1975, p. xiii). Hermeneutics is not primarily to be concerned with the development of a method for the human sciences, but with the philosophical question of what understanding and historicity actually are, and how the orientation, practice and aims involved in the study of human beings and human reality is to be understood and assessed.

Although Sartre insists on the importance of developing a method, his anthropology is characteristically concerned with many of the ontological issues discussed by Heidegger and Gadamer. A 'natural' background source for this orientation is that both Sartre and Gadamer continue on a line of reflection initiated by the ontological turn of phenomenology in Heidegger. As I shall show below, however, Sartre and Gadamer interpret and recast it in different directions.

Within a third orientation of hermeneutics I shall include both (3) Rorty's characterisation of hermeneutics in *Philosophy and the Mirror of Nature* (1980) as *edifying discourse* and John Caputo's idea of *radical hermeneutics* (1987). Although there are obvious differences between these two, what they have in common is the view that hermeneutics is neither concerned with methodology nor (to exaggerate slightly) with scientific progress at all (as may still be claimed of Gadamer). According to Rorty, hermeneutics is an attempt to set "... epistemologically centred philosophy ... aside" and establish an "... activity [which] is ... edifying without being constructive ... [and] *supposed* to be abnormal [in a Kuhnian sense], to take us out of our old selves by the power of strangeness, to aid us in becoming new beings" and "we must be hermeneutical where we do not understand what is happening but are honest enough to admit it" (Rorty 1980, p. 357, 360 and 321).

Caputo continues on a similar, but even more strongly 'existentialist' line. Caputo connects hermeneutics unconventionally to Kierkegaard, Heidegger and Derrida, while neither Gadamer nor Sartre plays any major part. Gadamer's *Wahrheit und Methode* is even described by Caputo as "... a reactionary gesture" and "... turn ... back to the fold of metaphysics" (Caputo 1987, p. 5). In contrast, Caputo understands hermeneutics to convey "... an attempt to stick with the original difficulty of life, and not to betray it with metaphysics ... [as] a radical thinking which is suspicious of the easy way out, which is especially suspicious that philosophy, which is always meta-physics, is always doing just that" (ibid. p. 1 and 3).

Thus, in contrast to Gadamer's insistence that hermeneutics is still concerned with "... what is feasible, what is possible, what is correct, here and now" (1975, p. xxv), Rorty and Caputo point towards a concern with what is existentially important, edifying and, according to Rorty, rather to "... destroy for the sake of [one's] ... own generation ... than to build for eternity" (Rorty 1980, p. 369).

Rorty links Sartre to hermeneutics. Rorty's interpretation of Sartre, however, is mainly based on EN, and he does not, for example, deal with Sartre's concerns with method.[3] Sartre's aim to constitute an anthropological method must surely have looked suspicious in Rorty's eyes. These differences raise some interesting questions: how are we actually to understand Sartre's concern with anthropology? As a 'reactionary' turn back to metaphysics, or not? As a turn away from what is most valuable in existentialism or as a real attempt actually to deepen it?

In "Sartre and Hermeneutics" Istvan Fehér, in my opinion, interprets the implicit hermeneutical stance of Sartre too restrictively in relation to this third line. Fehér thus claims that "... the basic hermeneutic comportment from Heidegger to Rorty ... [is] typically ... openness to the strange, to the unfamiliar" (Fehér 1994, p. 72). Fehér is probably right that one can find this Heideggerian idea of 'hermeneutical closure' in Sartre, but he neglects Sartre's concerns with the problem of method and with concrete historical-biographical interpretation.[4]

I shall primarily read Sartre in the light of the second, or the Heidegger-Gadamer, line of hermeneutics. It is, however, clear that his position cannot be understood as a rejection of the problem of method, and it is thus also closely related to the issues of the first line. Since I have set up my investigation on the basis of Sartre's concern with understanding and the human and social sciences, and not with his 'existentialism', I shall not make any extensive use of the third line. This does not mean that I would consider its problems and aims uninteresting or unimportant.[5] But as I read

Sartre, the gateway to a reflection on the relation between Sartre and hermeneutics primarily goes through Sartre's concrete interests to interpret human, situational reality and his ontology of human being-in-the-world.

Gadamer on Hermeneutics

I shall use the term hermeneutics in a wide but still quite specific sense. It is *wide* in that I do not limit hermeneutics to a concern with the interpretation of texts or text-like human expressions (linguisticality), nor to a question of the method, or solely on the basis of the specific way Gadamer generalises it and 'disconnects' it from the problem of method. I shall therefore understand hermeneutics neither *as unconcerned with the problem of method* nor *as exclusively concerned with the linguistic constitution of human being-in-the-world*. In this sense my employment does not fall strictly along either of the lines outlined above, but covers aspects of all of them.

The *specific* sense in which I shall use 'hermeneutics' can best be grasped by means of an outline of the themes I take to be central. The identification of these themes as central is itself partly rooted in the question of the relation between hermeneutics and Sartre. I thus underline that I neither understand my outline as exhaustive, nor as the only justified one, but as rooted in the questions I raise in this particular work.

My outline is primarily based on Heidegger and Gadamer. Since Gadamer is the initiator of the contemporary debate on hermeneutics, and since Gadamer and Sartre have a common background in Heidegger's ontological turn of phenomenology, my choice is quite uncontroversial.

Thus, I shall employ 'hermeneutics' to mean the following:

(1) Hermeneutical reflection is oriented towards questions concerning the *understanding* and *interpretation* of meaning.
(2) Hermeneutical reflection is a philosophical investigation that studies, questions and criticises *concretely lived human experience* and its *mode of being* (a phenomenologically biased reflection on, or ontology of, being-in-the-world).
(3) Hermeneutical reflection is based on the thesis that human experience is constituted by the kind of *preformative* dimensions characteristic of Heidegger's notion of being-in-the-world (temporality, care, pre-understanding, language, praxis, etc.).
(4) Hermeneutical reflection is based on the thesis that all experience is subjected to the condition of *historicity*.

(5) The hermeneutical dimension of reflection is an affirmation of (hermeneutical) *circularity*: (a) all interpretation is rooted in a more basic (pre)understanding, (b) human beings are reflexive, self-interpretative and self-monitoring beings, (c) knowledge of human beings is human beings knowledge of themselves, and (d) the study of human beings and human reality is a case of human beings studying themselves and their own reality.
(6) Since hermeneutics emphasises the participatory nature of the human and social sciences, a basic concern is *the discursive self-understanding of the human and social sciences*.

In order to make my intentions with this conception clearer I shall give an outline of Gadamer's conception, without, however, going too deeply into its details.

Gadamer locates the problem of *historical consciousness* (4) as central to the question of epistemological validity and to philosophical hermeneutics. According to Gadamer, the great achievement of Dilthey's was that he elevated the epistemological problem 'how a subjective consciousness can have knowledge of the objective world?' into the question 'how a historical consciousness can understand the historical world to which it itself belongs?' (1975, p. 195f). The problem is then no longer confined to a (Cartesian) inner subject gaining knowledge of an outside world, but concerns a *historically lived experience understanding itself in history*. In short, it has the characteristic of hermeneutical circularity (5). According to Gadamer, Dilthey's ideal was the *complete self-transparency* of understanding, a state that would *remove all alienation* from historical consciousness (6) (1975, p. 202).

By 'historical consciousness' might be meant at least two things. First, "... the noble and slowly perfected art of holding ourselves at a critical distance in dealing with witnesses to past life" (1976a, p. 5), that is, the attempt, typical of the science of history, to understand the past by means of the interpretation of documents. Second, one might mean the attempt *to understand the historical present* or *the historicity of present experiences*. This second form of historical consciousness does not refer us to the science of history, but to the more general problem of the intelligibility of experience as such. The latter is not only a question of scientific method, but it concerns something manifested in our everyday experiences of works of art (aesthetic consciousness), texts (hermeneutical consciousness in the traditional sense) and of ourselves and the world we live in (1976a, p. 4 and 7). It is thus more general in character.

In fact, according to Gadamer, this generalisation of the hermeneutical problem means that it becomes *universal* (1975, pp. 230-34). By 'the universality of the hermeneutical problem' Gadamer means the insight that the question of the mode of being of the *hermeneutical experience* is basic to all the three areas mentioned, and in general that "[hermeneutical experience] is the mode of the whole human experience of the world" (1976a, p. 15). According to both Heidegger and Gadamer, the experience present in our being-in-the-world is fundamentally characterised by an immediate experience of meaning, and not of bare things. On the basis of this, Gadamer claims that it is not so much our judgements, but our *prejudices,* or *pre-understanding*, that constitute our being (1975, p. 245).

This has consequences for the possibilities and scope of philosophical reflection. In *Sein und Zeit* Heidegger replaces Husserl's idea of *reflective intuition of essences* with that of *hermeneutical reflection*. Husserl distinguished between two kinds of *intuition*: empirical-individual and essential (Husserl 1962, pp. 48-50). Empirical-individual intuition is present in our encounter with objects in everyday experience; it is concerned with existing facts or entities. Essential intuition is radically different from this: it is not concerned with facts, but with essences and essential truths, and "... pure essential truths do not make the slightest assertion concerning facts" (1962, p. 51). Husserl believed it was possible for such eidetic judgements to have the character of apodictic certainty and generality (1962, pp. 53-56). The idea of *phenomenological reflection* is thus intended to capture the idea of a method whereby we study and reveal essences (1962, pp. 200-13), such as *intentionality*. By 'reflection' is thus not to be understood a vantage point situated outside of experience, but a reflexive account of the mode of being of experience as it appears from an *internal* point of view.

In contrast with this 'perspective of certainty', Heidegger characterises philosophical investigation as the *expression in discourse* (Auslegung) of what is *'always already' implicitly understood and presupposed* by human beings (in experience, speech and action): *the mode of being of their own existence*. Such an investigation is necessarily only an interpretation of a previously not clarified preunderstanding. In short, it is a *hermeneutic*:

> ... the meaning of phenomenological description as a method lies in *interpretation* (Auslegung). The logos of the phenomenology of Dasein has the character of a *hermenein*, through which the authentic meaning of Being, and also those basic structures of Being which Dasein itself possesses, are *made known* to Dasein's understanding of Being. The phenomenology of Dasein is a *hermeneutic* in the primordial signification of this word, where it designates this business of interpreting (Heidegger 1962, p. 62).

An essential result of Heidegger's hermeneutical phenomenology of being-in-the-world is that the essences revealed are not ahistorical in character and consequences, as might, perhaps, be said of 'intentionality', but they point towards historicity. Thus, the condition of experience is not only its directedness towards object, but that this directedness is necessarily always already filled with a *fore-structure* of understanding:

> In interpreting, we do not, so to speak, throw a 'signification' over some naked thing which is present-at-hand ... it is grounded in something we grasp in advance — in a fore-conception. Whenever something is interpreted as something, the interpretation will be founded essentially upon fore-having, fore-sight and fore-conception (1962, p. 190-91).

The fore-structure consists of certain orientations that are constitutive of experience. According to Heidegger, the fore-structure of understanding is threefold (1962, p. 191):

(1) Fore-having (Vorhabe). The practical orientation of experience. All experience is primarily dealing with entities in the world within the perspective of some practice, and not a pure observation. The attitude of observation is a secondary, thematised product of reflective thought.
(2) Fore-sight (Vorsicht). The meaning-filled orientation of experience or our way of seeing things in advance (the world as already meaningful).
(3) Fore-conception (Vorgriff). The conceptual or linguistic orientation of experience. All experience is primarily oriented to the world by the means of linguistic and conceptual schemes.

A philosophical investigation of this fore-structure is hermeneutical in the sense that the *fore-structure is itself a pre-condition* for philosophical investigation (1962, p. 193). The investigation thus becomes circular: "hermeneutics is the way this understanding enlightens itself" (ibid. p. 450).

The essential hermeneutical consequence of this standpoint is that the existence of a fore-structure point towards a previously acquired understanding, whose content and inclination is directly dependent on concrete cultural and social circumstances. That is, the fore-understanding is constituted by, as Sartre says, *internalised* ways of thinking, models of interpretation of the world and of action. Thus, although the concept of a pre-understanding itself is universal and ahistorical in character (all men at all times have a pre-understanding), any actual pre-understanding is an internalisation of the present, and thereby historical in its content.

There are then at least three conditions for philosophical reflection on experience and human reality: *internality*, *circularity* and *historicity*. They constitute necessary hermeneutical dimension of philosophical investigation. These conditions are rooted in the mode of being of human-being-in-the-world, or its facticity. Thus, according to Gadamer, "the main point of the hermeneutics of facticity [Heidegger] and its contrast with the transcendental constitution research of Husserl was that no freely chosen relation towards one's own being can go back beyond the facticity of this being" (Gadamer 1975, p. 234).

Gadamer interprets this threefold fore-structure of experience as fundamentally the *linguistic constitution* of human being-in-the world (3):

> Language is not just one of man's possessions in the world, but on it depends the fact that man has a world at all. For man the world exists as world in a way that no other being in the world experiences. But this world is linguistic in nature ... Thus the original humanity of language means at the same time the fundamental linguistic quality of man's being-in-the-world (1975, p. 401).

The universality of the hermeneutical problem is reinterpreted by Gadamer as a problem of "the universal phenomenon of human linguisticality..." (1976a, p. 19, see also 1975, p. 432). The motive for this focus on language is that Gadamer views language as the very *medium* through which the internalisation of culture and society takes place, and that also, for example, models of behaviour and action are internalisations occurring through the medium of language.

According to Gadamer, language is not primarily a tool but an *event*: "This structure of the hermeneutical experience that so totally contradicts the idea of scientific methodology itself depends on the eventual character of language ... language constitutes the hermeneutical event proper not as language, whether as grammar or as lexicon, but in the coming into language of that which has been said in the tradition: an event that is at once assimilation and interpretation" (1975, p. 420-21). Linguisticality communicates our primary belongingness to the world: it is situated on a level that precedes the distinction between subject and object (3). Since meaning, in this sense, is immediately co-existent with the appearance of something in experience, it does not primarily appear as imprinted on the world by a subject, but as the meaningfulness of the object itself as it is encountered in experience.

In order to illustrate this Gadamer draws an analogue between understanding, linguisticality and *play* (Spiel) (1975, pp. 91-92). When we play a game, the game is primary to the players. The idea is to play along with, conform to the rules and practices of the game, to assimilate oneself with it.

In the same sense, the meaning of a text is not primarily a product of the reader, but an event that takes place in the encounter with the text. Meaning rises gradually from the background of the linguistic meanings handed down by the tradition, and through the primary expectation of wholeness (the fore-conception of completion) present in all understanding (1975, p. 261).

Gadamer draws mainly four consequences from this hermeneutical standpoint. First, since all experience is constituted by linguisticality, human *experience is inherently historical* in nature (4) (1975, pp. 267-68). Through language, tradition and past are present in our everyday experience. Gadamer calls this *effective-historical consciousness*: "... the linguistic constitution of the world ... presents itself as the consciousness that is effected by history and that provides an initial schematisation for all our possibilities of knowing" (1976a, p. 13). This is a condition of all experience, and interpretative understanding cannot then simply delete the prejudices handed down by the tradition, it can only reflexively criticise and deepen our understanding of them and how they orient our thinking (2) and (5):

> Hermeneutical reflection fulfils the function that is accomplished in all bringing of something to a conscious awareness ... only through hermeneutical reflection ... can [I] deem freely what in my preunderstanding may be justified and what unjustifiable (1976b, p. 38).

Second, the linguisticality of pre-understanding implies that research within the human sciences must proceed on the basis of an internal process of *questions and answers* (6) (1975, pp. 325-26). No interpretation can fully overcome ones prejudices, but it is confined to asking its questions, and giving its answers, in relation to exactly that pre-understanding. All interpretation is thus historically situated and depends on the particular questions raised by the researcher.

Third, the interpretative process must be understood, not on the basis of a model of observation and testing, but as a *conversation* and *dialogue* (6) (1975, pp. 345-46). In the interpretation of a historical document, the dialogue primarily takes place between the interpreter and the text, where the text is seen to give a kind of conversational feedback in relation to the questions asked. In addition, no interpretation takes place in a social vacuum, and every interpretation take sup a relation with previous research and other contemporary research. It thus participates in a never-ending dialogue.

Fourth, Gadamer's insists that hermeneutics is not centred on the question of *methodology*, but on *truth* (1975, p. xi). The idea of scientific method conveys the idea of subjecting an object to some priory determined principles. But if the historically biased pre-givenness of meaning in experiential understanding is a condition of interpretation, and if understanding is an event that takes place in the encounter with the object, the very idea of interpretation is opposed to the idea of being guided by a method. Interpretation demands that one lets the text, and through that the effective-historical consciousness, speak for itself, without being predetermined by principles of method (1975, p. 420ff). According to Gadamer, the truth of historical objects does not primarily appear through a methodological filter, but in the encounter itself. The task of interpretation is to study the prejudices of meaning present in this encounter, and through that to deepen understanding and to deepen the truth of the object (whatever that might mean).

Interpretation is thus a process of *assimilation*. Furthermore, the reflexive process of immanent critique that takes place in the testing of ones understanding in interpretation (2) — that is, in scientific research within the human sciences — is not oriented towards freeing oneself from one's bonds with history. Instead, interpretation is necessarily *application* [Anwendung] (6): "... we consider application to be as integral a part of the hermeneutical act as are understanding and interpretation" (1975, p. 275). Thus, interpretative research necessarily *participates in contemporary history*.

In the essay "Die Universalität des hermeneutischen Problems" Gadamer specifies this view by explicitly grounding it on a *diagnosis of the times*. According to Gadamer, contemporary aesthetic, historical and hermeneutical consciousness are alienated. The reason for this alienation is the experience of a cleavage between the scientific investigation of art, texts and history and our everyday experience of them (1976a, pp. 4-5). He thus defines his task as "... to transcend the prejudices that underlie the aesthetic consciousness, the historical consciousness and the hermeneutical consciousness ... and to overcome the alienations present in them all" (1976a, p. 8). Gadamer in fact generalises this diagnosis to concern the whole of the present epoch. Again and again in his writings, he emphasises that the central task of our age is "... to reconcile the objective world of technology, which the sciences place at our disposal and discretion..." (1976a, p. 3-4) with our concrete experiences of the world in which we live, experiences which cannot so easily be considered in terms of technological practice.

Gadamer's contrast between science and hermeneutics culminates in his analogy of hermeneutical research with "moral knowledge [sittlichen

Wissen] ... [whose] purpose [is] ... to govern ones actions" (1975, p. 280). Gadamer's falls back on the classical ideals of learning as edification [*Bildung*] and practical wisdom (Aristotelian *phronesis*). In the final analysis then, Gadamer's claims are intended *to change the discursive self-understanding of the human sciences,* from the modern ideal of an objective and neutral knowledge, to a more classical ideal of a wisdom that participates in the self-formation of human history (6).

Language vs. Praxis

I have thus outlined some central characteristics of hermeneutics, and given an overview of Gadamer's standpoint. The two accounts go together in the sense that some version of all of (1)-(6) can be found in my account of Gadamer. My primary intention, however, is neither to discuss neither hermeneutics nor Gadamer as such, but to investigate the hermeneutical aspects of Sartre's anthropology. I shall thus consider my characterisation as a certain kind of generalisation, in the light of which the hermeneutical traits of Sartre's anthropology may become visible. It is thus tailored for the purpose to raise certain questions concerning the relation between Sartre and hermeneutics.

One such question concerns the relation between the paradigms of language and praxis. If Sartre's standpoint may be characterised as hermeneutical, it must be seen as a hermeneutics centred on *praxis*. But this initially appears to be a contradiction in terms. Modern hermeneutics is typically centred, not on the individual and practical goal-oriented nature of action, but on our *language*-mediated cultural, social and historical embeddedness in the given. The emphasis on praxis initially appears to blur this basic emphasise on cultural belongingness, and revert to a philosophy of the subject. To emphasise action is not to emphasise the historically transmitted and the socially given, but ones possibilities to influence and change ones own life, despite the circumstances. In this sense, hermeneutics and praxis-philosophy appears to be mutually exclusive options.

I claim, however, that Sartre's conception of praxis is to be interpreted in a fashion that is close to hermeneutics. First, Sartre's conception of praxis emphasises being-in-the-world. Second, according to Sartre, the meaning of praxis is never reducible to the intentions of the agent, but depends on the internal bond between action and the socio-material circumstances. Thus, although Sartre is keen to preserve a domain of freedom in human life, freedom cannot be understood, and not be authentic, outside its place in the material, social and historical present. I shall return to this issue below.

As I said, hermeneutics has traditionally been concerned with texts or text-like objects. The modern transformations of hermeneutics — first into a general problem of the human and social sciences and then into a problem of fundamental philosophical importance — have gradually loosened this connection with the paradigm of the text. In the contemporary debate the question of the text plays a minor role, outside of its self-evident status for example in literary interpretation. An exception is Paul Ricoeur, who still claims that "... the human sciences may be said to be hermeneutical (1) inasmuch as their *object* displays some of the features constitutive of a text as text, and (2) inasmuch as their *methodology* develops the same kind of procedures as those of Auslegung or text-interpretation" (1981a, p. 197).

Contemporary hermeneutics, from Gadamer to Rorty, focuses rather on *linguisticality* than on texts. The emphasis on linguisticality traces the presence of language, language skills, linguistic practices and historically transmitted interpretative models at the core of experience. According to Gadamer, language *is* "... the medium of hermeneutical experience" (Gadamer 1975, p. 345). Although this is the case, it is significant that Gadamer exemplifies this universality mainly with our encounter with *cultural artefacts*, such as works of art, documents and texts.

On the other hand, one cannot really charge Gadamer for neglecting the dimension of praxis. Quite the contrary, Gadamer's emphasis on *application* and *practical wisdom* places praxis at the centre of his conception. How is this co-presence of linguisticality and praxis to be understood?

Gadamer mainly discusses the relation between theory and praxis as a question concerning philosophy of science. He emphasises that interpretation is both theoretical and practical. He criticises the idea that science is pure theory, and, in his diagnosis of the times, that the practical dimension of science must necessarily be understood as technological output. The praxis of interpretation is not an external application of results to practical issues, but an internal feature of interpretation itself. Thus, he primarily discusses *the praxis of interpretation*, but not *the interpretation of praxis*, or praxis as an object of interpretation. In this sense Sartre's outlook differs from Gadamer's, for he focuses on the intelligibility of praxis, and not the intelligibility of human linguisticality, as the primary problem.

If the hermeneutical problem is to be truly universal, as Gadamer claims, linguisticality must be applicable to all the experiential domains of human reality. This seems to be exactly what Gadamer claims, for example, when he expands the domain of hermeneutics to the social sciences (1971, pp. 57-82 and 1975a, pp. 307-16). According to a dominant line of social science, however, their primary domain is not linguistically transmitted meanings, but *social action*. The question then arises whether the universality claimed by Gadamer is also applicable to the study of social action. If Gadamer's claim is interpreted to mean that 'linguisticality' equals 'meaningfulness', I have no other quarrel with him than the use of the word 'language' in this context. For even if one grants that the social sciences study social actions, they do not study actions as empirical objects found in the world, but as linguistically expressed narratives of actions. One could thus well claim that the linguisticality of experience is a universal condition for the interpretation of praxis.

However, as Habermas claims in *Zur Logik der Sozialwissenschaften*:

> An interpretative sociology that hypostatises language as the subject of life-forms and of tradition binds itself to the idealist presupposition that linguistically articulated consciousness determines the material being of life-practice. But the objective context of social action is not reducible to the dimension of intersubjectively intended and symbolically transmitted meaning ... *The objective context in terms of which alone social action can be understood is constituted conjointly by language, labour and domination* ... Sociology may therefore not be reduced to interpretative sociology (1988, p. 173-74).

An overemphasis on linguisticality risks neglecting the dimensions of labour and domination so central to social life.

Richard Bernstein, again, interprets the consequences of hermeneutics as a need to go *beyond hermeneutics towards praxis*, that is "... to the genuinely practical task of concretely realising in our historical situation what [Gadamer] has so nobly defended as being central to our humanity" (Bernstein 1985, p. 290), that is conversation and dialogue. In so far as this implies that we would have to leave philosophy and engage in practical issues (this is not something Bernstein says, but what he says can be interpreted in that way), I cannot see this as an argument that could lead *philosophy* beyond hermeneutics.

In the following I shall thus distinguish between *a hermeneutics of the text and language* and *a hermeneutics of human existence and praxis*. I place Gadamer in the first group and Sartre in the second. Although Sartre interprets praxis as inherently social, meaning carrying and linguistic, he nevertheless retains a primacy of praxis in relation to language. Or, to be more specific, Sartre understands the *nature of language exactly as a kind of praxis*: language is primarily communicative, and communication is a form of praxis. This rift between the paradigms of language and praxis is, of course, neither limited to the relation between Gadamer and Sartre nor to the problem of hermeneutics. Since the primacy of language is closely connected to a primacy of the given, of the past and of passivity, whereas the primacy of praxis emphasises action and future-orientation; the rift is characteristic of a much wider field within contemporary thought. It is a tension that cuts across 20th-century thought.

In summary then, my distinction between a hermeneutics centred on language and an attempt to view the *interpretation of praxis as a hermeneutical problem*, is not intended to construct a rigid dichotomy of paradigms, but to raise the issue of the relation between a perspective centred on language and one centred on the social dimensions of action to the foreground. This I consider to be a fruitful approach to a study of relation between Sartre and hermeneutics, as one important part of an assessment of the contemporary relevance of Sartre's anthropology.

Notes

1 See for example Sartre 1962, p. 24, BN, pp. 430 and 569, NE, p. 433-5. The passage in NE is one of the few places where Sartre explicitly discusses hermeneutics. The term itself is only mentioned twice, however. Notably Sartre here tries to answer the question "what is the structure of our society that provokes the appearance of this emphasis on hermeneutics?" (p. 435) by a discussion on the relation between action, creativity, realisation and failure.

2 Cf. Taylor 1971, von Wright 1971 and Dreyfus 1980. The second question asked by Dreyfus — "If there were ... a difference [between the natural and the human sciences], what personal and political difference would it make" (p. 3) — shows a clear shift of emphasise from the more narrowly formulated problems of the philosophy of science to broader issues, for example, in relation to Taylor's and von Wright's earlier contributions. The polemic contribution of Rorty (1980) is one obvious (philosophical) source for this shift.

3 See Rorty 1980, pp. 361-79. Rorty, it seems to me, does not as much base his characterisation of Sartre on a close reading of Sartre's writings, but on a kind of easily identifiable ground tone of Sartrean existentialism as it has been known since EN.

4 Fehér 1994, pp. 69-71. Fehér does observe that Sartre attempts "... to give a ... phenomenological-hermeneutical foundation to historical materialism" (p. 69), but he does not consider the methodological stance of Sartre as a hermeneutical trait.

5 I do, however, find the idea that Gadamer is unimportant for hermeneutics quite a strange reinterpretation of that term. The kind of turn to a radical kind of hermeneutics that is expressed by Caputo, through its connections with Derridean deconstruction, manifests a turn in a completely different direction

than what is the case with Sartre's later philosophy. Whereas Sartre turns his attention from the internal problems of the cogito, its being and self-understanding, to the task of making the socio-historical circumstances intelligible, exactly for the sake of understanding ourselves better, the Derrida-Caputo orientation (strongly inspired by Heidegger) constitutes a kind of 'second turn inwards'. This time, the turn is not concerned with consciousness, but with the inner complex of the relation between of being and discourse. This is of interest especially for the problem of the self-understanding of discourse and philosophy, but such issues are not immediate concerns for Sartre.

5 Sartre's Conception of Human Being and Philosophical Standpoint

General Features of Sartre's Conception of Human Being

In this chapter I do mainly two things. First, I discuss Sartre's *conception of human being*, mainly as it is expressed in CRD. In order to do this; I shall give a brief presentation of some of the main ideas in EN. Second, I examine the *philosophical standpoint* that stands at the basis of this conception. I bring forward especially Sartre's concern with *concrete human reality*, his focus on material and social *bonds of interiority between man and world*, and give an outline of the *hermeneutical* traits present in CRD.

Sartre's rejection of the idea of a universal human nature is not interpreted in a purely negative sense. That is, it does not imply the impossibility of an anthropological philosophy as such, nor of a conception of man, but indicates a need to transpose the problems of anthropology to another level of reflection. Thus:

(1) in the place of a theory of human nature, Sartre proposes a *method* by means of which the particular and unique features of human life can be made intelligible, and

(2) in a characteristically existential-phenomenological fashion, Sartre replaces the idea of a theory of human nature with an *ontology of human existence*. Whereas a theory of human nature seems to imply deciding what is and what is not essential to human beings on a generalising level, an ontology of existence is more limited in scope. It is oriented towards the discernment of general conditions and structures, on the basis of which human beings shape and reshape them and their reality. According to Sartre, in human life essence is always connected to the individual (the appropriation of past being, the constitution of a psychological character), whereas conditions may be common, even universal. Since this idea is reminiscent of the goals of a philosophical anthropology, although it rejects

the idea of a theory of human nature, I shall call it a *modified kind of philosophical anthropology*. It is important to recognise that this *forms only a part of* what Sartre means by anthropology.

These two tasks of an ontology of existence and a methodology are naturally closely connected with each other. In fact, *the ontology*, that expresses a conception of man, *is to form the ground of the method*. The ontology developed by Sartre, first in EN and then in CRD, emphasises both a certain level of *generality* (all human being shape their being by means of what they do) and *historicity* (what human beings do is internally dependent on historical reality).

Thus, according to Sartre, since Kierkegaard certain philosophers "... have succeeded in better describing what we might call the 'ontological region of existences'" (SM, p. 167 (124)). In a manner reminiscent of Heidegger's argumentation in *Sein und Zeit*[1], Sartre indicates that although ontology is not restricted to the being of the human, any philosophy must necessarily begin with a study of the human mode of existence:

> ... it is evident that the *presence-in-the-world* described by these ideologists[2] characterises a sector — or perhaps the whole — of the animal world. But within this living universe, man occupies, *for us*, a privileged place. First, because he is able to be historical; that is, he can continually define himself by his own *praxis* ... Second, because he is characterised as *the existent which we are* (SM, p. 167 (124)).

Sartre thus continues to affirm the importance of an ontology, although he now localises its nucleus in the *historical reality of praxis*. This modification also leads Sartre to emphasise, more clearly than before, the two tasks involved in dealing with the problem of understanding human beings and human reality: ontology is important as a ground, but it can only form a very abstract ground, what is needed in addition is a way of approaching *the concretely lived*. This concern was expressed especially in Sartre's method and in existential biographies.

In certain passages in QM Sartre indicates in outline the closest to what he ever comes to an expression of his later, modified ontology and conception of man. The notions he uses refer both to EN and indicates in which way that standpoint has been modified. First, he defines human existence as a *future-oriented project*.

> Man defines himself by his project. This material being perpetually goes beyond the condition which is made for him; he reveals and determines his

> situation by transcending it in order to objectify himself — by work, action or gesture ... This immediate relation with the Other than oneself, beyond the given and constituted elements, this perpetual production of oneself by work and *praxis*, is our peculiar structure ... our needs — like our passions or like the most abstract of our thoughts — participate in this structure. They are always *outside of themselves toward* . . . This is what we call existence, and with this we do not mean a stable substance which rests in itself, but rather a perpetual disequilibrium, a wrenching away from itself with all its body (SM, pp. 150-51 (113-14)).

By 'the mode of being of the project' Sartre thus means both individuals bonds of interiority with the world, and that human beings always surpass these conditions in their praxeis.

Second, from the point of view of the task to interpret concrete human beings and human reality, the *ontology of project* is limited. Although it defines the source of intelligibility of human beings, real life and history do not simply constitute a repetition of ontological categories, but are the result of concrete praxis: "The dialectic itself ... appears as History and as historical Reason only *upon the foundation of existence*; for it is the development of *praxis*, and *praxis* is inconceivable without *need*, *transcendence* and the *project*" (SM, p. 171 (126), my italics). That is, praxis indeed manifests the structure of existence, but the particularities of the real always outstrip categories.

Sartre then gives a more comprehensive account of the ontological structure at the background of praxis and history:

> Whatever the discipline considered, its most elementary notions would be *incomprehensible* without the *immediate comprehension* of the *project* which underlies them, of negativity as the basis of the project, of transcendence as the existence outside-of-itself in relation with the Other-than-itself and the Other-than-man, of the surpassing as a mediation between the given that is simply there and the practical signification, of *need*, finally as the being-outside-of-itself-in-the-world on the part of the practical organism (SM, p. 171 (126)).

These passages together thus indicate both the idea to base an investigation of historical human beings and human reality on a *general ontology*, and the imperative to focus any real attempt to understand on the (materially and socially) *real expressions of praxis*. An attempt to understand, according to Sartre, implies to study the real, and this again means to study how the general and universal conditions indicated by ontology *are concretely lived by particular human beings*. I shall proceed my exposition on the basis of this two-level model of an *ontology of the general structure of human existence* and an *interpretative concern with the concretely lived.*

Sartre's conception of human being, both in CRD and EN, is oriented by three basic ideas:

(1) A human being is *a being-in-the-world* that must be understood on the basis of his/her *bonds of interiority* with the world. Sartre criticises the atomisation of human being into non-social, self-sufficient individual units (Cartesian subject-philosophy). As is well known, this does not prevent him from claiming that human beings are individuals, free and responsible both for what they are and what they do.

The bonds of interiority with the world are both material and social, and in two senses. Human existence is itself a material (bodily) fact, and human beings stand in a concrete, internal relation to the material environment (conditions, instrumental possibilities, etc.). Furthermore, in the very internality of our consciousness, understanding and projects, we recognise the presence of other conscious and practical beings (being-for-others), and we always take up some concrete relation with others.

(2) A human being is *a free being of action.* Consciousness, behaviour and personal identity are, in the final instance, to be understood in terms of what we make of ourselves, that is, in terms of actions, undertakings, praxis, etc.

According to Sartre, we shape and reshape our life and character through what we do. This does not mean that it takes place in a planned, organised or reflective manner (although it may certainly be influenced by reflective thought). Sartre denies that we may have a complete overview of the totalising process whereby we shape ourselves, and that we shape ourselves autonomously. The real meaning of what we do, are and make of ourselves necessarily remains beyond a full self-understanding.

(3) A human being is *a whole.* Sartre's conception of human being is strongly *holistic*, although his holism neither implies the idea of an inner unity, nor that unity would be stable and exclude conflicts and tensions. On the contrary, a human person is a continuously on-going process of *totalisation*, whereby one constantly internalises and integrates the given (into experience), and externalises these internalisations in the singularities of actions, undertakings and the particularity of a life.

These — *bonds of interiority with the world*, *action* and *lived totalisation*

— make up the general features of Sartre's conception of human being.

I shall elucidate this conception beginning with an account of Sartre's ontology in EN. Before that, let me briefly restate, and slightly reconceptualize, the list of ontological categories found in the passages quoted above:

(i) project
(ii) negativity
(iii) transcendence
(iv) facticity (Other-than-man)
(v) intersubjectivity (Other-than-himself)
(vi) praxis
(vii) surpassing
(viii) materiality-instrumentality (the given as simply there)
(ix) signification
(x) need
(xi) inorganic materiality (the being-outside-itself of the organism)

In this one can quite clearly see what features of the philosophy of EN Sartre sticks with, and what modifications he wants. The first five are terms found in EN, while the last six are treated mainly in CRD and related works. Even a brief glance on the list, however, reveals that many notions that are here listed as different are similar in kind to each other. For example, it is clear that the categories of project, transcendence, praxis and surpassing repeat a similar figure of thought (the idea of a processual going beyond). The same is the case with the concepts of facticity, materiality-instrumentality and inorganic materiality (materiality).

In the following I shall use this list as an interpretative key for an outline of Sartre's conception of man. In order to clarify these categories I shall first give a brief introduction to the philosophy of EN. My exposition is oriented by the question of Sartre's conception of man. This means that I shall not give a covering account of the phenomenological ontology of EN as such, but pick out those issues that are particularly relevant for the questions asked. I shall also approach the list above in a slightly other order.

The Idea of a Phenomenological Ontology

The philosophical standpoint of Sartre can hardly be clarified without a treatment of the two main orientations that influenced Sartre: *phenomenology* and *ontology*. In an interview given in 1975, Sartre reaffirmed the twin presence of these. He declares that "philosophy is an inquiry concerning being and beings. Any thought that does not lead to an inquiry concerning being is not valid", and on Susan Gruenheck's question, "I have the impression that you continue to reflect as a phenomenologist. Have you ever left phenomenology?", Sartre answers: "Never. I continue to think in those terms" (1981a, pp. 14 and 24).

In my opinion, Sartre's understanding of phenomenology must crucially be understood in the light of Heidegger's transformation of Husserlian phenomenology into ontology. This has not always been taken for granted. For instance, Thomas W. Busch, although he criticises certain interpreters for neglecting phenomenology, almost completely neglects Sartre's incorporation of Heidegger's ontological turn (Busch 1980 and 1990). In my (and, for example, Chiodi's (1976, pp. 8-10)) opinion, CRD, even more strongly than EN incorporates the insights of Heidegger, although in a different way than the latter.

Phenomenology can be generally characterised as a philosophy concerned with the constitution, essence or mode of being of *our experience of the world*, taken as investigated from the *internal perspective* of this experience itself.[3] Indeed, phenomenology is based on the thesis that such an internal perspective is both (negatively) our *only possible access to this domain* and (positively) the *very fact that makes such an access possible*. The internal perspective is a *foundation*, not in the sense of a judgement of validity, but as the necessary vantagepoint of all philosophical reflection.

The *hermeneutical turn* of phenomenology largely consists in an attempt to carry through a *historized re-interpretation* of this thesis. If consciousness is internally related to its object, the object is historically situated, and, furthermore, if philosophical reflection cannot claim any stronger validity than to mirror historized consciousness, it must be understood as a historized mode of reflection. This, again, seems to remove any possibility for claims to universality and certainty, at least outside the certainty of historicity itself.

In EN Sartre conceives of phenomenology in a way that (uneasily) combines a Husserlian philosophy of *consciousness* with a Heideggerian *ontology* of human being-in-the-world and *existence* (BN, pp. xxi-xxxviii and 73-74, Sartre 1967, p. 132). Sartre follows Heidegger in his assertion of the primacy of the question of being. But he criticises Heidegger for his refusal to talk about consciousness in his attempt to overcome the language of dualism. Although Sartre also describes his work as an attempt to overcome the Cartesian dualism of subject and object, he did not believe that this would imply a total rejection of talk about consciousness. Sartre's solution is more Hegelian: he posits the idea of a processual 'dialectic' of subject and object, in which the internal relation between the two is affirmed.[4]

According to Husserl, phenomenology is "... the most fundamental region of philosophy" and "... *pure or transcendental phenomenology will be established ... as a science of essential Being* ... a science which aims exclusively at establishing 'knowledge of essences' and *absolutely no 'facts'*" (1962, pp. 37 and 40). Husserl's conception is based on a procedure of a series of reductions (or abstractions), considered the ultimate gate of access to the correct level of reflection (ibid., pp. 91-104). The object studied is *the essence of experience* or *consciousness*. Such an inquiry is not concerned with the facts of experience, but with its essence, and it is not an empirical science (ibid. pp. 45-57).

Husserl's phenomenology is transcendental in the sense that it studies the general and universal features of consciousness on a certain level of abstraction. For example, in what Husserl calls the natural standpoint, we simply assert the existence of what we perceive. In order to study consciousness as such we have to bracket all questions about the existence or non-existence of the phenomena encountered, along with all the truths established by the sciences (ibid. pp. 91-104). Since the sciences of fact presuppose experience as their foundation, the study of essence is more fundamental than all questions of fact. Husserl's transcendentalism differs from that of Kant in that Husserl does not inquiry into the conditions of *possibility* of experience, conditions that are, so to speak, located behind concrete experience. Instead he studies the internal structure of consciousness as such. The outcome is then not a series of abstract categories (relation, possibility, causality, etc.), but the structure common and inherent to all kinds of experience: *intentionality*, or that all consciousness is a consciousness of something, or directed towards an object. According to Husserl, 'intentionality' is a certain correlation between a noetic act of consciousness (perception, imagination, etc.) and a noematic or meaningful object (the blossoming apple-tree in the garden) (ibid. pp. 883, 200-1, 222).

The method employed by Husserl may be described as the reflection on the primordial intuitions present in concrete experience (ibid. pp. 105, 111-32). The possibility of such reflection is grounded in the inherent possibility of consciousness to study its own essence. Thus, reflective consciousness is able to reveal and express in language the fact that it is itself, in its essence, a being that posits or intends objects.

Heidegger's critique of transcendental phenomenology, and his turn to an ontological phenomenology, constitutes a rejection of the primacy of the question of knowledge and of Husserl's bracketing of the question of being (1962, pp. 61-63). Heidegger follows Husserl in adopting a phenomenological outlook in the sense of an investigation of essences, but he observes that human experience is to be defined, not in terms of a universal like intentionality, but in terms of its *mode of being*. According to Heidegger, the primary essence of human being, or Dasein[5], is not intentionality, but to be a *being-in-the-world* that is individually *concerned with its own being* (ibid., pp. 13 and 42). A human being is not primarily an inner subject, but a presence in the world. And the relation between an individual and his or her essence is not to be defined in terms of the specimen (this consciousness) of a universal (intentionality), but in terms of the universality that each one is individually concerned with his or her own being. For human beings, being is not a given and self-evident fact, but implies the possibility of different ways of living this mode of being. Heidegger thus describes human beings in terms of *project* (Entwurf) and *care* (Sorge): a human being is *thrown out in the world* and his being is a *task* to care for (ibid., pp. 358-82).

Heidegger interprets these possibilities in terms of two basic modalities: *inauthentic* (Uneigentlich) and *authentic* (Eigentlich) being (ibid., p. 68). In our inauthentic being we simply perform our everyday practices and busy ourselves with things in the world as given, whereas in an authentic mode of existence we understand ourselves in terms of our fundamental mode of being: individuality, possibility, wholeness, etc. Heidegger, however, rejects an ethical interpretation of these terms.

Heidegger's investigation is an attempt to overcome two perspectives which he finds constitutive for Husserl and the tradition preceding him: the dualism between subject and object and the primacy of epistemology (ibid., pp. 28-49, 87-90, 122-34). By regarding human experience as the intentional positing of things in the world, and by studying this problem on the level of knowledge, Husserl falls along the line of these two prejudices. The ontological perspective of Heidegger, on the other hand, posits experience in terms of our activities in the world, and our preoccupation with our own being.

Whereas phenomenology for Husserl was mainly motivated by *epistemological* concerns, and Heidegger's turn to a phenomenological ontology was mainly motivated by his concerns with *ontology*, for Sartre phenomenology is turned into a concern with *concrete human reality*. Thus, in one of his first accounts of phenomenology, the essay "La Transcendance de l'ego", Sartre claims that:

> The phenomenologists have plunged man back into the world; they have given full measure to man's agonies and sufferings, and also to his rebellions (1957, p. 105).

In EN, again, Sartre interprets the shortcomings of dualism, and the corresponding worth of Heidegger's idea of being-in-the-world, exactly as a thesis about concreteness:

> ... consciousness is an abstraction since it conceals within itself an ontological source in the region of the in-itself, and conversely, the phenomenon is likewise an abstraction since it must 'appear' to consciousness. The concrete can be only the synthetic totality of which consciousness, like the phenomenon, constitutes only moments. The concrete is man within the world in that specific union of man with the world which Heidegger, for example, calls 'being-in-the-world' (BN, p. 3 (37)).

Sartre defines concreteness, borrowing from Laporte, in terms of *what may be said to exist by itself alone*: "... an abstraction is made when something not capable of existing in isolation is thought of as in an isolated state. The concrete by contrast is a totality which can exist by itself alone" (BN, p. 3 (37)).

In retrospective comments Sartre observes that this concern in EN with the concrete misses its goal. In fact, he now explains the difference between EN and CRD exactly as a shift from the abstract to the concrete: "EN is a general point of view, a fundamental point of view. And CRD is a point of view that on the contrary is social and concrete. The one is abstract, studies general truths, and the other is not so concerned with that and places itself upon the plane of the concrete" (Sartre 1980, p. 225). In QM, again, Sartre claims that he has finally understood that the concrete is neither just an existential structure, nor individual "... man and things in their 'concrete' existence ... [but] history and dialectical action" (SM, pp. 20-21 (30)).

These differences in orientation are clearly present in Sartre's critique of Heidegger. First, Heidegger's way of situating understanding immediately on the level of the internal bond between experience, existence and world should not, according to Sartre, neglect that understanding is a form of consciousness: "Heidegger ... begins with the existential analytic of the Dasein without going through the cogito. But since the Dasein has from the start been deprived of the dimension of consciousness, it can never regain this dimension ... how could there be an understanding which would not in itself be the consciousness (of) being understanding?" (BN, p. 73 (111-12)). An important motive for Sartre is that, without the concept of consciousness, it is difficult to uphold a distinction between pre-reflexivity and reflection, and to affirm our responsibilities for what we do (see Scott 1981 and Haar 1980). Heidegger's concept of understanding overemphasises our bond with the world, and neglects the idea of reflective intervention.

Second, Heidegger has neglected the dimension of authentic action as a real intervention in the world. Although Heidegger indeed declares that doing is a cardinal category of existence, his views on action are mainly situated on the level of the inauthentic. According to Scott (1981, p. 286), whereas enlightenment for Heidegger is oriented toward the thinking being, his care of self, being-toward death and the possibility of wholeness, enlightenment for Sartre is oriented towards the possibility of undeceived and non-alienated action in the social world. Sartre thus criticises Heidegger for his conception of inauthenticity as 'loosing oneself in the world' and to see authenticity as 'contemplative':

> It is not the through inauthenticity that human reality loses itself in the world. For human reality, being-in-the-world means radically to lose oneself in the world ... that is, to be referred without respite ... from instrument to instrument with no recourse save the reflective revolution (BN, p. 200 (242)).

According to Sartre, 'the reflective revolution' should not lead to a contemplative care of self, but to active and responsible engagement in the world.

Third, on similar grounds Sartre criticises Heidegger's conception of intersubjectivity. Heidegger has indeed affirmed sociality (Mitsein), but he still focuses on the opposition between the social being of inauthentic everyday existence (das Man) and the individuality of authentic existence. Authenticity is seen as the surpassing of oneself towards ones own innermost possibilities, in a non-social sense. The analysis of intersubjectivity, although a step in the right direction, is not able to affirm intersubjectivity strongly enough (BN, p. 247ff).

In summary then, in Sartre phenomenological ontology becomes gradually transformed, from a concern with the issues of epistemology and ontology, to a concern with *understanding concrete human reality*. This transformation is only partly completed in EN, more fully so in CRD. In the remainder of this chapter I shall first give an account of some of the themes of EN, and then of the hermeneutisation of this standpoint in CRD.

Consciousness as Transcendence

Sartre's theory of consciousness in EN is intended to remove all traits of an (Cartesian or Husserlian) idealistic philosophy of an inner and primarily epistemic subject, and (in a Heideggerian fashion) to replace it with an existential philosophy centred on consciousness' bond of interiority with the world. In order to achieve this Sartre raises the notion of *transcendence* to the foreground. Sartre reinterprets Husserl's thesis that consciousness is intentional in character to mean that *the mode of being of consciousness is transcendence*.[6]

The technical notion of transcendence means 'being beyond' or 'going beyond' (see Morris 1985, pp. 182-84). Whereas in Kant the transcendent is what experience cannot possibly reach — something genuinely beyond experience (e.g. the transcendence of God) — Sartre uses the notion to describe human experience as such. Thus, by 'transcendence' Sartre means 'to be beyond oneself in the world' and 'to pass beyond objects towards their meanings, one's aims, the future, etc.' (BN, pp. xxxvii-xxxix).

Sartre actually uses the notion of transcendence in two senses: as the *structural feature of consciousness seen as active* and in order to describe the *relation between object and consciousness*.[7] Beginning with the latter, Sartre's notion repeats Heidegger's concept of *being-in-the-world* on the level of consciousness. It emphasises that consciousness is not a substantial, inner subject, but that consciousness is primarily a relation with the world:

> The first procedure of a philosophy ought to be to expel things from consciousness and to re-establish its true connection with the world, to know that consciousness is a positional consciousness *of* the world. All consciousness is positional in that it transcends itself in order to reach an object, and it exhausts itself in the same positing. All that there is of intention in my actual consciousness is directed toward the outside (BN, pp. xxvii-iii (18)).

Sartre consequently reinterprets the phenomenological thesis of intentionality as a thesis affirming the worldliness of consciousness:

> All consciousness is consciousness of something ... This means that transcendence is the constitutive structure of consciousness; that is, that consciousness is born *supported by* a being which is not itself. This is what we call the ontological proof ... for consciousness there is no being outside of that precise obligation to be a revealing intuition of something — *i.e.*, of a transcendent being (BN, pp. xxxvi-ii (27)).

According to this first use of 'transcendence' (opposed by Morris to 'immanence'), consciousness is neither autonomous nor separated from the world. The primary reality of consciousness is to be a being-in-the-world; it is *in* the world, its directedness is *of* the world and it does not have any independent being outside of such a positing-revealing. This may be read as a defence of *realism*, since it postulates the primacy of the real world (and existence) to consciousness and ideas: "... consciousness is an abstraction, since it conceals within itself an ontological source in the region of the in-itself" (BN, p. 3 (37)).

Sartre also uses 'transcendence' in order to communicate that the relation between consciousness and world is fundamentally *active* or *processual* in character. Thus, by 'the transcendence of consciousness' Sartre also means that consciousness necessarily passes beyond the given (BN, p. xxix). For example, in the perception of a chair, consciousness spontaneously passes beyond the physical features of the object and the particularity of the perspective, towards meanings like 'chair' or 'something to sit on': "the perceived is originally the surpassed" (BN, p. 192 (233)). In imagination, again, consciousness passes beyond the given towards the absent, the non-existent, etc. (an imagined chair, a unicorn). And in action, the goal is posited as 'something to be realised in the future'. Thus, Sartre emphasises that in perception, imagination and action one is both dependent on the given (the actual chair, the present world, the circumstances and possibilities of action), and passes beyond it. That is, being-in-the-world precedes but does not determine active transcendence: transcendence implies both *facticity* and *freedom*.

As is well known, Sartre posits the category of *negativity* or *nothingness* (le néant) as the ontological 'source' of consciousness and its freedom (BN pp. 3-70). The (necessarily always present) possibility for us to take up negative attitudes in relation to the world is a condition of the possibility of consciousness. It also implies freedom, although neither social freedom nor the moral freedom to do whatever one likes (see e.g. BN, p. 483). In this work I shall not make any extensive use of Sartre's philosophy (metaphysics) of being and nothingness. It is not, in my opinion, kernel for Sartre's views on anthropology in CRD, although he has in no way abandoned the use of 'concepts of negativity'.[8]

Pre-reflexivity and Reflective Consciousness

The interpretation of consciousness as a kind of arrow-like directedness towards objects is not sufficient to define consciousness. What makes directedness into a conscious directedness? A robot that transforms a plate of metal into the side-door of a car may be claimed to be directed in a transcending sense (even if one recognises that these meanings are human): it grabs something and changes its form. Nevertheless, we would not call the robot 'conscious'. What is, then, the essential characteristic of human consciousness?

Sartre's answers by introducing the crucial notion of *pre-reflexive, non-positional self-consciousness* (BN, pp. xxvi-xxxii, 73-79). He defines pre-reflexive consciousness as a consciousness of self that does not posit the self as an object. According to Sartre, all modes of consciousness (unreflective and reflective) are pre-reflexive, and it is pre-reflexivity that makes directedness into *conscious* directedness. This co-presence of transcendence and pre-reflexivity Sartre calls *being-for-itself*, and he opposes it to the *being-in-itself* of thing-like objects.

Sartre gives several examples of pre-reflexive self-consciousness. When I count items that lie on the table, I am pre-reflexively aware of 'the activity of counting', without needing a reflective plan in order to be able to count. The activity of counting belongs to my repertoire of capacities. But this does not mean that it is done unconsciously. When I count, I am fully aware of what I am doing. Similarly, when I speak I am fully aware of the act of speaking, and when I run in order to catch the tram I do not have reflectively to think about running in order to do it consciously. All such examples communicate the presence of a pre-reflexive, conscious but not contemplative, awareness of the kind of activity one is involved in.

Sartre distinguishes between *consciousness* and *knowledge* (BN, pp. xxvi-xxvii and 172-80, Sartre 1967, pp. 121-25). Pre-reflexive consciousness is the revelation of something as something, but it not a knowledge. The object is revealed as endowed with a certain meaning, and as encountered in a certain mode of consciousness (perception, imagination, etc.), but this awareness does not constitute a propositional knowledge or a presence to truth. Consciousness is a condition of possibility of knowledge, but it is primarily a mode of being. Here Sartre follows in the footsteps of Heidegger's critique of Husserl (Heidegger 1962, pp. 41-49).

Our immediate consciousness of the world thus necessarily encompasses a dimension of self-consciousness. Such self-consciousness is neither positional nor intentionally directed, nor does it constitute a reflective knowledge of self. Crucially, the kind of 'content' or 'self' revealed in pre-reflexivity is not the same as my personal character, the Ego or my true self (see Morris 1985). What one is aware of in pre-reflexive self-consciousness is the *specific act* in which one is involved (counting, speaking, running, imagining, etc.) and their respective objects (1957, pp. 38-42 and BN, pp. 162-70). That is, not *only* the modality of the act ('to run', etc.), but the *concrete act in question*: 'running in order to catch the train', 'seeing the beautiful apple-tree in my neighbours garden a sunny afternoon', etc. This is why Sartre calls this self *impersonal*.

According to Sartre, the immanence of pre-reflexivity is what is usually meant by *subjectivity*. This already points towards the possibility of integrating Sartre with hermeneutics. For such subjectivity implies both the necessity of a pre-structured understanding of the world, and that it constitutes the basis for how I relate to the world. Subjectivity implies a relation to the world of which only I am aware myself, but it does not imply a justified knowledge of the world.

Reflection, or reflective consciousness, is a specific modality of consciousness in which consciousness posits itself as an object (BN, pp. 150-62). Reflective consciousness is both a transcendence and pre-reflexive: it is a positional consciousness of an object (immediate consciousness, which in turn is directed towards the outside) and a pre-reflexive consciousness (of) itself as reflection (Morris 1985, p. 181). Reflection is not, however, necessarily always active, only an inherent possibility of all consciousness.

Sartre posits two different kinds of reflection: *impure* and *pure reflection* (BN, pp. 155-70). By 'impure reflection' is meant an attitude in which consciousness hypostatises a certain kind of object: an Ego or I. Impure reflection is thus an *objectifying consciousness of self*. It does not reveal our true selves, but constructs an object-like Ego (on the basis of the processual flux of immediate consciousness). On the basis of my repeated feelings of hatred towards A, impure reflection objectifies a character such that 'I hate A' or 'I am a person that hates A'.

Pure reflection is an attitude that reveals the *truth* of consciousness. For instance, pure reflection discloses the attitude of objectification as a false hypostatisation, and the Ego as a construction. It discloses the true contingency of my present feelings of hatred, and reveals my thesis that I hate A as unfounded. Pure reflection is thus the mode of investigation characteristic of *philosophical thinking*. It enables us to reveal to ourselves the innermost character of consciousness: transcendence, pre-reflexivity, etc. It may thus be called *interrogative reflection*, in contrast to the *introspective-constructive* mode of impure reflection.

This has at least two consequences. First, it constitutes a thesis of the existence of a consciousness that is able to reveal its own nature, presumably with apodictic certainty and universality. In this sense, Sartre's phenomenology is *Husserlian*. Second, since pure reflection is purifying only in relation to an 'always already' immediate (pre-reflexive) consciousness of the world (and impure reflection), it is bound to work on the basis of a world-embedded pre-understanding. This points towards a *hermeneutical* dimension of Sartre's conception of consciousness, a dimension that Sartre does not, however, explicitly reflect on in EN.

Or does he? Sartre in fact develops two slightly different interrogative perspectives in EN. On the one hand, ontology investigates the general structure of consciousness and reveals certain categories in relation to this (transcendence, pre-reflexivity, reflection, being-for-others, etc.). On the other hand, Sartre posits an investigation of real human beings, which he calls *existential psychoanalysis*. Existential psychoanalysis is typically not interested in the abstract structure of consciousness, but in *the coherence of a life* in terms of the presence of a *fundamental project* (see below), and this kind of investigation, again, Sartre explicitly calls hermeneutical. I shall return to this issue below.

In Figure 1 I have illustrated the basic ideas of Sartre theory of consciousness so far. I have marked the positional directedness of consciousness with a straight-line, and pre-reflexive, non-positional self-awareness with a semicircular line. The curved lines are intended to illustrate the movement of transcendence.

Intersubjectivity as Being-For-Others

Sartre's theory of consciousness is thus grounded in a reflective investigation, which claims to reveal *with certainty* the essential structure of human consciousness. Continuing on this line, Sartre's discourse on intersubjectivity attempts to establish with equal certainty *the necessity of intersubjectivity* at the very heart of consciousness (BN, pp. 221 and 302). In the following I shall focus on Sartre's arguments for certainty, but on the general form of this theory seen as a *descriptive characterisation of intersubjectivity*.

The discussion of intersubjectivity or *being-for-others* appears relatively late in EN. This fact should in my opinion mainly be understood as rooted in the phenomenological order of investigation applied by Sartre. Due to the strongly methodological disposition of the investigation, the

Figure 1. Sartre on the Structure of Consciousness

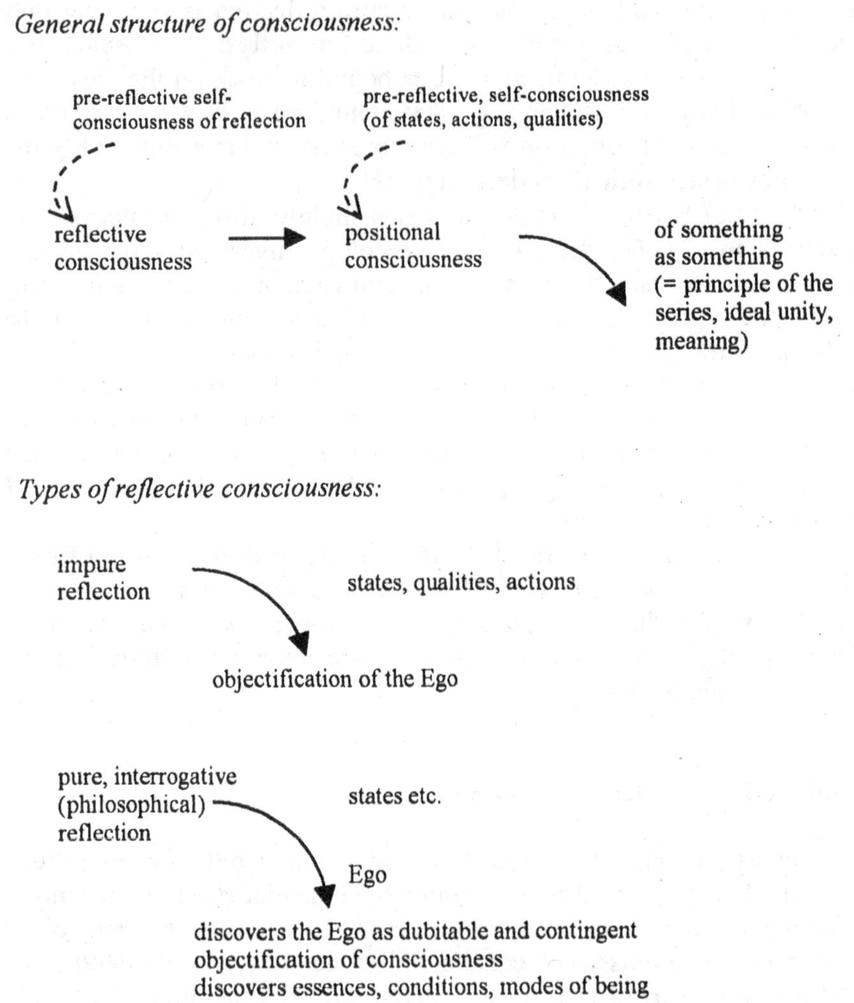

problem of intersubjectivity cannot, according to Sartre, be posed until the general structure of consciousness has been clarified. If one accepts this, it is clear that intersubjectivity has both a strong and important position in Sartre's ontology. *Intersubjectivity is* in fact *constitutive* of Sartre's *conception of man*:

> ... our human-reality must of necessity be simultaneously for-itself and for-others ... It would perhaps not be impossible to conceive of a For-itself which would be wholly free from all For-others ... But this For-itself simply would not be 'man' ... it is found — and this is indisputable — that ... the being which is revealed to the reflective consciousness is for-itself-for-others (BN, p. 282 (329)).

That is, to define human being as being-for-itself (as some commentators do) would grossly distort Sartre's conception.[9]

In line with the phenomenological mode of investigation employed, intersubjectivity must first be dealt with on the level of consciousness. Sartre's argument is intended to establish that intersubjectivity is a *necessary feature of all human consciousness*, that is, of our experience of the world and of ourselves. By this Sartre situates himself within a tradition which affirms primary status to our relations with other human beings: Hegel, Marx, Heidegger, Mead, etc.

According to Sartre, human consciousness has basically three ways of 'being beyond' or 'standing out of' itself (BN, p. 298). First, it stands out of itself by its relations with *objects in the world* (in perception, imagination, emotions, etc.). Second, human beings have the capability to take up reflexive relations with themselves (reflective consciousness). Third, human consciousness stands out of itself by being conscious of *other conscious beings* (being-for-others).

Sartre's discourse on intersubjectivity deals mainly with four phenomena:[10] (1) the being-for-others *inherent in my experience* of the world and myself, (2) my experience of *my own body*, (3) the intersubjectivity of the *meaningful world of things* and (4) the intersubjectivity of *social formations*. I shall here focus on (1), and comment only briefly on (3). I shall not discuss Sartre's conception of the body, and I postpone discussing (4) to Chapter 8. Sartre was himself later particularly dissatisfied with the discourse on social formations in EN (1981a, p. 13), and the theory of 'ensembles pratiques' and the conception of human relations as mediated reciprocities developed in CRD make some important modifications to Sartre's standpoint on intersubjectivity and sociality.

As Theunissen observes, the most original point in Sartre's discourse on intersubjectivity is the way he turns the problem itself around its axis (Theunissen 1984, pp. 200-1 and 211-16). Traditionally the question of other minds has been raised as an epistemological issue of how we can know that there are other minds, so to speak, inside their bodies. Sartre, in contrast, locates the primary form of intersubjectivity at the level of *my own experience of myself.* Intersubjectivity is not primarily found in a perception of the other as conscious body, but in my consciousness of *myself as an object for others* (BN, pp. 221-23 and 251-82). This is why Sartre chooses the term *being-for-others*.

Although Sartre does not set himself the task to prove the existence of other minds, his argument is intended to remove the relevance of the problem of solipsism (BN, p. 250-51). He argues that "without going outside our attitude of reflective description, we can encounter modes of consciousness which seem to ... point to a radically different type of ontological structure [than being-for-itself]" (BN, p. 221 (265)). Certain modes of subjective consciousness are unintelligible without reference to the existence of other conscious beings in the world. These cannot, furthermore, possible have been constructed by the imaginary power of reflection, but themselves point towards the existence of other conscious beings.

The best known examples in Sartre are deeply personal emotions like shame and pride (BN, pp. 221-22 and 259-64). I lean over to look through a keyhole in order to see what is going on in the room. Suddenly I hear a noise. Has someone seen me? I immediately feel ashamed of what I am doing. According to Sartre, such a feeling of shame (or pride) is "... an immediate shudder which runs through me from head to foot without any discursive preparation" (BN, p. 222 (266)). It is also inconceivable without an immediate presupposition that there are other conscious beings in the world; shame has a meaning that refers to others: "... shame is shame of oneself before the other" (ibid.).

The basic experience of being-for-others is my experience of the other's *look*, which makes *me* into an *object for another consciousness* (BN, p. 257-82).[11] In impure reflection I posit myself as an I, in being-for-others I am conferred with objective, social meanings, which appear as immediate, but not as the result of reflection. When I lean over the keyhole and experience myself as looked at, I do not only experience myself as curious (reflection), but also as immoral, bad, shameful, etc. (before others).

Thus, the basic point is to show the presence of intersubjective consciousness *at the very heart of subjectivity.* Already at the level of deeply personal emotions, others are implied. This has important consequences for what may be said to constitute the point of departure for *phenomenological reflection.* The other cannot fall before the phenomenological reduction: consciousness of others is an immanent feature of individual consciousness and of subjectivity.

The exact nature of the relation between reflective consciousness and being-for-others remains largely unspecified. In certain passages Sartre indicates that being-for-others is a *condition* for the possibility of reflective consciousness (BN, 95, 154-55, 298-301 and 349), or at least, a condition for a reflection in which we judge and evaluate ourselves: "... the other is the indispensable mediator between me and myself ... By the mere appearance of the other, I am put in position of passing judgement on myself as on an object, for it is as an object that I appear to the other" (BN, p. 222 (266)). In other passages, he situates reflection *between* immediate consciousness and being-for-others: "... the reflective ekstasis is found on the path to a more radical ekstasis — being-for-others" (BN, p. 298 (346)). That is, reflection would be possible even without being-for-others. Sartre does not, however, take any definite standpoint on this issue.

I shall briefly mention two other features of Sartre's theory of being-of-others. First, the relation between conscious beings is characterised as *an internal relation of reciprocal recognition* (BN, p. 284). He contrasts this both with the internal relation between consciousness and world, and the external relation between objects. The experience of the other as a conscious beings implies the recognition of the other as an *Other of the Same* (conscious being). However — and this is probably the best known feature — reciprocal recognition is not, on its most basic level, primarily a genuine relation of positive mutuality, but a *conflict*: "conflict is the original meaning of being-for-others" (BN, p. 364 (413)). The motive for this interpretation is found in the theory of consciousness itself. Since consciousness is transcendence, my being-for-others is an experience of myself as transcended by another consciousness (BN, p. 263). When the other objectifies me in his look, it transcends both my own objectification of myself (impure reflection) and my own transcendence. Sartre argues that two attitudes are possible: either I submit to the other's objectification, or I respond by trying to objectify the other (BN, pp. 363-412). Positive and non-conflictual mutual recognition thus appears to be impossible.

The moral implications of this pessimistic description have been discussed extensively. As Flynn observes, some have concluded that 'hell is other people' — a phrase taken from Sartre's play *Huis clos* — is "... a fitting epitaph for Sartre's social philosophy" (Flynn 1981, p. 345).[12] Later Sartre emphasised the distinction between the phenomenological description of EN and the problem of morality. EN describes the level of spontaneous and unreflective human existence, but the problem of morality must be discussed as a reflective existence. Thus, the question of the possibility of mutual human relations of recognition is not even breached in EN. I shall return to this issue in Chapter 9.

Sartre's theory of intersubjectivity in EN is not limited to these general theses about being-for-others. Another important level discussed is the social nature of the thing-world and meanings:

> To live in a world haunted by my fellowman is not only to be able to encounter the Other at every turn of the road; it is also to find myself engaged in a world in which instrumental-complexes can have a meaning [*signification*] which my free project has not first given to them. It means also that in the midst of this world already provided with meaning [*sens*] I meet with a meaning [*signification*] which is mine and which I have not given to myself (BN, pp. 510-11 (567)).

Objects encountered in the world may appear useful to me from the point of view of my projects. It is, however, equally clear that I encounter phenomena in the world whose meanings are independent of myself. A hammer, a railroad sign, a work of art, my nationality and race are instrumental-complexes and meanings, which are given independently of how I conceive of them. The hammer remains a hammer, even though I temporarily use it as a doorstopper. As the latter example indicates, however, this does not determine how I am to make use of given meanings; whatever meaning something has, it is always possible for me to conceive of it differently within the perspective of my projects.

According to Theunissen, "in comparison with Husserl's theory of intersubjectivity and with Heidegger's analysis of being-with, Sartre's social ontology ... comes a good bit nearer to the essence and reality of inter-human encounter" (1984, p. 199). The theory of being-for-others succeeds quite well to describe experiential intersubjectivity. In my opinion, it is, however, limited by being grounded in an incomplete conception of consciousness. Whereas Sartre moves on quite well grounded territory in his descriptions of the experience of the other, the interpretation of human relations as originally rooted in the look and as conflictual appears to be more based on his theory of consciousness than on reality. Sartre would have to reconsider more fully the consequences of the presence of being-for-others already in his discussion of transcendence, pre-reflexivity and reflection, instead of adding it on the former. I shall not, however, here discuss the details of such a critique.[13]

Project and Action as the Basis of a Conception of Man

The conception of man in EN is thus based on a philosophy of consciousness whose basic ideas are:

(1) that consciousness has the character of *transcendence*, implying both that it is *active* and that it constitutes a *bond of interiority* with the world
(2) that consciousness is defined by *pre-reflexive self-awareness*, which is neither the construction of an Ego nor a genuine knowledge of self
(3) that consciousness is in its innermost character a *consciousness of other conscious beings*.

In addition Sartre also claims that:

(4) transcendence, pre-reflexivity and reflection constitute *temporal* awareness (BN, p. 107-70), or consciousness of having a past, of being in process and of future-orientation
(5) consciousness, through its continuous possibility to posit the negative, is constituted as *freedom*.

In the last part (before the conclusion) of EN, Sartre finally gets to the heart of the matter. Ontology reveals that the major distinction at stake is between the categories of *Doing* and *Being*. Dependent on how one looks at the situation, these can or cannot be understood dualistically. The being of human reality is revealed as a doing (transcendence as an act). On the other hand, doing is dependent on and unintelligible without the primacy of being (transcendence as being-in-the-world). Both the phenomenological ontology of EN and the philosophy of praxis and practico-inert in CRD are serious attempts to make this scheme intelligible.

A temporal concept of transcendence implies that consciousness is a practical and processual orientation toward *ends* and the *future*. 'Going beyond' is revealed as temporal surpassing, or *project* and *action*. This has important consequences for a conception of man: "Cause [*motif*], act and end constitute a *continuum*, a *plenum* ... Human-reality is free because it *is not enough*. It is free because it is perpetually wrenched away from itself and because it has been separated by a nothingness from what it is and from what it will be ... Man is free because he is not himself but presence to himself ... Freedom is precisely the nothingness which *is made-to-be* at the heart of man and which forces human-reality *to make itself* instead of *to be*" (BN, p. 440 (495)). That is, "... for [human reality] ... being is reduced[14] to doing" (p. 476 (532)).

The task to understand a human being thus implies to make him or her intelligible in terms of his/her projects and actions. But here Sartre's discourse gradually shifts ground. If a human being does not have a nature, but is constituted by his or her own projects, the universalisations of phenomenological ontology cannot reach any deeper. The task to interpret human projects is an empirical-interpretative task concerned with the concrete and not an issue of ontology, although it must surely be based on it.

In EN Sartre in fact claims that phenomenological ontology may take one additional step. Within the perspective of what Sartre calls *existential psychoanalysis* — a method for the interpretation of individuals — Sartre introduces the concept of a *fundamental project* (BN, pp. 479-80 and 557-615, see Howells 1988, pp. 145-65). It is intended to replace the static idea of a *personal character* or *identity* with the idea of a moving unity that changes through time. By a 'fundamental project' Sartre thus means a kind of enveloping or totalising *meaning* or *orientation* in terms of which a person is intelligible in totality. By this is not meant a reflectively posited life-plan, but an orientation that a person seldom or never is fully aware of. It implies the task of an existential psychoanalysis, not as Freudian psychoanalysis aimed to bring forward some unconscious forces that govern the person, but to interpret him hermeneutically. To understand Flaubert means to integrate his life situations, major choices, actions and their results into a narrative in which a single meaning can be deciphered as constitutive of his life.

But this idea of a fundamental project refers us to concrete individuals, not ontology. In EN there is, however, a certain tension between two kinds of fundamental projects. As a conclusion of the ontology of being-in-itself and being-for-itself Sartre claims that human beings are oriented towards a certain, unrealisable value or ideal: the harmonious reconciliation of being thing-like and being conscious, or the *in-itself-for-itself* (BN, pp. 88-92, 451 and 564-66). That is, the fundamental project is something universal. In other passages, again, he seems to refer to the particular project of some individual. The relation between these two kinds remains rather unclear. But by posing the problem in this way, we reaches the gateway to the idea of a *hermeneutics of praxis*: the co-presence of *an ontology* centred on *the project* and *the interpretation of concrete human reality in terms of praxis*, that is, Sartre's *method* in CRD.

I have thus given an account of Sartre's views in EN on man as a being-in-the-world and as a free being of action. I have also discussed the notions of project, negativity, transcendence, facticity and intersubjectivity, that is (i)-(v) in the list given above. I shall now turn to the modifications and additions made by Sartre in CRD (and related works), modifications which I claim justify my use of the phrase 'a hermeneutics of praxis' to characterise Sartre's conception.

The Hermeneutical Dimension of CRD

A basic thesis of my work is that CRD accomplishes a shift in Sartre's discernment of realm of study and philosophical standpoint that has much in common with hermeneutics. However, if this conception is to be characterised as hermeneutical, it must be seen as a hermeneutics that preserves a *certain level of universality*. Of course, Gadamer also claims that the hermeneutical problem is universal, so this does not as such represent an unhermeneutical trait.

In QM Sartre briefly clarifies *the status of the philosophical claims of ontology*. One may interpret Sartre to say that phenomenological ontology proceeds on the basis of a method of *immanent reflection*. It studies the mode of being of consciousness from the point of view of reflective consciousness. Although the theoretical categories (transcendence, pre-reflexivity, negativity, being-for-others, project) appear to be universal and ahistorical features of the human condition, the standpoint that reveals them (pure reflection) is in no way external. Thus, ontological knowledge is characterised as a form of *indirect knowing* (*connaissance indirecte*), which is "... the result of reflection on existence" (SM, p. 171 (126)). Such interrogative reflection reveals necessary ingredients of the human mode of being, although in a (hermeneutically) *circular* manner:

> The very employment of these vocables to designate existence ... indicate that it is capable of *denotation*. But the relation of the sign to the signified cannot be conceived of here in the form of an empirical signification. The signifying movement ... is itself a project. This means that the existential project will be in the word which denotes it, not as the signified — which on principle is outside — but as its original foundation and its very structure ... The word 'project' originally designates a certain human attitude (one 'makes' projects) which supposes as its foundation the pro-ject, an existential structure ... In this sense the word by itself manifests the project from which it derives ... (SM, pp. 171-72 (127)).

That is, the known is itself presupposed in the very act that reveals this knowledge: the category of project is itself revealed in 'a project of revelation'. This circularity cannot, furthermore, be overcome, it "... is the very ambiguity of a discipline in which the questioner, the question, and the questioned are one" (SM, p. 174 (129)).

Second, the ontological categories themselves, if understood as lived by human beings in a concrete context (that is, in history) imply *historicity*. Insofar as transcendence, freedom and project are beings-in-the-world, on a concrete level they are particularised and situated: "... human reality eludes direct knowledge to the degree that *it makes itself*. The determinations of the person appear only in a society which constantly constructs itself by assigning to each of its members a specific work, and relations of production with the other members ..." (SM p. 170 (126)). In CRD Sartre, thus, directs his interrogative outlook away from ontology and consciousness to the *concretely lived* and *historically embedded experience*:[15]

> ... we are not concerned, at this point, with interrogating consciousness about itself: the object it must give itself is precisely *the life*, the objective being, of the investigator in the world of others, in so far as this being totalises itself from birth and will continue to totalise itself until death (CDR, p. 51 (167)).

In EN Sartre insisted that consciousness has *no content*: that it exhausts itself in its bond with the outside and contain no Ego. In CRD the abstract vocabulary of consciousness is replaced with a concrete vocabulary of experience. By 'experience' Sartre means human consciousness taken on a (hermeneutical) level of embeddedness in the world, where it is 'always already' filled with content (through the internalisation of culture, social relations, childhood experiences, etc.). Sartre does unfortunately not clarify his conception of experience very much. Or rather, he takes another experiential notion as central: *comprehension* (see Chapter 8). By focusing on this concept of understanding, Sartre explicitly situates himself within the tradition of hermeneutical thinking.

The distinction between consciousness and experience shall not be understood in a rigid sense. Sartre has not rejected his philosophy of consciousness, but it is reinterpreted from another point of view. Thus, the categories of consciousness stand at the core of 'experience' and 'comprehension'. Both are forms of transcendence (bond with the world and surpassing of the world), they are pre-reflexive and might become reflective, they are beings-for-others, etc. However, Sartre now prefers to introduce a parallel vocabulary to that of EN: parallel with the abstract notion of transcendence, for example, Sartre introduces the concrete and dialectical (Hegelian) notion of *surpassing* (*depassément*) in order to discuss real processes of going beyond.

In CRD Sartre also re-interprets the place and status of consciousness in a way that better suits a *materialist* outlook. Thus, he claims (mainly indirectly) that *need* is more a fundamental category than consciousness (CDR, p. 80-88): "Need is the first totalising relation between the material being, man, and the material ensemble of which he is part" (CDR, p. 80 (194)). The relation between the organic reality of the human body and the inorganic conditions of life forms the primary bond of interiority with the world, and the first motive for surpassing. In a sense then, since need appears to be situated beneath consciousness and praxis, Sartre now sees it as the most fundamental level of consciousness.[16]

The method of inquiry is no longer described in terms of pure reflection, but, playing on the double meaning of 'expérience' as both 'experience' and 'investigation', as *a reflexive self-critique* of *the experience and life of the investigator* himself: "the critical investigation [experience] ... is the very life of the investigator in so far as it reflexively criticises itself" (CRD, p. 51 (167)). Sartre is here neither concerned with understanding "... the *content* of [the investigators] life ..." (CDR, pp. 51-52 (167)), nor of understanding any other individual as such. This investigation is concerned with "... the *Truth of History*" (ibid.). It should thus accomplish the aim to move *from individual experience* to the *intelligibility of the historical situation*. In order to do this, it must:

> ... bear on *the nature of bonds of interiority* [liens d'intériorité] (if they exist), on *the basis of the human relations* which define the investigator. If he is to be totalised by history, the important thing is that he should re-live his membership of human ensembles with different structures and determine the reality of these ensembles through the bonds which constitute them and the practices which define them (CDR, pp. 51-52 (167), my italics).

According to Sartre, the basic (metaphysical?) assumption that underlie such an investigation, and the very thesis that it must be able to prove, is that:

> The link of our critical investigation is none other than the fundamental identity between an individual life and human history (or, from the methodological point of view, the 'reciprocity of their perspectives'). Strictly speaking, the identity of these two totalising processes must itself be proved ... critical investigation proceeds exactly from this hypothesis and each moment of the regression (and later of the progression) directly calls it into question. The continuity ... would be interrupted at every level if ontological identity and methodological reciprocity did not in fact appear both as a fact and as necessary and intelligible Truth (CDR, p. 70 (184)).

By the 'ontological identity' between individual life and history Sartre means (i) that both a life and history are *lived totalisations* — they have 'an identity in the mode of being' — and (ii) that they reciprocally refer to each other: the concrete individual is historical, and history is concretely lived and made by individuals. By 'methodological reciprocity', again, Sartre means, on the one hand, that an individual must be studied towards the background of society and history and, on the other hand, that society and history must be studied through the way individuals live, shape, make and remake them.

Sartre here again emphasises the internal bond between individual and environment. But instead of describing it abstractly in terms of being-in-the-world, Sartre now introduces the concrete categories of *internalisation* and *externalisation*[17]. These communicate both that human being is a process, and imply a level of *necessity and universality*: "necessity asserts itself, as an inevitable and irreducible moment, in the internalisation of the external and in the externalisation of the interior" (CDR, p. 71 (185)). *Internalisation* (assimilation, acquisition, etc.) is the experiential moment by which an individual makes the environment and situation his own (in learning, the acquisition of skills (language), through human relations, childhood experiences, etc.). Even in internalisation the individual is still an active and free interpreter, and the process is unique in everyone. *Externalisation* (adaptation, action, etc.) is the praxis-centred moment whereby a person makes use of what he has internalised in concrete solutions and actions. Naturally, externalisation might imply anything on the scale from adaptation to creative activity and revolt. It does not imply that internalised experiences are simply translated into schemes of actions, but externalisation is likewise an active, free and innovative process. Thus, the possibility to affirm *freedom* is preserved on both levels.

Thus, in a manner reminiscent of the hermeneutics of Gadamer, Sartre's approach strongly affirms *the historicity* of both *understanding* and *praxis*:

> I find myself dialectically conditioned by the totalised and totalising past of the process of human development: as a man of culture (an expression which applies to *every* man, whatever his culture, and even if he is illiterate) I totalise myself on the basis of centuries of history and, in accordance with my culture, I totalise this experience. This means that my life itself is centuries old, since the schemata which permit me to understand, to modify and to totalise my practical undertaking ... have *entered the present* (CDR, p. 54 (170)).

That is, the intelligibility of experience, as an understanding of the present, is located exactly at the meeting point between acquired skills, models of interpretation (or what Gadamer calls effective-historical consciousness) and the movement of surpassing in the freedom of individual projects. It is not only individual experience that is historical. *The investigation itself*, although expressed on a general and formal level, must necessarily be seen as both *particular* and *participatory* in nature:

> The dialectic reveals itself only to an observer situated in interiority, that is to say, to an investigator who lives his investigation both as a possible contribution to the ideology of the entire epoch and as the particular *praxis* of an individual defined by his historical and personal career within the wider history which conditions it (CDR, p. 38 (156)).

In order to emphasise the distinction between (non-hermeneutical) science and his own historically situated investigation, Sartre now characterises his investigation as a *notional approach* in distinction from a *conceptual* one.[18] In an interview Sartre thus answers the question whether IF is to be considered a scientific work:

> No ... 'Scientific' would imply rigorous concepts. As a philosopher I try to be rigorous with notions ... A concept is a way of defining things from the outside, and it is atemporal. A notion, as I see it, is a way of defining things from the inside, and it includes not only the time of the object about which we have a notion, but also its own time of knowledge. In other words, it is a thought that carries time within itself ... The distinction I make between concept and notion is similar to the distinction I make between knowledge and understanding (1978b, p.113, see Chapter 8 for the distinction between knowledge and understanding).

Notions (i) define things from an *internal perspective* and (ii) *incorporate time* and the *possibility of change*. Sartre, on the other hand, understands concepts, as expressing general ideas or universal essences seen as common to the particulars that fall under the concept. Concepts are used by the sciences to express objective knowledge (Savoir), and these take an external perspective to the object.[19] Notions constantly underline internality of perspective and historicity. The distinction itself actually stems from Hegel, for whom "... the notion organises and fuses concepts together in the organic and living unity of concrete reality", and "dialectical enrichment lies in the transition from the abstract to the concrete, that is, from elementary concepts to notions of greater and greater richness" (Sartre 1955a, p. 195).

These shifts or changes in emphasis imply a different conception of *concreteness*. By 'concrete' cannot be meant only the synthetic whole of consciousness and its object (see above), but concreteness must be seen as *historical*. Thus, according to Sartre:

> Immediate experience reveals being at *its most concrete*, but it takes it at its most superficial level and remains in the realm of abstractions (CDR, p. 95 (208)).

What appears to us in everyday experience as the most concrete, the here and now of object, the world and self-experience is, in fact, an abstraction. *Immediate experience does not understand itself* (hermeneutically) *in terms of the totality of its real bonds with the social and historical world* in which it appears, and is thus not fully concrete. By this claim Sartre actually *identifies concreteness* with something as taken in terms it's *full truth*, where truth is defined in terms of the *totality of* some phenomena's *relations with the world* (including other human beings), and these understood as a process *in movement* (see Chapters 7 and 8 for Sartre's conception of truth).

Thus, a second level of concreteness can be reached only by means of what Sartre calls *regressive understanding* and *regressive investigation*, which:

> ... will set out from the immediate, that is to say from the individual fulfilling himself in his abstract *praxis*, so as to rediscover, through deeper and deeper conditionings, the totality of his practical bonds with others and, thereby, the structures of the various practical multiplicities and, through their contradictions and struggles, *the absolute concrete: historical man* (CDR, p. 52 (167), my italics).

The *absolute concrete* is a *human being taken on the level of his or her embeddedness in culture, society and history*.

But, importantly, such concrete historicity must not be limited only to a set of conditions, or the social setting of an individual. Such a setting only makes up the *milieu* in which the real movement of the historically concrete occurs: "... [regressive investigation] enables us to reach the concrete at last ... We now confront, not the real concrete, but the set of formal contexts, curves, structures and conditionings which constitute the *formal milieu* in which the historical concrete must necessarily occur" (CDR, p. 671 (753)). Thus, the task of *progressive understanding* and the *progressive moment* of the investigation are to make intelligible (theoretical investigation) and reconstruct (empirical-interpretative investigation) this *historical concrete* on the level of *reality in movement*.

In summary then, Sartre's idea of a critical investigation of historically embedded experience takes the bonds of interiority between the individual and his times as its point of departure and object of study. This, however, does not lead Sartre simply to an empirical study of the present. Instead, Sartre believes that *situationality* as such opens itself to *theoretical investigation*. The task of CRD thus becomes to carry out such a *philosophical-theoretical* investigation of the principles of *intelligibility of human sociality, culturality and historicity*. The outcome of this investigation is *the regressive-progressive method*. As a second task, Sartre both proposes and realises a series of *empirical-interpretative* investigation of particular persons, groups, social situations, etc., which function as tests and applications of the method.

Sartre's Conception of Man in CRD: the Notions of the Lived and Totalisation

In so far as the task to understand a human being is understood as oriented towards the understanding of an *individual as a whole*, an action-theoretic framework is not as such sufficient. In the first place, a human being is much more than a product of his own actions: a sensitive, organic body, a being of emotions, a man of needs, a socially situated being, etc. It is clear, especially from the existential biographies, that Sartre does not reduce these realms to action, although he does insist that intelligibility in the final analysis depends on projects, activities and actions.

In the second place, as is often recognised, a human being is not only a being of action, but also a *unitary whole*. Sartre's conception is explicitly constituted as an attempt to deal with this assumption. Already in his discoursen on existential psychoanalysis Sartre declares that "the *principle* of this psychoanalysis is that man is a *totality* and not a collection. Consequently he expresses himself as a whole in even his most insignificant and his most superficial behaviour" (BN, p. 568 (628), my italics). This claim is repeated in QM: "... on whatever ground, at whatever level, one is considering him, the individual is always a *whole*" (SM, p. 139 (106), my italics).

In this sense, Sartre's conception is *holistic* in character, although it neither indicates the harmony of a system in equilibrium, nor a unity independent of it's environment (the philosophy of the subject). On the contrary, he emphasises that unity constitutes a continuously on-going *process* that typically is characterised by internal *tensions and conflicts*, and that it is realised through processes of *internalisation* (making the environment mine in a unifying sense) and *externalisation* (the singularity of solutions and decisions).

I have already introduced the notion of a *fundamental project*. This integrates the possibility of *change*. By 'the unity of a fundamental project' is not meant something reflectively laid down beforehand, or a project that can be finished in a lifetime. How is this unity actually to be understood? Sartre hastens between the position that the fundamental project is settled at a certain, crucial time of a persons life, and that it continuously changes. However, instead of treating this issue in terms of this notion, I shall examine the similar idea of a *lived totalisation*, introduced by Sartre in CRD and IF.

The idea that persons are to be understood in terms of a *project* is sustained in CRD. The life — or, even, the meaning of life — of a person is not fixed by a pregiven essence, but is constantly made and remade. In CRD Sartre adds that this process must necessarily be understood in relation to "... a society which constantly constructs itself in a never-ceasing totalisation", although "... these determinations are themselves sustained, internalised and lived (whether in acceptance or refusal) by a *personal project* ...", which, furthermore, "... cannot under any circumstances be defined by concepts" (SM, p. 170 (105)). In CRD, but more clearly in later writings and interviews, Sartre replaces the notion of a fundamental project with the notion of *the lived* (le vécu).[20] This is explicitly introduced in order to overcome some of the shortcomings — or, what Sartre calls, idealistic and rationalistic traits — of his earlier conception of consciousness. Regardless of Sartre's emphases on the contrary, 'consciousness' and 'project' both connote reflective awareness. 'The lived', on the other hand, more clearly conveys the *co-presence of the conscious and unconscious aspects of life* (Sartre 1974b, pp. 35-42, Howells 1988, pp. 150-64).

'The lived' is a typical phenomenological-hermeneutical concept. It is *a construction* intended to capture descriptively a certain reality or mode of being. The reality in question is a certain complex whole, which everyday language often refers to in a piecemeal fashion (the self, etc.). Sartre introduces the notion as a replacement of his earlier conception of consciousness. It is intended to integrate the two dimensions of the unconscious and consciousness in human experience. The specific way in which this solution to dualism is to be understood remains quite unclear.

The notion of the lived incorporates three domains of human life. First, it is of a consciousness-, experience- or understanding-type (*the lived as experienced*): the lived is the life of an individual taken as understood, experienced and monitored by the individual himself. Second, it carries the idea of being actively lived, as distinguished from being passively experienced (*the lived as activity*): action and project as basic features of human life. Third, it is intended to communicate that concrete life constitutes an internalisation (*lived in the world*) that is also a *totalisation*.

By 'totalisation' Sartre means a 'continuously on-going process of synthesis or integration' (CDR, pp. 44-48, see also Flynn 1984, pp. 85-89). It implies the two ideas of *unification* and *constant change*. Sartre distinguishes between a totalisation and a totality. A totality is a unity of an object-kind (a being in-itself), while a totalisation is a unity of a processual kind. Thus, for example, a thing (a stone), a situation (a field of action or environment) or a particular society (the law, type of government, etc.) may be said to form totalities, while actions, the temporal process of history and the life of a person (at the moment when it is lived) constitute totalisations.

Sartre introduces the notion of totalisation as a replacement of the scientific idea of *universalisation* (see for example SM, pp. 25-28). In order to avoid relativism, Sartre affirms the need of a monism of interpretation, but this cannot consist in the discovery of universal laws that govern history (CDR, pp. 15-21). To interpret human beings does not imply to eliminate the unique, subjective and individual, as in the natural sciences, but, on the contrary, exactly to render this uniqueness as such intelligible. The idea of totalisation connotes the idea of *a synthetic integration of facts* that makes facts intelligible in their unique constellation. Sartre also importantly characterises such a totalisation as a *singularisation*:[21] it does not simply cover the whole with an overall scheme, but it interprets facts in the light of a singular (narrative) pattern: what may be called the disclosed *meaning*.

On the basis of this co-presence of the covering notion of totalisation and the particularising notion of singularisation, we may better understand what Sartre means by 'the ontological identity' and 'reciprocity of perspectives' between individual life and history. The integrating aspect of totalisation must in fact be understood in two ways. First, in our interpretations, choices and undertakings, the whole of the environment is integrated, but always in a particular way. Second, such integration does not imply that everything, so to speak, is taken in by the subject, but that the singular way of integrating, in its full intelligibility, should be seen as referring to the totality of the environment. Thus, by 'totalisation as a singularisation' are both meant *synthetic integration* and a *referential relation to the whole*.[22]

These ideas are summarised by Sartre in IF when he claims that an individual constitutes a *universal singular* (a Hegelian term):

For a man is never an individual; it would be more fitting to call him a *uni-*

> *versal singular* (universel singulier). Totalised, and for this reason universalised, by his epoch, he in turn retotalises it and reproduces himself in it as singularity. Universal by the singular universality of human history, singular by the universalising singularity of his projects, he requires simultaneous examination from both ends (FI 1, p. ix (7)).[23]

A human being must be understood as both totalised by the epoch in which he lives (internalisation), and as a being that totalises and retotalises the epoch by living it in a singular way. These are the two levels of *the lived as a totalisation*.

The notion of the lived communicates a process in which the person himself necessarily lacks a complete overview of what he is doing, or a full self-knowledge. The lived is a process that is "... obscure to itself because it is a constant totalisation, thus necessarily a totalisation which cannot be conscious of what it is" (Sartre 1974b, p. 41, see also SM, p. 97). One reason for this is that this process is defined by its orientation towards the future. That is, in the lived we are oriented towards what is not yet, what is still to be done, etc., and the future is something of which cannot strictly *know* anything. The idea of complete self-knowledge would then imply that the process has been completed, in other words, that the person is dead.

This totalising process of integration shall not, as I said above, be understood as harmonious. According to Sartre, unity is primarily an ontological necessity, and not a pre-established harmony. That is, also situations which do not allow of a harmonious integration (what Sartre calls contradictory situations, see CDR II, pp. 3-6) must be integrated in concrete reality. One may even claim that the very idea of contradiction and conflict presupposes a unity within which something is contradictory. Since the individual is always a whole, everything that is experienced, regardless of whether it does or doesn't fit in with other experiences, must be lived by the individual as internally related to these other experiences. According to Sartre, even contradictory situations must, thus, necessarily *be lived in a single way*, that is, they must necessarily have a singular solution in the persons choice and decision. Sartre makes use of this idea in his interpretation of Flaubert (see Chapter 8).

So far I have presented the different dimensions of Sartre's anthropology, discussed his conception of human being and some major traits of his philosophical standpoint. These already give us an indication of what kind of solution Sartre gives to the problem how we are to understand and study human beings and human reality.

According to Sartre, a human being is fundamentally to be understood through an interpretation of *projects* and *praxis*. But Sartre's concept of praxis (see Chapter 7), like his philosophical standpoint, is conceived as an attempt to overcome the dualism between, on the one hand, the objective and not directly experienced aspects of human behaviour, and, on the other hand, the world as experienced and lived by subjects. Sartre's conception (both in EN and CRD) emphasises that a human being is primarily to be seen as a synthetic totality or a being-in-the-world, and is to be studied on the basis of how he or she (i) (immediately and temporally) continuously internalises the circumstances and (ii) (individually, adaptation and innovation) reshapes the world and him/herself through his/her actions. Thus, Sartre's conception constitutes an attempt to combine *a thesis of historicity* (the full truth of a human being, action, etc.) with *a philosophy centred on action* (the final locus of intelligibility).

According to Sartre, this points to the task to formulate *the principles of a method* for how human beings and human reality is to be studied. As I shall show in Chapter 6, it also points to an even more fundamental task: a conception of rationality as the foundation of the method.

Sartre's idea of a method shall not be understood as a set of rules, which is simply to be *applied* in a straightforward manner to an empirical object, and which would *rationally test* the validity of one's hypotheses. The progressive-regressive method *orients* research: it indicates from where we are to begin (immediate experience, the circumstances), what is to be studied (the bonds of interiority of experience, the person, etc.) and in terms of what the reality studied is to be understood in the final analysis (praxis and totalisation).

Thus, the *regressive*, analytical moment orients us to study the socio-historical setting in which persons live, and the process whereby these circumstances are internalised. It moves regressively and analytically, from the concrete whole of individual experience to the enumeration and description of the material and social relations that make up the situational reality of this experience. The *theoretical task* involved in this moment is to judge and decide on how such an *analysis of the situation* or an *interpretation of the times* is to be carried out.

The *progressive*, synthetical moment orients us to study and reconstruct the very movement whereby human beings in their actions, undertakings and involvement reshape their world, lives and themselves. It moves along with the very movement it attempts to reconstruct, and it synthesises the differentiated relations and significations found in the regressive analysis, through how they are bound together in individual solutions. The *theoretical* task involved in this moment is to judge and decide how and on what grounds such a *totalising interpretation of reality in process* is to be carried out.

There are several possible ways to interpret and make use of this scheme. Perhaps the most obvious, and most safely Sartrean, is to interpret it as a description of how one is to study the life of an individual human being. I shall call this *the biographical interpretation*. By calling it 'the most safely Sartrean' I mean that the task to reconstruct the life, fundamental project or lived totalisation of an individual human being preoccupied Sartre himself to a very large extent. The point of culmination of this preoccupation is, of course, the study of Flaubert. The principal aim of that work is outlined already in QM:

> The problem is to recover the totalising movement of enrichment which engenders each moment in terms of the prior moment, the impulse which starts from lived obscurities in order to arrive at the final objectification — in short the *project* by which Flaubert, in order to escape from the petite bourgeoisie, will launch himself across the various fields of possibilities toward the alienated objectification of himself and will constitute himself inevitably and indissoluble as the author of *Madame Bovary* and as that petit bourgeois which he refused to be (SM, p. 147 (111)).

Sartre obviously used this scheme and the method for other kinds of investigations and interpretations also. Thus, the regressive and progressive modes of investigation are present in Sartre's approach to the theory of practical social formations and the study of the intelligibility of history in CRD and in his later notes on a second ethics (see Chapter 9). Sartre also uses similar schemes in his studies of anti-Semitism (1948c), colonialism (1964), the intellectual (1974c), etc. Although this is the case, it remains true that the most comprehensive use of this scheme is found in Sartre's existential biographies.

I investigate Sartre's anthropology on the basis of another interpretation than the biographical. It does not as such quarrel with the biographical interpretation, as one possible orientation of Sartre's ideas. But instead of following Sartre on this point, I seek ways to make use of and discuss Sartre's contribution that are not limited to, or primarily interested in, the task to reconstruct an individual life. I thus regard this as only one possible way to understand Sartre's conception of how we are to understand human beings and human reality. I instead focus on the question *how Sartre's conception of the intelligibility of praxis*, and of the social meanings of actions and socio-historical processes, *can be used for* the study of *historical events and situations*, the structure and evolution of *societies*, *social practices*, etc.

Notes

1 Heidegger 1962, pp. 31-32, 37-38, 47, 71-75. Heidegger argues that fundamental ontology, or the investigation of the question of the meaning of Being from the perspective of Dasein, is both ontologically and ontically prior to anthropology.

2 By using 'ideologists' instead of 'philosophers', Sartre emphasises that existentialism, at its present stage of development, only constitutes a partial truth, which is anyhow justified as a reaction against objectivism, etc. Since this distinction presupposes Sartre's thesis that real philosophers are those who expresses the truth of an epoch (see SM, 3-8), and I do not accept this, I shall not make use of Sartre's distinction.

3 For the indirect confirmation and support of this, not unproblematic, characterisation, cf. Husserl 1977, pp. 27-31, and Heidegger 1962, pp. 50-55. See also Chapter 4.

4 In EN Sartre does not describe his conception as dialectical (see Sartre 1981a, pp. 9-10). A few years later, however, he is prepared to redescribe the philosophy of EN in terms of the dialectic (1967, p. 132).

5 I am well aware of Heidegger's insistence on distinguishing between Dasein and human being (1962, pp. 36-40 and 67-75). I do not, however, find it important to uphold that distinction in this context. It is anyway clear that at least some, although not necessarily all, human beings are Dasein. If Dasein is to characterise *the mode of being of the ontological investigator him- or herself* (the primary point of departure), it includes such things as self-understanding, linguistic competence and the possibility of authentic existence, and these possibilities are not necessarily present to all human beings at all times of their life (for example, infants and gravely mentally ill).

6 As a consequence Sartre almost completely refrains from using the notion of intentionality itself. In EN 'intentionality' reappears mainly in the context of *action* (BN, pp. 433ff). One may of course claim that it is still present in Sartre's use of the phrase "all consciousness is consciousness of something" (BN, p. xxxvi). My claim does not imply that Sartre has come to reject the *idea* of intentionality, which would be absurd, but that he makes a point out of re-interpreting intentionality as transcendence.

7 Cf. Morris 1985, pp. 182-84. Morris, correctly I think, distinguishes between three uses of the term in Sartre. I prefer to group them into two in order to avoid unnecessary complexity.

8 The concepts of negation and nothingness appear in CRD mainly in the discourse on need (CDR, pp. 80-94). Sartre uses the dialectical scheme of a negation of a negation in order to describe the transformation from a static way to a dynamic way of describing need. As a scheme of intelligibility it is interesting, but it is not crucial for making Sartre's philosophy of praxis intelligible. For a discussion of Sartre's philosophy of being and nothingness, see any

general introduction to Sartre (Warnock 1965, Caws 1979, Saarinen 1983, Howells 1988).

9 Sartre is keen to emphasise that the mode of being implied by being-for-itself (transcendence, project, action and freedom) is kernel for the intelligibility of the human. But being-for-itself is defined as the mode of being of *consciousness*, not of human being (BN, 33-45, 52-54, 307-8, 433).

10 The most thoroughful expositions of Sartre's theory of being-for-others is found in Theunissen 1984 and Schroeder 1984, esp. pp. 176-217. Schroeder, however, limits himself largely to the first and fourth of these themes, and he might be criticised for neglecting especially the third. In addition he does not, as Theunissen does, consider the changes in Sartre's conception developed in CRD. For the latter issue, see also Flynn 1981 and 1984.

11 Sartre does not claim that my experience of being looked at is dependent on the factual existence of another at the exact time and place of the experience. He only claims that the existence in myself of an experience of being-looked at shows that my own being is being-for-others. The factual possibility of such an experience is that one has sometimes encountered concrete others, not that a concrete other is present in all experiences. Sartre is not, however, very clear on this issue.

12 For example, both Aron (1975, esp. pp. 25-53) and Stack (1977, p. 113) makes a moralising point about Sartre's 'pessimistic' and violent descriptions.

13 This echoes Merleau-Ponty's critique of Sartre in *Phenomenlogie de la perception* (1962).

14 Sartre's use of 'réduit' here is yet another place where he vacillates between dualism and anti-dualism. On the basis of what I have said above, the use of 'reduce' must not be taken in a formal, but in a metaphorical sense: Sartre does not want to reduce the being of man to pure activity: activity is the core but not the whole of Sartre's conception of human being.

15 As I indicated above, one may argue that this distinction is already present in he distinction between ontology and existential psychoanalysis in EN (BN, 568). But in EN it mainly functions to distinguish the general from the individual, whereas concrete experience is not made into a major object of study. The presence of this distinction in EN confirms continuity, it does not affect the importance of re-emphasising it in CRD.

16 The introduction of the category of need does not, in my opinion, bring any major changes to the overall conception. In his discussion of need Sartre in fact repeats the thought-figures of being-in-the-world, pre-reflexivity, negativity and surpassing on the level of the relation between organism and material environment. Need is thus characterised dialectically as a negation of a negation, and this is one of the few contexts in which Sartre explicitly makes use of this classical dialectical scheme. The first negation is the organisms lack of self-sufficient permanence (automatic nutrition), the second negation

(which negates the first) is the attempt by the organism to sustain itself by means of the same environment (food). Thus, lack of permanence is transformed into instrumental use, and the relation between organism and environment is transformed into a processual relation of surpassing: the organism surpasses its condition by making use of it in order to preserve itself.

17 I prefer to use 'internalisation-externalisation' instead of 'interiorisation-exteriorisation' as a translation of 'intériorisation-extériorisation'.

18 This distinction is not as such found in CRD, but mainly in Sartre 1955a, p. 195), 1978b, p. 113 and IF (FI 4, p. 42). See also Flynn 1984, p. 90 and 228n.

19 The distinction between concept and notion is then actually not rooted in an interest to account for the nature of concepts as such, but in an observation on the place of concepts in science. The distinction between science and philosophy is not intended to reject research for the sake of pure philosophy, but to speak for another type of research: a philosophically enlightened research of an interpretative kind.

20 I prefer to translate the French term 'le vécu' as 'the lived', and not use the more common term 'lived experience'. The latter is quite well established within phenomenology as an English translation of the German *Erlebnis*. 'Lived experience' has the disadvantage that it seems to refer only to an experience or mode of consciousness, whereas Sartre's notion is clearly intended to express the active, practical and processual nature of experience and life. Howells decision to leave it untranslated (Howells 1988, p. 150) is unsatisfactory, since there are suitable English expressions. In CRD the notion of *le vécu* appear mostly in passing (CDR, p. 39). It is especially in "Sartre par Sartre" (1974b, pp. 35-42) where Sartre indicates a shift from 'the fundamental project' to 'the lived'. On the other hand, the notion itself is already used in EN in the chapter on existential psychoanalysis (BN, p. 570, 'vécu' is there translated into English as 'experienced').

21 This notion is mainly found in CRD II (pp. 3-4) and IF (FI 1, p. ix). In this context I prefer to translate 'particularisation' as 'singularisation' in order to conform with Sartre's use of Hegel's term 'universel singulier' (IF 1, p. 7).

22 This idea is expressed already in *Esquisse d'une théorie des émotions*, where Sartre explains the connection between individual modes of consciousness (actions, emotions, etc.) and the general structure of existence by the idea that singular attitudes express and refer to the whole of human reality: "... an emotion signifies in its own manner the whole of consciousness, or, if we take our stand on the existential plane, of human reality" (1962, p. 27).

23 I have changed the translation slightly. The English original has 'resumes' as a translation of 'retotalise'. I prefer 'retotalises', since it directly connotes with Sartre's view of truth as a totalisation. One may note that Sartre here uses of the concept of universality. But it is not used to refer to scientific universalisation, but to the enveloping nature of history.

6 A Critical Investigation of Reason

A Non-Foundationalist Foundation?

The outline of a method for the study of human beings and human reality presented in QM is based (i) on a certain conception of what human beings are like (being-in-the-world, project and action, the lived as totalisation) and (ii) on certain principles for how an empirical-interpretative investigation of concrete human beings and human reality shall proceed (regressive analysis and progressive synthesis). However, In the time between QM and the set up of what is to become the main body of text of CRD, Sartre has come to recognise that the principles outlined actually appear "... merely as one option among others..." (CDR, p. 15 (135), see also p. 822). Sartre is not satisfied with the conjectural nature of his claims, and observes that their *truth* and *validity* must be *demonstrated*:

> I have proposed certain methodological developments; but they cannot be valid, in fact they cannot even be discussed, unless the materialist dialectic can be assumed to be true (CDR, p. 15 (135)).

On the basis of this observation, Sartre sets himself the task to investigate the very foundation of his standpoint. This task he now understands as a *critical investigation of reason*. More specifically, since he assumes that the intelligibility of the basic domain of human reality — praxis, social relations and history — is *dialectical* in nature, the investigation is to be of *dialectical reason*: "so we must take up the whole problem once again, and explore the limits, validity and extent of dialectical Reason" (CDR, p. 21 (140)).

This recasting of major theme, *from methodology to rationality*, has at least two important consequences from the point of view of an assessment of Sartre's standpoint. First, the problem of rationality transgresses that of methodology by posing (i) the question of the *intelligibility of concrete human reality* as such, which is far more extensive and fundamental problem than that of a method for the human sciences, and (ii) a problem that is inherently *normative*, which make possibility the reconnection of epistemological and ethical-political issues. Second, since one may claim that the value of a method depends on whether anyone finds it useful (and very few has in fact made any use of Sartre's method[1]) by posing an issue that transgresses the problem of method, *the contemporary relevance and value* of Sartre's standpoint does not stand and fall with whether the method is considered useful or not.

Sartre thus sets up his investigation as a *critique of reason*, in a Kantian sense of critique (Kant 1934): it is intended to investigate the *limits, scope* and *validity* of a certain conception of reason. It is also, as in Kant (Hume's relatively legitimate empiricist attack on rationalism, see Kant 1953, pp. 5-14), motivated by "... the real need to separate the true from the false ... " (CDR, p. 50 (166)). By 'the real need' Sartre primarily means both the *theoretical deviations* (Marxist dogmatism) and *social abuses* (Stalinism) made, during the 20th century, to the Hegelian-Marxist conception of human reality as intelligible in a historical-dialectical manner (CDR, p. 50 and 823).

Although the mode of investigation is primarily set up as Kantian, both Sartre's conception of reason and his views on the status of the results are informed by the Hegelian-Marxist tradition (and, one may retrospectively say, by its continuation in hermeneutical phenomenology). Thus, contrary to a Kantian critique, it cannot be oriented towards the discernment of a transcendental and ahistorical level of synthetic a priori categories (CDR, p. 27 and 35):

> we cannot deny that a *critique* ... of dialectical Reason can be made only by dialectical Reason itself; and indeed it must be allowed to ground itself and to develop itself as a free critique of itself, at the same time as being the movement of History and of knowledge ... if there is such a thing as a dialectical reason, it is revealed and established through human *praxis*, to men in a given society at a particular moment of its development ... Consequently, [it] ... can be *true* only within the limits of our social universe (CDR, p. 21 and 33 (141, 151)).

The principles revealed by the investigation, furthermore, must be seen as "... attempts at abstraction and universalisation [which] can only result in schemata which are continuously valid *for that* process" (CDR, p. 49 (165)).

In this sense, Sartre poses the problem of rationality and foundation on a *non-foundationalist* level: the investigation constitutes an *immanent, reflexive investigation* and it *affirms historicity*. However, a problem for the assessment of the status of Sartre's claims is that he does not altogether refrain from the language of *metaphysical foundationalism* or *first-philosophy thinking*. It seems that Sartre is caught in a dilemma, and he has not really attempted to solve it. On the one hand, he *rejects non-historical conceptions* of rationality, on the other hand, he wants to *fight relativism* and set up a monism of interpretation (CDR, p. 15-18).

In my opinion it is especially the threat of relativism that makes Sartre reintroduce a foundationalist language of *universality*, *a priori*, *apodictic certainty* and *necessity*: "... we are confronted once again with the need to establish the dialectic as the universal method and universal law of anthropology. And this amounts to requiring Marxists to establish their method *a priori*". In addition, "... knowledge of such scope would be a mere philosophical dream if it did not have all the marks of apodictic certainty (évidence)". It must therefore be built on "... the absolute requirement *that there must be* a necessity in History at the very heart of its intelligibility" (CDR, pp. 18, 21 and 72 (138, 140 and 187)).

There is thus a tension in Sartre's text between his declared antifoundationalism, a standpoint that might well be characterised as hermeneutical, and his attempt to provide a universal foundation for such historical thinking. Unfortunately Sartre himself largely neglects discussing this crucial problem. It seems that Sartre's solution is based on grounding rationality on *the intelligibility of concrete human reality*, an intelligibility that by itself, or internally, *affirms the necessity of historicity*.[2] That is, universality concerns the primacy of praxis, freedom and our embeddedness in culture and society. This again implies that an intelligibility of the concrete must be focused on how these universals are manifested and lived by individuals in specific, historical circumstances. This twofoldedness corresponds with the two dimensions of an (universal) *ontology of being-in-the-world* and a (historical) *methodology* present in Sartre.

In this context it becomes important to recognise that the concept of rationality implies both *theoretical* (the validity of our understanding of human beings and human reality) and *practical reason* (the justification of our actions). Significantly (and, perhaps, symptomatically) Sartre's investigation is focused on *reason as intelligibility*, that is, on the epistemological issue. But the concept of reason itself is inherently practical: *reason is embodied in praxis*. Thus, one may expect that the normative issues involved extend way beyond the validity of our interpretations and into the ethical-political questions of the goodness and justification of what we do. In CRD, however, this latter issue is pushed to the background. Sartre only returns to it afterwards, in his post-CRD work on an ethics. I shall return to it below and in Chapter 9.

The Problem of Rationality and the Dialectic

Sartre's investigation is an attempt to demonstrate the validity of basically the following five hypotheses:[3]

1. (historical materialism): it is *human beings* that (through their actions) *make history*, but this can only be understood on the basis of how they *internalise and act on the basis of the given circumstances*. Sartre identifies this scheme as fundamental to the historical materialism of Marx.
2. (dialectical Reason): the principle of intelligibility of this scheme is *dialectical* in character.
3. (totalisation): the dialectic is primarily the intelligibility of constantly on-going, temporal processes of *totalisation*.
4. (the ontological primacy of praxis): dialectical rationality, and totalisation, exists if and only if *human praxis is dialectical and totalising* in character.
5. (the methodological primacy of praxis): the study of human beings and human reality is basically a *study of human praxis* and *its bonds of interiority with the material and social world*.

In my account of Sartre's conception of rationality I shall proceed on the basis of an initial, reconstructive distinction between the *problem of rationality* as such and the *question of the dialectic*. It is Sartre's explicit aim to prove the validity of what he calls *dialectical* rationality. The principle orientation of *my* investigation, however, is not to study the *dialectic*. I shall discuss the Sartrean dialectic primarily from the point of view of the *problem of rationality*. My motives for this distinction are that:

(1) whereas I find Sartre's views on rationality interesting and important (also in a contemporary perspective), in my opinion his strong claim that rationality is dialectical in nature does not in fact as such bring very much in addition to what he says about rationality in general (see below).

(2) I also claim that there is a tension between what Sartre says about rationality, and his strong thesis that rationality necessarily is dialectical in character. A major example is his claim that both human *praxis* (project)

and *human relations* (mediated reciprocity) are dialectical in character, and that these two dialectics are one and the same (see Chapter 7). Thus Sartre will have to claim that the intelligibility of *project* and that of *mediated reciprocity* are identical.

(3) Sartre never reached that part of his investigation where he should have discussed the question whether he actually has proved the validity of the hypothesis of dialecticality. He abandoned the investigation long before the final question of dialectical rationality was breached.

(4) In my opinion too many interpreters tend to get stuck on the notion of 'dialectical', whereas both Sartre's views on reason and the idea of a critique of reason are largely neglected.[4] I argue — in opposition, for example, to Caws[5] — that Sartre's conception can be made more intelligible if we focus on the problem of rationality, rather than on the dialectic. In addition, in a contemporary perspective, the concept of a dialectic, due to its long and controversial history (Hegel, Marx, etc.), raises more problems than clarifications.

I do not quarrel with the obvious fact that much in Sartre may well be characterised as *dialectical in a general sense*. I criticise the implementation by Sartre of the dialectic as a covering scheme intended to secure the unity of reason by reducing the different dimensions (action, human relations, etc.) to a single scheme (totalisation).

Sartre's own motives for his focus on the dialectic are of course important in this context. There are, I think, mainly two such motives. First, dialectics, dialectical method and dialectical reason are inherently connected to the Marxist perspective Sartre adopts in CRD. Second, the notion of a dialectic, as developed by Hegel and Marx, inherently contains the germ of a synthesis between phenomenology and an existentialist philosophy of action and Marxist historical process thinking. In the end, however, I think the basic motive why Sartre chooses to organise his investigation around the dialectic, is his choice of the framework of Marxist thought. The second reason mentioned does not of itself demand such a choice: no conceptual necessity obliges Sartre to identify all he says about praxis and human relations with such a 'strong' conception of the dialectic.

These differences in outlook — in combination with a recognition that there is much in Sartre of interest and importance — paves the way for reopening the question of foundations and validity in Sartre. On the basis of these observations one may distinguish between:

1. Sartre's theses about the intelligibility of the human world
2. The foundations of his theses as a question of rationality
3. The thesis of rationality as dialectical.

By separating the issues in this manner, we may raise at least the following questions.

A. (1-2). Is what Sartre says about the understanding of human beings and human reality as such well justified, internally consistent and valid?
B. (1-3). Is what Sartre says about the understanding of human beings and human reality completely dependent on the thesis of dialectical rationality?
C. (2-3) Is what Sartre says about rationality completely dependent on the specific thesis of the dialectical character of rationality
D. (3). Is what Sartre says about dialectics internally consistent and valid?

In the following I shall employ the strategy that there is no initial reason for us to accept and adopt Sartre's strong thesis of dialecticality, and proceed with this distinction in mind.

The True Contradictions of Realism

Sartre recognises that the starting point of his investigation must be "... *the true contradictions of realism*" (CDR, p. 21 (141), my italics). Sartre thus understands his own standpoint as a kind of *realism*, or rather a *situated or historical realism*. But by 'realism' shall not be understood a ready-made position that Sartre simply adopts. Instead his task becomes to develop such a valid realism. But if the starting point must be certain 'contradictions' that are in some sense 'true', the investigation cannot simply criticise non-realist conceptions and adopt realism. For by 'the true contradictions of realism' Sartre means that the realism he accepts is historically built up of a series of contradictory options. Thus, all the positions criticised by Sartre contain a germ of truth, just as Kant gave Hume's attack on reason relative legitimacy (1953, pp. 5-10).

These inner contradictions of realism can thus best be illustrated by an exposition of the positions Sartre criticises and their relative legitimacy. We may sift out at least four such positions:

1. Empiricism (CDR, pp. 17-21 and 28, Hendley 1991, pp. 14-15). A conception according to which all knowledge claims are to be based on sense-

observation and empirical testing. If by 'matter' is understood 'the physical ground from which emanates the content of our observations and which 'responds' in empirical research', empiricism is also a kind of *materialism*. Sartre's own *historical* materialism is critical of this understanding of materialism.

2. Idealism. Conceptions which are either subjectivist (subjectivist idealism) or which must be assessed as products of thought rather than founded on reality (rationalist idealism), e.g. the transcendentalism of Kant and dogmatic Marxism (which subjects reality to political imperatives).[6]

3. Analytical Reason or positivism (SM, pp. 68-74, CDR, pp. 17-21, 26-32, CDR II, pp. 7-11). An approach that divides reality into its constituent parts, primarily studies the parts and the relations between them, and which is oriented towards the discovering of ahistorical and universal laws. The employment of analytical reason is characteristic of the natural sciences, but can also be found within then contemporary human and social science. Although Sartre often opposes analytical to dialectical reason, he also emphasises that analytical reason is not irrational, only a limited form of rationality.

4. Relativism (CDR, pp. 15 and 25). A conception affirming that rationality and truth are relative to particular life forms and historical circumstances. The option of relativism suggests itself through the rejection of the absolutisms of empiricism, idealism and analytical reason, but Sartre refuses to accept it.

All of these options contain a limited truth and legitimacy:

(ad 1) empirism contains a germ of truth in that it conveys the demand to rely on experience, but it becomes illegitimate if reduced to a philosophy of empirical observation (=empiricism). According to the Sartre-realist position, experience also constructs our representations, it is social and practically oriented. This, again, refers us to idealism.

(ad 2) idealism is true in the sense that an investigation of human reality must be based on an internal perspective (which refers us to relativism), but it becomes illegitimate when turned into either a transcendentalist or a subjectivist position.

(ad 3) analytical rationality is true in the sense that it conveys the (existentialist) demand to affirm the specificity of events and the irreducibility of different layers of reality, but it becomes illegitimate when turned into an atomism that denies the existence of internal relations, and when it rejects the synthetic demand to totalise.

(ad 4) relativism is true in the sense that human reality must be studied from the internal perspective of this reality itself, but it becomes illegitimate when an absolute line is drawn between different interpretative perspectives and the differences between cultures, societies or historical periods. According to Sartre, the specificities of internal perspectives do not deny the possibility of transhistorical conditions and schemes of intelligibility.

The Domain and Intelligibility of Dialectical Reason

The basic thesis of Sartre's *realism* is communicated in terms of his agreement with the conception of Marx:

> Marx demonstrated that History *is in development* ... that material existence was irreducible to knowledge (*connaissance*), that praxis outstrips Knowledge (*Savoir*) in its real efficacy. Needless to say, this is my own position (CDR, pp. 23-24 (142-43))

According to Sartre, this implies the need not to reduce being (that is, existence and praxis) to knowledge, but still to affirm the presence of a dialectic in both, and to affirm the interconnectedness of these two dialectics: to "... assert simultaneously that the process of knowledge is dialectical, that the movement of the object ... is itself dialectical, and that these two dialectics are one and the same" (CDR, 20 (140)).

Thus:

> Reason is a certain correspondence between knowledge [connaissance] and Being. From this point of view, if the correspondence between the historical totalisation and the totalising Truth is possible, and if this correspondence is a double movement in both knowledge [connaissance] and Being, we shall be justified in calling this changing relation Reason (CDR, 823 (14)).

By 'reason' or 'rationality' Sartre means a certain kind of relation of *correspondence between knowledge and being* (see also Hendley 1991, pp. 17-

24) Within the perspective of science, this conception seem quite unambiguous: scientific rationality, it may be claimed, consists in the correspondence between the object and our knowledge of it (theory), rationality is the ground, principles or foundation, which makes our knowledge claims justified.

When this line of thought is transferred to the domains of praxis, sociality and history, the relation of correspondence appears differently. In this case, by 'knowledge' is meant the understanding of praxis and the historical process, by 'being' is meant praxis, its bonds of interiority and the historical process itself. The relation of correspondence thus concerns *a correspondence between our understanding of praxis and praxis itself* and *between our understanding of history and history itself.*

In my opinion, however, such a correspondence must be understood in *two ways*: both *epistemologically* and *practically-morally*. That is, besides the epistemological correspondence between a certain praxis and our (retrospective) understanding of it (the science of history), it also concerns the correspondence between our understanding of the situation and our practical decisions and their (perhaps moral) justification. That is, legitimacy and moral-political value of what we do. In a parallel fashion, it concerns not only the special case of individual praxis, but also the two-way correspondence between historical knowledge and the practical-moral problems of the historical process itself (CDR, pp. 823-24).

As I mentioned above, in his negative critique of *analytical reason* and positivism Sartre does not argue that the analytical conception of rationality is totally false, as long as it is applied within its proper domain: *physical nature* and *external relations* (CDR, pp. 19-21)[7]. But this condition implies that the principles of the sciences of nature (causality, lawfulness, etc.) are not exclusively grounded on their object alone. Instead, according to Sartre, the application of these principles ".. is the condition and fundamental structure of scientific *praxis* ... the scientist, in his activity, assumes that reality will always manifest itself in such a way that a provisional and fluid rationality can be constituted in and through it" (CDR, 19 (139)).

The rationality of analytical reason in fact stems from the internal relation between a particular praxis (scientific research) and a specific domain (of physical nature). Within the perspective of this praxis, rationality implies, first, that research should subordinate itself to the demands of the studied object, and, second, to eliminate the human and subjective element to as large a degree as possible. It is only through these principles that it can posit the existence of universal laws of nature. In summary, that scientific research is a praxis does not, according to Sartre, have any decisive, practical implications for the rationality of natural scientific research. But it has critical implications for any attempt to adopt a similar attitude in relation to other domains of reality, such as praxis and sociality.

This has several consequences. First, the rationality of praxis (dialectical reason) is more extensive in scope and a more fundamental issue than the natural scientific problem of rationality (analytical reason). Second, since analytical rationality is justified from the point of view of the study of physical reality, it is not irrational but only limited (CDR, pp. 20-21, CDR II, pp. 7-11). Third, since analytical rationality is relatively legitimate, it is possible that some areas of research within the human and social sciences may use analytical methods. In fact, Sartre himself delimits such a domain within the regressive, *analytical* moment of his method.

That is, the domain of dialectical rationality is more fundamental than analytical rationality, but it is not itself completely un-analytical. Sartre encircles the real *domain of dialectical rationality* to embody mainly three domains of human reality: *human actions* or *praxis*, *human relations* or *sociality* and *the temporal process of history*.

The existence of dialectical reason, however, is due to the dialectical nature of *praxis*, even of *individual praxis*:

> The entire historical dialectic rests on individual *praxis* in so far as it is already dialectical ... If the results of the investigation are positive ... we shall finally be able to prove the strict equivalence between *praxis* with its particular articulations and the dialectic as the *logic of creative action*, that is to say, in the final analysis, as the *logic of freedom* ... (CDR, 80 and 69 (194 and 183, my italics).

By this Sartre ties the presence of a dialectic in reality and the problem of rationality to the question of the intelligibility of praxis.

Sartre's concepts of reason and praxis are to be *dialectical*. By 'dialectics' one might, however, mean several different things. In the Hegelian-Marxist tradition, by 'dialectics' is most typically meant 'a process of surpassing or *Aufhebung*' (cf. Hegel 1991, pp. 59-60, Taylor 1975, pp. 76-80 and 127-34 and Bubner 1988a). A dialectical *Aufhebung* is a process that synthetically goes beyond the given (transcendence) and simultaneously preserves it as its condition and ground of intelligibility (facticity).

Sartre emphatically rejects the dogmatism of Engels conception of a dialectics of nature (CDR, p. 31), and retraces the original idea of dialectics as it is found in Hegel and Marx: dialectics is the logic of a synthetic Aufhebung (*dépassement*). Sartre chooses his own term to characterise such synthetic Aufhebung: *totalisation*:

> ... *the basic intelligibility of dialectical Reason*, if it exists, *is that of a totalisation*. In other words ... a dialectic exists if, in at least one ontological region, a totalisation is in progress ... (CDR, p. 44 (161), my italics).

Dialectical reason is thus posited as *the intelligibility of totalisation* and *totalisation as inherent in praxis*.

I shall return to Sartre's conception of praxis in Chapter 7. As for the intelligibility of totalisation, I have already mentioned in Chapter 5 that a totalisation is both *a continuously on-going process* (in opposition to a totality) and *a singularisation* (in opposition to a universalisation). In CRD II Sartre extends his concept of dialectical intelligibility by adding *contradiction*: "... totalisation, particularisation and contradiction are the three factors of dialectical intelligibility ..." (CDR II, 4 (11)). Since a totalisation is singularising in the sense of being embodied in a particular process, it is manifested as one particular totalisation (or action) to the exclusion of others (other projects and solutions). This has, at least, two implications. First, the notions of totalisation and praxis are inherently connected to the idea of *a particular and real intervention in the world*, and this may raise a contradiction in relation to material restraints. Second, a practical field consists of a plurality of praxes, and these may come to stand in *conflictual* relations with each other.

As I indicated above, totalisation is, importantly, both an *epistemological* and *ontological* notion. By 'totalisation' Sartre refers both to the synthesising nature of human reality as such (being or praxis), and to the synthetic nature of our interpretations (knowledge). As an epistemological notion, it conveys the demand that an interpretation must enable us to integrate all the facts into a single framework. This implies that interpretations that do not fulfil this imperative can not be final, that is encompass a *full understanding*. As an ontological concept, again, it conveys the idea that praxis, the lived, the historical process, etc. are totalising *in their mode of being*: they constitute practical integrations and internalisations of the circumstances and singularise in the mode of a specific solution or series of events.

Sartre's investigation is thus centred on the problem of *intelligibility*: the "... fundamental characteristics [of dialectical Reason] imply that it appears as apodictic experience in its very intelligibility. It is not a question of simply asserting its existence, but rather of directly experiencing its existence through its intelligibility, independent of any *empirical discovery*" (CDR, 44 (160)). 'Intelligibility' connotes 'that which makes something understandable or coherent to thought in a comprehensive manner'. To delimit the intelligibility of physical nature is to refer to principles or laws in terms of which it is understood. To delimit the intelligibility of concrete actions, however, is to refer both to basic features of actions *in general* (goal-orientation, means to the end, conditions) and to the problem of the *meaning of specific actions* (the actual result, historical significance, etc.).

Sartre thus understands the problem of intelligibility as two-fold (CDR, pp. 43-44 and 57-58). First, the formal principles of dialectical rationality (totalisation, etc.) must as such be intelligible (*primary intelligibility*). Second, the concrete reality studied must itself appear as intelligible in its very uniqueness (*secondary intelligibility*). It would thus not be sufficient just to focus on a concept of rationality (rationalism): reality itself must be made intelligible in a way that demonstrates the practical fruitfulness and validity of the concept. The question of the validity of dialectical rationality is then not only a theoretical issue, but it depends on empirical-interpretative investigations.

This also means that the ordering into primary and secondary intelligibility must not be understood to imply that primary intelligibility (the principle) is the foundation of secondary intelligibility (concrete reality). On the contrary, Sartre supports a *nominalist* conception: the universals and generalities presented must be grounded on reality itself (CDR, p. 37). Thus, secondary intelligibility is both the foundation and test of primary intelligibility.

Historical Bonds of Interiority as Non-foundationalist Foundation

Sartre thus again and again emphasises the importance to think in terms of *praxis* and *being-in-the-world*, rather than the opposition between subject and object. The investigation of praxis as totalisation should not be understood as a study of agent-intentionality as such, but a study of *the bonds of interiority* that make up the *reality of concrete praxis*:

> we are proposing ... the critical investigation of *bonds of interiority*, or, in other words, the discovery ... of the answer to this all-important question: in the process of human history, what is the respective role of relations of interiority and exteriority? And if this total investigation ... establishes that the *bond of exteriority* (analytical and positivist reason) is itself *interiorised* by practical multiplicities ... we will find ourselves situated, through the investigation itself, at the very heart of a developing totalisation (CDR, pp. 56-57 (172)).

This means, for example, that neither totalisation, praxis, freedom nor dialectical reason are intelligible in abstraction from their 'opposites': totality, the practico-inert, necessity and analytical reason.

Although in the quotation above (6.4), Sartre (idealistically) characterises the dialectic as the *logic of freedom*, this logic must in fact be understood in terms of the *bond of interiority between freedom and necessity*: "... dialectical rationality ... must be seen as the permanent and dialectical unity of freedom and necessity" (CDR, p. 35 (154), see also 79 and 671). This unity-in-motion has two aspects. First, as Sartre claimed in EN, human beings — through their inherent power to posit the negative (néantiser) — are condemned to freedom, or in other words, they are *necessarily free* (BN, p. 439). Second, ontology demonstrates that freedom is necessarily bound to the restrictions of *the material situation*, to the necessities of *bodily existence* and to the *real results* of what one does (CDR, pp. 36 and 671).

Sartre observes an initial contradiction between *necessity* and *intelligibility*: "intelligibility provides the perfect certainty (évidence) of the new on the basis of the old; it enables us to witness the transparent practical production of the new on the basis of previously defined factors and in the light of a totalisation" (CDR, p. 73n (187n)). That is, intelligibility refers to the teleological project of an action. *Necessity*, on the other hand, "... appears within certainty as the formal inertia of intelligibility ... the intelligibility of praxis comes to depend on the result of the praxis ... and this result ... will appear as incapable of being different than it is" (ibid.). Such necessity "... asserts itself, as an inevitable and irreducible moment, in the internalisation of the external and in the externalisation of the interior" (CDR, 71 (185)).

By 'a *necessity* in History at the very heart of its intelligibility' Sartre thus primarily means the necessity that human beings internalises their situation and that their externalisations are embodied. Sartre importantly adds that this experience of necessity is not a pure experience of matter, but an experience of *other human beings* and their praxes:

> ... the first practical experience of necessity occurs in the unconstrained activity of the individual to the extent that the final result, though conforming to the one anticipated, also appears as radically other, in that it has never been the object of an intention on the part of the agent ... Necessity appears in experience when we are robbed of our action by worked matter, *not* in so far as it is pure materiality [solitary action] but in so far as it is materialised *praxis* ... it is the experience of the Other ... in so far as his dispersed praxis, totalised by matter, turns back on me in order to transform me (CDR, pp. 223-24 and 226, (332-35).

Thus, by 'necessity' Sartre does not mean a universal law of history, but the untranscendable fact that history is embodied in materiality.

It is this bond of interiority between the existence of free praxis and necessary materiality and sociality that make up the level of *universality* and *apodictic certainty.*[8] Furthermore, this is a universality and certainty that immediately throws us into particularity (history) and uncertainty (future-orientation). In this way Sartre simultaneously poses the *transhistorical* and *transcultural* validity of certain principles of intelligibility (primary intelligibility), and affirms the historicity of the intelligibility of concrete human reality (secondary intelligibility).

So far, so good. I shall, however, argue that Sartre's conception suffers from an unresolved tension. In a way that somewhat deviates from the main emphasis on praxis, Sartre claims that "... dialectical Reason has to be grasped initially through human relations" (CDR, p. 44 (160)). In this, and other, passage Sartre implies that *human relations* also are to be understood as dialectical in character, and thus in terms of the notion of totalisations and praxis.

In his actual argumentation, however, Sartre emphasises what appears to be a different kind of intelligibility than totalisation for human relations: *mediated reciprocity.* By 'reciprocity' is meant 'mutual recognition', or a relation where person A recognises the existence of another which is the Same in kind as himself (human being, praxis, etc.). By claiming that both praxis and mediated reciprocity are dialectical in nature, and that these dialectics are one and the same, Sartre implies an *identity in the mode of being* between the *totalisation involved in actions* (the relation between an interpretation of the world, an end of action and the action itself) and *intersubjective reciprocity* (the recognition of the other as the Same).

Sartre attempts to solve this by positing the existence of *mediating factors* in human relations. Sartre, again, conceives these mediations, in terms of *praxis*: the conditions of praxis and the project of a praxis itself are the basic forms of mediation (see Chapter 7). By this Sartre is both relatively successful in showing that human relations may be seen as dialectical in nature, and that human relations depend on praxis, but he does not, in my opinion, demonstrate that the relation of reciprocity and the understanding-means-end relation are identical in their mode of being.

My criticism is partly informed by Habermas theory of communicative action, although I do not follow Habermas in his solution. Habermas would probably claim that Sartre fails to distinguish between *work* and *interaction*, or between teleological action and communicative action (Habermas 1978, p. 62 and 1984, pp. 273-337). A difference between Habermas and

Sartre, then, is that Sartre finds it important to keep a unified concept of praxis, instead of distinguishing between sociality and action. An alternative criticism would then claim that Sartre fails to show how work and interaction are different aspects of the same reality.

The presence of this unresolved tension is one reason why I chose to distinguish between Sartre's conception of rationality and his views on the dialectic. That is, one may well claim that both praxis and human relations are dialectical in character, but Sartre fails to provide grounds for the implied claim that they are dialectical in exactly the same way. I shall return to this issue in Chapter 7.

Notes

1 As exceptions to this general trend one may mention Craib 1976, Douglas and Johnson (eds.) 1977, Østerberg 1988 and 1993. In the latter Østerberg proposes to study the thought of Sartre by means of his own regressive-progressive method, that is, in terms of the relation between his thoughts and the circumstances (pp. 13-14).

2 Hendley calls such an attempt at a foundation non-theoretical since it is neither grounded in a generalisation of empirical facts, nor on some kind of transcendental deduction of conditions of possibility (Hendley 1991, pp. 111ff).

3 This list must be seen as a reconstruction since one cannot find such a list anywhere in Sartre. In CRD Sartre gives different lists of more specific things which are to be 'proved' by the investigation (CDR, pp. 15, 34ff, 79 and 822).

4 See for example Caws 1979, pp. 146-54, Flynn 1984, pp. 84-123, Howells 1988, pp. 105-13. Although Flynn's account of Sartre's dialectical conception of reason is thorough, he does not pose the question 'what does Sartre mean by 'reason'?'.

5 Caws 1979, p. 149. Caws tend to suspect that the Kantian twist of Sartre's investigation is an attempt to sound clever or a typically French type of literary play.

6 The issue of idealism in its multitude of forms can be found discussed by Sartre in many different works. This is natural since Sartre continuously posits the reality of non-observable entities (like freedom, transcendence, project etc.) but is simultaneously keen to emphasise the primacy of concrete reality to ideas. See for example BN, pp. xxi-xxiv and 223-32, SM, pp. 14-23, 68-74, 125-7, CDR, pp. 21 and 26-32.

7 See also Claude Lévi-Strauss critique and misrepresentation of Sartre's distinction between analytical and dialectical reason (1966, pp. 245-70), Sartre's answers (1966 and 1972a) and Caws 1992.

8 As for the 'a priori', Sartre observes that his investigation may appear contradictory. First, "the failure of dialectical dogmatism has shown us that the dialectic as rationality must be open to direct, everyday investigation" (CDR, p. 35 (153)). On the other hand, the requirements of an internal, reflexive investigation (opposed to empiricism) "... forces us to the conclusion that dialectical universality must be imposed *a priori* ..." (ibid.). 'A priori' does not, however, here imply some "... constitutive principles which are prior to experience", but, in a phenomenological fashion, "it relates to a universality and necessity which are contained in every experience but which transcend any particular experience" (ibid.).

7 Praxis and Social Theory

Sartre's Concept of Praxis

The concept of *praxis* stands *at the core of Sartre's anthropology*. CRD is also characterised by Sartre as aiming at *a deepening of praxis*:

> ... the deepening [*approfondissement*] of our experience/investigation [*expérience*] must also be the deepening of *praxis* (CDR, p. 160 (271)).

Especially in the light of Sartre's later concerns with an ethics of praxis, this should in my opinion be understood in two senses: to deepen our understanding of the nature of human action (*the intelligibility of praxis*), and to investigate the grounds of reasoning in practical, ethical and political matters (*practical reason*). Sartre in CRD does not, however, explicitly treat this connection between epistemic and ethical-political issues. I shall return to it in Chapter 9.

Sartre sets up his philosophy of praxis on the basis of a critique of two misconceptions: (1) *the reduction of the intelligibility of human action to the intentional project of an individual agent*: "... the translucidity of individual *praxis* as the free, re-organising surpassing of particular conditionings, is really an abstract moment..." (CDR, p. 160 (271)), slightly modified translation). The main argument against this traditional understanding is that it is *limited* and *abstract* since it does not account for the contextual, social and historical meanings of action.

(2) *The reduction of socio-historical events and processes to impersonal and mechanistic processes*. According to Sartre, contemporary thought has difficulties with connecting the concepts of action and process: "today, everyone finds a true intelligibility in the objective process ... today everyone understands, or can understand, how machines ... *create men* ... [but our] strange language ... which we have no difficulty in understanding ... links finality to necessity so indissolubly that it is impossible to tell any longer whether it is man or machine which is a practical project" (CDR, pp. 159-60 (270)). For instance, due to this difficulty the important question of *historical* or, as Flynn (1984) says, *collective responsibility* becomes blurred.

Thus, already in the immediate time following the Second World War Sartre sets himself the task to develop *a philosophy of action* emphasising both that history is made by actions, and that no action is decipherable in abstraction from the circumstances. The concept of praxis is intended by Sartre to (hermeneutically) grasp human action as both 'a *teleological* orientation towards goals' and 'a *being-in-the-world*'. In CM Sartre characterises *praxis* in the following manner:

> The movement of *praxis* does not consist in defining a world over against oneself but in plunging into a world that closes in around you. The world which is the object lays siege from all sides to the subject who unveils it and returns his image to him (NE, p. 356 (370)).

And in CRD Sartre the underlying notion of *project* is characterised as follows:

> The most rudimentary behaviour must be determined both in relation to the real and present factors which condition it and in relation to a certain object, still to come, which it is trying to bring into being. This is what we call *the project* (SM, p. 91 (76)).

The discourse on praxis in CRD is set up around a distinction between the two levels of *meaning* that such a solution must be able to connect: (1) *agent-meaning*, or what Sartre calls the *imaginary praxis* or the *project*, and (2) the *objective* (or socio-historical) *meaning*, or what Sartre calls *real praxis* or the *truth of a praxis*. In order to avoid teleological idealism Sartre is keen to define the *meaning of action* primarily in terms of it being a *real intervention in the world*:

> *praxis* ... is a passage from objective to objective through internalisation ... the objective truth of the objectified subjective [the result] must be considered as the only truth of the subjective ... An action cannot be judged by the intention behind it... (SM, p. 97-98n (80)).

This primarity of real intervention to intention parallels that of the primarity of the *text* to the *author* in contemporary hermeneutics, and by this Sartre's conception of praxis becomes more closely related to Gadamer's conception of language (see Chapter 4).

In QM Sartre describes the main orientation of his solution in little more detail:

> Imagine an actor who is playing Hamlet and who is caught up in his role. He

> crosses his mother's room to kill Polonius hidden behind the arras. But that is not *what he is actually doing*. He crosses a stage before an audience and passes from 'court side' to 'garden side' in order to earn his living, to win fame, and this real activity defines his position in society (SM, pp. 45-46 (46-47)).

Furthermore:

> One cannot deny that these *real results are present in some way in his imaginary act*. One cannot deny that the movement of *the imaginary prince expresses*, in a certain indirect and refracted manner, *the actor's real movement* ... Thus we may speak simultaneously of a subjective drama (the simple play of appearances which hides nothing, which contain no 'unconscious' elements) and of an *objective, intentional* organisation of real means with a view to achieving real ends — without any organisation of all this by a consciousness or a premeditated will ... The truth of the imaginary *praxis* is in the real *praxis*, and the real ... includes implicit references to the imaginary *praxis* as to its interpretation (ibid., my italics).

The *imaginary praxis* is the agent's own interpretation of what he is doing or aiming at (the project 'Hamlet kills Polonius'). The *real praxis* contain all the *truths* of what is done (acting in order to earn a living, etc.), it informs about the conditions and social reality that makes up the real contextual meaning and significance of some behaviour. Since the truth of a praxis is grounded, not in the intention, but in the real relations of the action with the circumstances, this facticity returns the image (that is, originally the project) to the agent in the form of a description of what he actually was doing.

At the basis of this stands a distinction between the *epistemological starting point* and the *task of a critical investigation*. Thus, on the one hand

> ... the epistemological starting point must always be consciousness as prereflective apodictic certainty [certitude] (of) itself and as consciousness *of* such and such an object. (CDR, 51 (167)).

The starting point for all interpretation is the agent's own immediate, prereflective and experiential understanding of what is done, or, concerning other's actions, our immediate assumptions about what others are aiming at. In the example above, the starting point is the agent's consciousness of himself as 'an actor' and as 'acting Hamlet'. Concerning other's actions, if I, for example, see A walk towards the window and open it, I spontaneously understand his behaviour, for example, as an act of 'opening the window, because the room is to hot' (SM, p. 153-56). The behaviour of A is meaningful to me independently of the actual intentions of the agent.

It might still be the case that A is walking in his sleep, that he is opening the window because he has seen a friend outside or that he is in fact a robot. The point is thus not that our immediate understanding would be correct, but that such pre-understanding is a necessary starting point. As I showed in Chapter 5, pre-reflective awareness does not imply a full understanding of what someone (or oneself) is really doing. The task of an *interpretative investigation* is thus to decipher the real meaning on the basis of this pre-understanding.

In the example of the actor acting Hamlet, we might assume that the agent himself is well aware of the real meanings mentioned, and the situation does not as such constitute a genuine interpretative problem. In most cases, however, we are not fully aware of all the meanings of what we do. An important task then is *to interpret action* with the goal in mind to *decipher its truth or real meaning*. According to Sartre's conception, *truth implies the imperative to totalise*: it is only through the contextual bonds of interiority of an action with the circumstances that the full intelligibility of 'a concrete action in history' can be understood in a way that raises claims to validity. Sartre's conception of history as a totalisation means that there are *connections between individual acts* and *the historical process as a whole*, and it is exactly these connections that make up the domain of historical interpretation.

It is exactly this task that forms the set up of Sartre's critical investigation of reason understood as a study of the intelligibility of praxis. For according to Sartre, striving for the truth of man and reason in history implies the task to carry out a *critical investigation of the conditions of the historical intelligibility of praxis*. This investigation is concerned with *the concrete truth of praxis*, and it is motivated by the fact that this concrete truth most often appears *hidden* or *unintelligible*. Thus:

> ... critical investigation will reveal actions without an agent, productions without a producer, totalisations without a totaliser, counter-finalities and infernal circularities. We shall also discover multiplicities producing totalised thoughts and acts without reference to the individuals composing them, indeed without their even being aware of it ... Vagabond and authorless, these free actions, which can overturn a society or its dead institutions ... cannot remain foreign bodies within a developing History ... [The investigation] ... must be able to grasp ... the source of such things, the reasons ... for their inhumanity and for their accessibility ... to a totalising anthropology (CDR, 76 (189-90)).

This presence of (real) meanings that are not rooted in the actual (imaginary) projects of individuals has two implications for Sartre. Besides the task to deepen the understanding of what we do in terms of a study of the material, social and historical *bonds of interiority*, the investigation should engage in the normative task to disclose the sources of *alienation*. History is made by actions, but the orientation of the historical process is not an explicitly defined or individualised human project that is set up by individuals. According to Sartre, at the present time of history, we are continuously robbed of the meaning of what we do. Our praxis is necessarily alienated.

Sartre's theory of praxis coincides with *social theory*. The social theory of CRD discusses mainly three themes:
(1) to make intelligible the relation between what we do and the material circumstances. This theme is mainly discussed by means of the conceptual double of *praxis* and *practico-inert* [*pratico-inerte*] *fields* and *processes*. (2) To make intelligible different types of social praxis. This, by far the most extensively treated issue in CRD, is dealt with in the form of a *theory of social formations* [*théorie des ensembles pratiques*]. The generalisation of the concept of praxis to encompass any historically situated future-orientation — fully comprehended or largely uncomprehended by the agents, or unspecified as to its real meaning — implies the task to study the *different types of social praxis* that may be manifested as *real* in a *historical process*. In CRD Sartre gradually introduces other types of praxis than individual action: *passivity* or *active passivity*, *serial praxis*, *common praxis*, *institutionalised praxis* and the *praxis-process*. (3) To make intelligible social fields in movement, or history. This Sartre mainly discusses under the theme of a *theory of the intelligibility of conflict*, which is Sartre's *key to the intelligibility of history*.

Since CRD is thus also intended to provide the foundation for sociological and historical knowledge (CDR, p. 69), Sartre raises praxis as the paradigm for sociology and history. In this way, Sartre places himself within a tradition of social theory that builds on an action-theoretic framework, alongside Marx and the Marxists, Weber (1947), Parsons (1951) and, today, such thinkers as Habermas (1984) and Bourdieu (1990).

If Sartre's concept of praxis is turned into a paradigm for *social* theory, we may ask what is it's actual relevance for the general question how we are to understand human beings and human reality, and for the more specific question how we are to understand individuals. That is, what is actually the relation between Sartre's theory of social formations, conflict and history and the biographical-interpretative task outlined in EN and IF?

Is not 'praxis' rather a concept relevant for social theory than applicable to the individually lived? This is partly true. But the way Sartre defines praxis as a general concept of actions and undertakings and as emphasising concreteness in fact makes it usable to both kinds of investigation. More importantly, according to Sartre social theory is of uttermost importance for the understanding of individuals, and vice versa.

In summary then, Sartre's concept of praxis, by emphasising the dimension of real intervention and inscription in socio-material reality, implies that the question of the intelligibility of what we do is to be answered by means of an investigation of *the dimensions of real meaning* of praxis. By 'real', again, Sartre means both material reality and the social reality of meanings, intersubjective recognition and conflict. Sartre's concept of praxis thus has basically three dimensions: (i) it is a concept of action, (ii) it constitutes a bond of interiority with the material world and (iii) it constitutes a human relation or a bond of interiority with other human beings and praxes. It thereby fulfils the three demands of Sartre's anthropology to be a philosophy of *action*, *materiality* and *sociality*.[1]

Materiality and Sociality: Praxis and the Practico-Inert vs. Praxis as Language

Sartre's concept of praxis, by its simultaneous emphasis on the *material* and the *social*, contains a certain unresolved tension and vacillation concerning what the core of praxis actually consists of. This leads to a parallel tension in Sartre's conception of rationality between the structures of *totalisation* and *reciprocal recognition*. Sartre's ambition is clearly that these two dimensions are to be combined in a single concept of praxis and dialectical reason, but he does not in my opinion fully succeed in this.

In CRD Sartre first claims, in his discourse on need, that "... *praxis*, in the first instance, is nothing but the relation of the organism, as an exterior and future end, to the present organism, as a totality under threat; it is function exteriorised", and that "... *human labour* [is] the original *praxis* by which man produces and reproduces his life" (CDR, pp. 83 and 90 (197, 203). Praxis is also described as a "... a *totalisation* [my italics] whose movement toward its own end *practically* makes the environment into a totality" (CDR, 85 (199)).

On the other hand, praxis is neither to be reduced to manual work nor to the totalisation involved in physical realisations. Sartre continuously, although not in every section, emphasises the necessary intersubjective and social dimension of praxis. He even intriguingly compares praxis to *language*:

> ... *praxis* is always language (whether truthful or deceptive) because it cannot take place without signifying itself (CDR, 99 (212)).

This implies that praxis is not only a *totalisation*, but also equally well a *signification*. Or rather, Sartre's notion of totalisation is intended to incorporate signification or meaningfulness. This also means that the dimensions of *singularisation* and *contradiction* I mentioned in Chapter 6 encompass both a material and an intersubjectively signifying aspect.

By being a socially recognisable form of reality, and by being a real intervention in social reality, praxis constitutes a meaning-carrying relation to other human beings. By 'meaningful' and 'signifying' one may mean both (i) that an action may be described in different ways by different persons and (ii) that actions may be more, less and differently significant for other persons. The latter dimension often contains moral implications. For example, if I solve a problem by hitting someone in the face instead of discussing the issue, this does not only imply different descriptions, but also a different impact (hearing a word vs. being punched) and different moral connotations (agreement vs. violence).

A totalisation is comprehensive in a singularising and not in a covering sense: totalisation implies a reference to the whole. This relation may now be understood as signifying. Take, for example, language. When A expresses his opinion to B, the sentences he uses are significations. The chosen expression contain lexical signs and conforms to grammatical rules. In this sense a linguistic expression may be described as a singularising totalisation: it refers to the whole of language (lexicon and grammar) and to the contextual background which makes the sentence meaningful at this time and place.

This example may also be used in reverse to illuminate the notion of totalisation. In analogue with the significations involved in linguistic expressions, praxis refers to the whole of the environment, in two senses. First, praxis is internally connected to the environment (as the sentence is to the whole of language). Second, through its internal bonds of sociality it refers to the social environment by necessarily being meaningful for others (as the sentence refers to the contextual background of dialogue). It is perhaps in this sense that a praxis (or the life of a human being) may be said both to *totalise the epoch* (to integrate all its meanings and express them in a single undertaking) and to *be totalised by the epoch* (the epoch is the context which brings forth the real meaning of the action) (cf. Flynn 1992).

This analogue between praxis and language is, self-evidently, significant for my distinction between a *hermeneutics of language* and a *hermeneutics of praxis*. We can now see that Sartre in fact intends to combine an action-perspective with a language-perspective, or rather, to incorporate the language-perspective within the action-perspective. Sartre does not then deny that human reality is inherently linguistic in character, quite the contrary. However, Sartre insists that linguisticality is only intelligible as a certain dimension of praxis. According to Sartre, the original mode of being of language is communication, and communication is fundamentally a specific kind of praxis. This implies that meaningfulness (of linguistic expressions and actions) is not reducible to linguistic relations, but is much wider (being punched, social identity, etc.).

This attempt to develop a solution in which an action- and a language-perspective are necessarily always co-present implies that Sartre's conception of *material reality* should show a similar duality. First, from the point of view of a philosophy that describes human reality primarily in terms of project and action, material reality ought to be redescribed as both *thing* and *instrument*. Already in EN Sartre reformulates, in a Heideggerian manner, what he first calls being-in-itself as *instrumental-thing*: "The thing is not first a thing in order to be subsequently an instrument; neither is it first an instrument in order to be revealed subsequently as a thing. It is an instrumental-thing [*chose-ustensile*]" (BN, 200 (245)).

In CRD Sartre introduces the notion of the *practico-inert* in order to describe this feature of our encounter with the world (CDR, especially pp. 320-24, Flynn 1984 pp. 72-84 and 93-104). From the point of view of praxis, the material world appears both as an *inertial system* governed, for example, by the laws of physics, and as a *practical field* of possibilities. For example a hammer is both a physical object with certain inert characteristics (made of wood, steel, etc.) and a practical object whose properties is defined in relation to some project (useful or not for hitting a nail). By such expressions as 'the practico-inert', 'practico-inert fields' and 'practico-inert processes' Sartre thus means the co-presence of (i) objective laws of inert materiality and (ii) a perspective of practicality that defines such objective phenomena as 'useful', 'obstacles', etc.

The concept of the practico-inert must not, however, be limited to physical materiality (CDR, pp. 318-42). Thus, for example, social institutions and language as a system share the character of being practico-inert. Furthermore, within the practico-inert must be included such social 'lawfulness' and alienation as, for example, 'breaking a law leads to police intervention' and 'using meaningless words may lead to a diagnosis of mental illness and confinement in a hospital'. Practico-inert sociality is rooted in the dependence of social practices on materiality and in institutionalisation.

I shall give a brief exposition of Sartre's conception of the practico-inert — also describes as the necessity present at the heart of intelligibility and as the anti-dialectic (CDR, p. 320) — by the means of a division into five aspects of the practico-inert: (i) the past, (ii) objective possibility, (iii) scarcity of resources, (iv) inscription of results and (v) counter-finality.

In QM Sartre claims that "the given which we surpass at every instant by the simple fact of living it, is not restricted to the material conditions of our existence; we must include in it ... our own childhood" (SM, p. 100 (82)). The traits of character we inherit from our own past are of uttermost importance for the understanding of a human beings, and consequently for an individual's understanding of his/her actions (i). Personal character, as Sartre shows in the example of Flaubert (see Chapter 8), may thus form both an orientation and obstacle which is a part of the given. It is thus practico-inert.

In addition, "the project must of necessity cut across the field of instrumental possibilities" (SM, p. 111 (89)). The objective possibilities (ii) of the given material and social field makes up a practico-inert condition for praxis (cf. Flynn 1984, pp. 72-84). Furthermore, the results of praxis are necessarily inscribed into the practico-inert (iv). If praxis is to be seen as a real intervention in the world, it necessarily has a dimension of materiality. The practico-inert is the destiny of praxis: "... in so far as praxis is process, goals loose their teleological character. Without ceasing to be genuine goals, they become destinies" (CDR, p. 663 (746), see also Flynn 1984, pp. 102-4).

In a field consisting of a multiplicity of practical agents, or indeed in any situation, the possibilities and resources present are limited or *scarce* (iii) (CDR, pp. 122-52, see also McBride 1981, pp. 620-24 and 1991, pp. 109-11). Sartre in fact makes the scarcity of resources a major source of intelligibility in our kind of history: "*Scarcity* is a fundamental relation of *our* History and a contingent determination of our univocal relation to materiality. Scarcity [is] ... the lived relation of a practical multiplicity to surrounding materiality within the interiority of that multiplicity itself" (CDR, p. 125 (237)). Besides scarcity of food, Sartre also mentions other kinds of scarcity: time, given linguistic expressions, etc.

A fifth example of a dimension of the practico-inert is *counter-finality* (v) (CDR, pp. 162-96). Praxis is characteristically defined by its teleological goal-orientation. But in so far as praxis necessarily becomes inscribed in the practico-inert (in processes which are not goal-oriented), and in so far as the practical agent never can have a complete overview and knowledge of the situation, the actual result may appear as the opposite of what was intended. Sartre takes the example of deforestation in China. By turning more and more forest into cultivable soil, Chinese peasants in actual fact, through the practico-inert mediation of geological and hydrographical regularities, created first drought and then flooding. The finality involved in the praxis to increase cultivable soil made useless even the land that was already in use.

According to Sartre, the intelligibility of practico-inert field and processes is to be defined in terms of the bonds of interiority between the teleology of actions, their inscription in socio-material objectivity and the plurality of agents in the field (CDR, pp. 318-24). Through the mediation of laws of physical nature and other's actions, the results of our projects may lead to processes that appear to be relatively independent of and even contrary to our aims. This is counter-finality.

The notions of project, intervention and totalisation make up the action-theoretic core of Sartre's concept of praxis. Together they convey the co-presence of goal-directedness with a hermeneutical emphasis on the bonds of interiority between action and world. The concept of practico-inert, again, is introduced in order to describe the material dimension of this bond.

The crucial dimension for the interpretation of the *real meanings of praxis* and of the *intelligibility of practico-inert fields* is, however, *sociality*. It is of course possible for us to do things individually and in isolation, but according to Sartre, isolation appears on the ground of a more fundamental sociality: "... we must not assume that there are no such things as isolated workers. Isolated workers, in fact, exist wherever the social and technical conditions of their work require that they work alone. But their very solitude is a historical and social characteristic" (CDR, p. 95 (208). For example, a gardener working alone in his garden stand — through a series of mediations — in relation to other workers and non-workers in the field, to social institutions and the socio-economic framework of society at large. These dimensions belong to the truth, although not necessarily the project, of gardening.

In addition, the intelligibility of practico-inert fields and processes depend on the social bond. The presence of "... the *necessity of the existence of this field of inert activity*" as a "... *necessity within certainty* [évidence] ... at the heart of free individual *praxis* ... rests on ... the univocal relation of interiority as a basis of individual praxis and of the plurality of agents within the practical field" (CDR, pp. 319-20 (425-26)).

Human Relations as Mediated Reciprocities

In order to make the social bonds and levels of sociality intelligible; Sartre develops a theory of human relations. Within the perspective of CRD, the problems involved in a study of social reality may be limited to two: (i) the general character of intersubjectivity and (ii) how social formations, social interaction and societies are to be understood. I shall not go into the details of this complex, highly sophisticated and important investigation, but focus on some of its central features. I limit my exposition to: (1) Sartre's *theory of human relations* as *mediated reciprocities*, (2) his *typology of social formations* and their corresponding *types of praxis*, and (3) his *theory of conflict* as basic for his theory of history. Since my investigation primarily deals with Sartre's hermeneutics of praxis, I focus on the consequences of his views on sociality for the intelligibility of praxis.

As I mentioned above, Sartre defines praxis both as *action* and *language*. The latter communicates the necessity of the social dimension, as did the *theory of being-for-others* in EN. The theory of being-for-others, however, is basically modelled on a *philosophy of perception*. The primary characteristic of our consciousness of other conscious beings is manifested in *the look*.

Already in this theory certain traits point towards Sartre's latter developments towards a theory of *mediated reciprocity* and its inherent *linguisticality*. First, although Sartre insists that conflict is the meaning of being-for-others, he also claims that "... the internal negative relation [to the other] is a relation of reciprocity" (BN, 284 (331)): the other is encountered as the Same in kind (human being, freedom, transcendence, etc.) as myself, and not as a being-in-itself (other in kind). Second, Sartre indicates that the theory is not strictly bound to the model of perception, but reminisces a model of language: "language is not a phenomenon added on to being-for-others. It *is* originally being-for-others; that is, it is the fact that a subjectivity experiences itself as an object for the other" (BN, 372 (422). Third, Sartre does not reduce sociality to the concrete encounter with others: it may also imply "... to find myself engaged in a world in which instrumental-complexes can have a signification which my free project has not first given to them" (BN, 509-10 (567)).

The theory of mediated reciprocity describes *the fundamental mode of the human relation*. It does not engage in the classical task to prove the existence of others, but attempts to characterise the general form of our relations with others. Sartre does unfortunately not present any strong arguments why exactly this model, and no other, is to be accepted as a correct description of intersubjectivity.

At the core of the theory of mediated reciprocity stand the notions of *reciprocity*, *mediation* and *signification*. By (intersubjective) 'reciprocity' is meant a relation where person A stands in a relation to person B such that both affirm or recognise the other as similar in kind (although different in existence). For example, (i) if A recognises B as another human being and (ii) B recognises A as a human being and, furthermore, (iii) that A and B both recognise that the other recognises himself as a human being, their relation may be said to fulfil the condition of reciprocity. Mutual recognition implies both an experience of the other, a reflexive experience of oneself as related to the other and a hypothesis about the other's similar experience of myself.

According to Sartre, the recognition involved does not actually have the form of an experience of the other as a human being as such. Instead, the reciprocity of human relations is basically a recognition of the other as *project* and *praxis*. In CRD Sartre thus defines 'reciprocity' in terms of four conditions (CDR, pp. 112-13 (224-25):

(1) "... that the Other is a means to the extent that I myself am a means...". If a human being is treated as a means, reciprocity demands that both the other and myself are seen as means to the same end.
(2) "... that I recognise the Other as *praxis*...". Reciprocity implies that the other is recognised as the Same in kind as I experience myself.
(3) "... that I recognise his movement toward his own ends in the same movement by which I project myself towards mine...". Reciprocity is an experiential recognition, which is fulfilled if my experience of my own project immediately implies that the other is a being of projects.
(4) "... that I discover myself as an object and instrument of his ends through the same act which constitutes him as an objective instrument of my ends". If I treat the other as means, then reciprocity demands that I experience myself as a possible means for the other.

It is important to notice that Sartre with 'reciprocity' means both a condition of *intelligibility* and an *ethical ideal* or value (see Chapter 9).

Although reciprocity is a basic feature of all human relations, it is possible to take up different attitudes to it: "... reciprocity can be either positive or negative" (CDR, p. 113 (225)). For example, in exchange and in an action oriented toward a common aim, reciprocity is affirmed, whereas "in the case of negative reciprocity, the four necessary conditions are fulfilled but on the basis of a reciprocal refusal" (ibid.). In the most extreme cases, refusal may lead to conflict and struggle, but negative reciprocity may also have less violent forms (e.g. seriality, see below).

A second necessary feature of human relations is *mediation*. By 'mediation' is meant 'in between' or 'passing through'. It thus stands in opposition to 'directness' or 'immediacy'. On the crudest level, intersubjective reciprocity is mediated by practico-inert materiality: the relation of reciprocity between two praxes is necessarily mediated by the material circumstances, the instrumental means employed and the material result achieved (CDR, p. 113). As I mentioned, practico-inert mediation may also be understood in a non-physical sense: e.g. the meaning embodied in a linguistic sign.

Language is one of the clearest examples of a relation of mediated reciprocity. The meaning of a word is simultaneously embodied in the lexical sign (practico-inert mediation) and reciprocally recognised by all that understand it. According to Sartre's conception of language, the signification is the act of expression, whereas the internal relation between signifying and signified is a feature of the practico-inert mediation of the act (CDR, p. 98-99, Morot-Sir 1986).

There are two kinds of possible mediations: *praxis and practico-inert* (CDR, pp. 366-82). Practico-inert mediations are mediations of an object-like type. However, the important thing, especially in a normative-ethical perspective, is that reciprocity may also be mediated by praxis. In a genuinely common action, the reciprocity of the participants is each participants reciprocal recognition of a single common project that orients the action of each. Such recognition may either be explicitly stated in communication or implied in the undertaking itself. In addition, the definition of the common project may be relatively vague or mute.

The theory of mediated reciprocity posits the necessity of social meanings in praxis. It also gives some indication of how such meanings are to be understood: differences between types of mediations, the analogy with language, etc. According to Sartre, an investigation of such mediations and meanings must account for the different ways in which human beings are involved with each other. This seems to imply mainly three things: (1) on the sociological and socio-psychological plane, an investigation of social formations, (2) on the ethical plane, an investigation of the moral-evaluative meanings involved in such encounters and (3) on the psychological plane, an investigation of the place and relevance of others in a persons life. In the following I shall focus on the first of these, and return to the second in Chapter 9. The third is constantly at play in Sartre's writings, but an attempt to systematise it would fall outside the scope of this investigation.

The Theory of Social Formations: Collective, Group and Institution

Almost 2/3 of the first volume of CRD is dedicated to a *theory of social formations*. It investigates the different types of social bonds and unities that make up a social field, community or society. The theory is formal in nature: it does not study real social formations, but attempts to sift out the principles by means of which real formations are to be made intelligible. The typology presented is based on a differentiation between *types of social unity, types of human relations* and *types of social praxis*. In relation to Marxism, Sartre's theory functions both as a *specification* and as a *critique* of the *theory of social classes*. Sartre introduces a different set of types than socio-economic classes as basic, although the theory is also intended to shed light on the intelligibility of class-formation itself.

The theory is based on the differentiation between types of mediations. Mediations function as what *unifies* a plurality of individuals into a social formation. Sartre criticises the hypostatisation of groups as some kind of hyper-organic wholes, which would function independently of the individuals of which it consists (CDR, p. 345). According to Sartre, social formations must be made intelligible on the basis of *individual praxis* and *human relations*, and it is exactly the *mediating* factor of human relations that functions as the bridge between these two frameworks of action and reciprocity.

Sartre initially distinguishes between two basic types of social formations (CDR esp. pp. 253-55, 363-82 and 576-79): (1) the *collective* or *series* and (2) the *group*. The distinction parallels that of the practico-inert and praxis as mediation. In addition Sartre introduces a third type of formation in which the mediation is both praxis and practico-inert: (3) the *institution* or *institutionalised group*. Since the institutionalised group is a certain combination of collective and group, some have preferred a division into two types. Although this is not unjustified, I find a division into three more elucidating. For one thing, it only by means of a three-fold distinction that two of the most important dividing lines in Sartre's social theory becomes visible: (i) that between serial and group-like human relations, and (ii) that between non-hierarchic and hierarchic human relations within a group.

Thus:

(1) A social formation in which human relations are mediated by a practico-inert object is called a *collective* or a *series*. Collectives can be more generally defined as a social bond, rather than as constituting a genuine social interaction.

(2) A social formation in which human relations are mediated by a praxis or a project is called a *group*. By a group Sartre means a social formation which is defined by a genuinely common undertaking.

(3) A group in which the mediating project that orients the common project has been transformed into a certain kind of practico-inert object is called an *institution* or *institutionalised group*.

According to Sartre, by means of this typology we are able to make any concrete social field, real constellation of social formations or any society intelligible. However, the theory of social formations describes society only as a static field, and not on the level of practices and history in process. In the final instance then, the *intelligibility of concrete social fields* depends on the *historical intelligibility* of *actual practices* set up by *real formations*.

The formal mode of Sartre's investigation has another important implication. Some interpreters, like Aron (1975), tend to read Sartre's (regressive) investigation as a description of a chronological movement, whereby a serialised society is turned over by a revolutionary group and gradually deteriorates into a institutionalised society. This interpretation violates Sartre's own self-understanding; it also misinterprets theoretical categories for empirical ones. According to Sartre,

> A social field is constituted … by structured ensembles of groupings which are always both *praxis* and practico-inert, although either of these characteristics may constantly tend to cancel itself out; only experience permit us to determine the internal relationships of the structure of interiority of a definite group and of a definite moment of its interior dialectic ... I have claimed that the inert gathering with its structure of seriality is the basic type of sociality. But I have not meant this in a historical sense, and the term 'fundamental' here does not imply temporal priority. Who could claim that collectives come before groups? No one is a position to advance any hypothesis on this subject (CDR, pp. 254 and 348 (362 and 452)).

For instance, a socio-economic class may simultaneously consist of a collective (the socio-economic bond of wage-labourers), groups (militant combat groups) and institutions (the trade union).

To these three types of social formations correspond certain kinds of *praxis* and certain kinds of *human relations*: (i) collective or serial praxis and human relations of separation and alienation, (ii) genuinely common action, commonly — even democratically — organised undertakings and human relations of co-operation, solidarity and non-alienation, (iii) hierarchically organised common undertakings and human relations of leadership and subjugation. These descriptions already suggest a moral reading: the group appears to be a kind of ethical ideal (cf. Aron 1975, pp. 54-59, Flynn 1984, pp. 113-19 and 190-96). But since the group also, according to Sartre, contains the fruits of terror and oppression, its status is rather ambiguous. I shall return to this issue below and in Chapter 9. In the following I shall characterise the types of formation and praxis in little more detail.

A social formation does not constitute 'a melting of individual consciousness" into a collective consciousness, or a hyper-organism. The existence of social formations depends on the actual relations between real human beings. The being, continuity, unity or social bond of a social formation is something that continuously must be made, remade, taken care of an organised by human beings.

A *collective* or *series* is a type of social formation, where the human relations are mediated by a social, practico-inert object: "I call the two-way relation between a material, inorganic worked object and a multiplicity which finds its unity of exteriority in it *collective*. It defines a *social object*" (CDR, p. 269 (376)). The praxes of the individuals participating in a collective are not oriented towards the collective, but towards the object. It is the collective object that makes a plurality into a collective.

Sartre gives many examples of collectives (CDR, pp. 256-318, see also Sartre 1978c): the direct gathering of persons queuing to a bus, the indirect gathering of radio-listeners or viewers of the same TV-program, buyers and sellers on a common market, persons with a similar socio-economic status (employers, employees, the unemployed), the population of a certain nation-state (citizenship), voters in an election, etc. What these have in common is the mediation of a pre-structured, collective object, and it is the existence of the practico-inert object and not the wills of the persons which constitutes the collective: the bus, the system of collective traffic, radio and television, a market economy, the socio-economic system, the law, a constitution and geographical borders.

The praxis of an individual in a collective is characterised by Sartre as *serial praxis*. In case a number of persons take, let's say, the 8.12 bus from a certain stop into the centre of town, the individual praxis of person A 'to take the 8.12 bus from nearby his suburban flat in order to get to the Department of Philosophy at the centre of town' may be redescribed on a social level to form a part of 'the collective praxis of a plurality taking the 8.12 bus from point a to point b'. *Seriality* consists in the fact that A does the same as everybody else, not in co-operation. Serial praxis thus constitutes a *collective undertaking* (project) carried out in *separation* (serially) by a plurality of individuals. The social relation of seriality encompasses a kind of parallel, side-by-side identity of aspects of the concrete actions of individuals (CDR, p. 261). They do not co-operate, but sustain a certain project, which none of them could sustain by himself. This means that seriality is only an aspect — or a description from a particular point of view — of a concrete action, and it does not exhaust its concrete reality: the same action may simultaneously be individual, collective and common.

Sartre emphasises the bond of interiority between consciousness and its object, between experience and the world. This also implies that to the serial relations of a collective corresponds "... serial behaviour, serial feelings and serial thoughts; in other words *a series is a mode of being for individuals both in relation to one another and in relation to their common being* and this mode of being transforms all their structures" (CDR, p. 266 (373)). These behaviours, feelings and thoughts stem from the fact that it is primarily the structure of the object, and the rules that belong to this structure (queuing, not to disturb others, etc.), which orients the action and one's understanding of it.

The *group* is a social formation defined by a common undertaking or a common praxis (CDR, pp. 345-404). In a group, human beings act in genuine co-operation. That praxis is the mediation means basically two things. First, the praxis in question cannot be solitary defined by any single individual, but must be set up by a plurality. Second, since human beings are fundamentally to be defined in terms of their praxis, the mediation is *human*. That is, whereas serial human relations are characterised by Sartre as relations between persons as Others, the human relations in a group constitute relations between persons as Thirds. By a *mediating Third* Sartre means that aspect of the person, where he or she autonomously defines his own praxis in terms of the common praxis (cf. Flynn 1981 and 1984): "... I am *amongst* third parties and I have no privileged status. But this operation does not transform me into an object, because totalisation by the third party only reveals a free praxis as a common unity which already qualifies him" (CDR, 379 (481). Sartre gives numerous examples of common group-praxis (CDR, pp. 351-63, 450-51): a revolutionary group (the storming of the Bastille), a football team, etc.

Common praxis thus constitutes a co-operation between individuals in the realisation of a certain aim. In this case each individual must totalise the project so it becomes common to all. So far I have discussed the notion of *totalisation* mainly as an individual's comprehension of his project. The totalisation at play in common praxis must be both *practical*, in that it is defined by a project, and *social*, in that it must *integrate* all the individuals in question. Importantly, such a totalisation, because it is always particular, may in fact consist either in *social integration* or in *social exclusion*. For example, the members may integrate some individuals and exclude others, and these excluded others either constitutes another group, an enemy group, a series of non-members, etc. (CDR, pp. 346-48, 564-75).

Consequently two different kinds of *conflict* are possible: integrative and exclusive. In social integration the project must be defined as common, and this may give rise to a debate on the actual content and direction of the common project (CDR, 410-12 and pp. 576-77). In social exclusion, again, the project is explicitly defined in relation to an outside, and this may give rise to conflicts in relation to the projects of other groups, and to the projects of individuals that do not belong to any group.

A group is thus not a natural, but an *artificially constructed unity*. As we saw, the collective is also an artificial unity, but in this case unity is preserved by the object itself. In the group, however, the members must themselves actively *take care of their unity*, that is, of the *ontological status* of the group. This problem of unity may be divided into two: the problem of *permanence*, or continuity of existence, and the problem of *organisation*, or the structure of this unity.

According to Sartre, the permanence of a group depends on the existence of a (implicit or explicit) *pledge* (CDR, p. 417-44) or, if you like, a contract. By means of a pledge, the members commit themselves to participating in the common undertaking over a longer period of time. In the case of a spontaneously formed new group, or what Sartre calls a *group-in-fusion*, unity and permanence are directly and solely dependent on the common praxis itself (CDR, pp. 351-405). Parallel to his description of serial behaviour, feelings and thoughts, Sartre claims that "at this level, there is group behaviour and there are group thoughts in that the common *praxis* is self-elucidating" (CDR, p. 405 (505)).

The common undertaking may be of such kind that it needs long-term planning, patience and many years of work in order to be realised. It is in order to secure such continuity that the pledge is needed. By the introduction of a pledge, however, there arises a new dimension of *sanctions* and *rewards* by means of which the pledge is sustained, and this raises the possibility of internal terror.

The pledge certifies the existence of the group, but it does not secure the content and organisation of the project: the group needs *organisation* (CDR, pp. 445-62). An organised group may be structured by means of a division of labour between jobs and functions assigned to different persons, and perhaps a forum of decision-making concerning the content and direction of the common undertaking. An organised group needs not be hierarchically organised or have specified leaders, but it may constitute what may be called a radically democratic group.

In summary, the common praxis of a group must be oriented both towards the *definition of a project* and towards the *care taking* and *organisation* of the human relations of the group. In an ethical perspective, it is important to recognise that human beings in this type of social formation may define themselves simultaneously as *autonomous agents*, *authentic individuals* and *socially common*. The group thus constitutes an opposite to serial alienation (CDR, pp. 396-98, 458-63, 615), and it is in this sense that it functions as a kind of socio-political ideal.

The intelligibility of the *institution* is found in the extension of the group, at a time when serial relations are reintroduced into the group. An institution, institutionalised praxis or institutionalised group is a group where the pledge has been transformed into a practico-inert object, or an *institution*, and the organisation has been transformed into *hierarchy*. The institution is defined by an objectification of the common undertaking, for example, in terms of a written constitution, written rules and the assignment of leaders and subjugated employees.

From the point of view of normative and ethical questions, it is important to recognise two dividing lines in Sartre's theory of social formations, and especially to be clear about exactly where these are to be drawn. The first is easy: in opposition to seriality, the group constitutes an overcoming of alienation. But Sartre's investigation of the group continues to discuss praxis and its bonds of interiority with the world. Thus, in the regressive investigation I have outlined above the group gradually seem to deteriorate into a hierarchical institution. The institution is a social formation where seriality and alienation is reintroduced on another level.

But exactly where is the 'turning point' in this second case? Does the main dividing line go between the group-of-fusion, which is defined purely in terms of praxis, and the pledged group, which introduces terror (sanctions) into the human relations? Or does it go between the organised group, which constitutes non-hierarchically organised long-term projects, and the hierarchical institution, which introduces subjugating leadership? The answer to this difficult question depends on whether one chooses to emphasise *purity of form and anarchism*, on the one hand, or *concreteness and the possibility of an ideal society*, on the other, as the major ingredient of Sartre's ethical thinking. That is, in the first case, already social organisation would be seen as a first step towards alienation, whereas in the second case, one would imply that Sartre believed in the value of a common organisation (at least as a first step towards an ideal society). I shall return to this issue in Chapter 9.

The Intelligibility of Conflict

The typology of social formations is intended to enable us to make social fields intelligible in their internal, structural and static aspects. It also informs us about different types of social praxis. But such a regressively denoted typology does not as such provide us with the means to make *historical processes* (the field in movement) intelligible. In approaching this question Sartre proceeds in a similar manner as in the theory of social formations. He studies the intelligibility of the moving relations that constitute the temporal dimension of a plurality of praxes and social formations. This study is begun but never finished in the second volume of CRD: the intelligibility of history.[2]

Already towards the end of the first volume Sartre indicates the orientation of his answer:

> The conclusion of this [regressive] investigation is that *the only possible intelligibility* of human relations is dialectical and that this intelligibility, in a concrete history whose true foundation is *scarcity*, can be manifested only as antagonistic reciprocity (CDR, p. 805 (881)).

The history in which we live is a process of antagonisms, conflicts, social contradictions and social struggle, between different praxes and between different social formations. This conclusion leads Sartre to pose the problem of *the intelligibility of conflict* as the leading theme of the second volume. Or, alternatively, since the theory of social formations enables us to make social bonds and intersubjective co-operation intelligible, the task to make social conflicts intelligible remains.

In the simplified case of two antagonistically related undertakings, the situation and problem:

> ... involves a twin-headed temporalisation, of which each moment represent *at the same time* a *praxis*, its negation by the other *praxis* and the beginnings of a transformation of the former in order to outwit [déjouer] the latter and of the latter in order not to be outwitted by the former. But even if this strange reality, the practice of no one, can be related, in a divergent double intuition, to the two agents when two individuals are involved ... can there be a dialectical comprehension of it? (CDR, 805-56 (882)).[3]

From the point of view of each praxis, both one's own and the other's praxis are intelligible in the light of their own ends. This would imply two different frameworks of intelligibility. But according to Sartre, the problem of historical understanding is whether we are able, in a justified manner, to grasp the totality of this process in a singular way (totalisation), that is, as an intelligibility that transgresses the twin-headed perspective of the two antagonists. Thus, the problem of historical intelligibility cannot be reduced to the strategic rationality of the respective participants:

> The historical problem is not just to know if operation x was the best possible in the given historical circumstances, but also to know why it did not correspond — and could not correspond — to the practical and totalising schema which summarises it in the lessons at the War Academy. In fact, the historicity of an action consists in the fact that it is *never* assimilable without further ado to the best possible solution, since the best possible solution can be found only if you possess all the elements of the solution, all the time required to assemble them into a synthesis which transcends them, and all the calm and objectivity necessary for self-criticism. Science is a necessary moment of action, but action is necessarily transcended ignorance since it determines itself as the far side of knowledge ... *If then, the dialectical intelligibility of the struggle must be able to exist*, it is *at the actual level of the concrete, when the adversaries ... know and do not know what they are doing* (CDR II, p. 10, my italics).

To posit the problem in this manner becomes a little more intelligible if one realises that the outcome or concrete result of a real antagonism is always common to both parties. Two praxes in conflict produces a single result, although it may be that neither succeeds to bring about exactly what they intended. The problem is then: how is this *unity in conflict* to be understood?

In CRD II Sartre thus investigates the intelligibility of antagonistic social relations, in a way that transgresses the internal perspectives of the combatants. If such an investigation is to satisfy the conditions of a study of the intelligibility of history, it must be able to demonstrate how a certain conflict can be claimed to totalise (or signify) the historical process in it's entirety. That is, according to Sartre, if history is a totalising process, a particular conflictual situation both realises this unity and signifies the different levels of the unification. Thus, the problem of the intelligibility of conflict is concretised into mainly two (CDR II, pp. 17-50, Aronson 1987, pp. 54-75): (i) how can a concrete conflict be understood as a singularisation of a more general antagonism, and (ii) how are we to understand the objective process of the antagonism.

Sartre's investigation starts from the concrete example of boxing (two individuals fighting each other at a certain time and place) and then moves on to other level of sociality: antagonism between groups, and their relations to collectives, institutions, society as a whole, etc. Sartre's study of boxing appears to be relatively finished, while the rest is largely unfinished. I shall restrict myself to illuminating a few aspects of Sartre's conception.

A perspective in which a particular antagonism expresses a more general, societal conflict would provide a scheme which both transgresses the perspectives of the combatants (and is thus more 'objective'), and emphasises the bonds of interiority between different levels of social life. That is, Sartre's study of boxing is unsatisfactory if one would expect that it intends to make boxing intelligible as such. Sartre's focus is on the general problem of the intelligibility of conflict.

Sartre aims to show how a boxing-match, or indeed any particular antagonism, can be claimed to *incarnate* and *singularise* the violent situation of a certain society as a whole: "The violent 'game' *incarnates* the type of violence characterising the society in question: but this characteristic ... which refers back to practical *mediations*, must not prevent us from seeing that the public combat is an embodiment, if front of everyone, of the fundamental violence" (CDR II, p. 25 (34)). If a society is ridden through with conflict, the general conflict must necessarily become manifest in particular conflicts. This means that even a violent 'game' like boxing may be said to incarnate and refer to the general conflict.

In addition, if this is accepted, the particular conflict constitutes an *outcome*, or even concrete *solution*, of the general conflict. This does not mean that it actually manages to solve or resolve the fundamental conflict: "... this particular conflict will find its solution *in boxing* but that boxing *is not a solution* ... The violence of the participants is simultaneously unleashed and de-realised. It becomes a show, without ceasing to be lived in its explosive power" (CDR II, p. 46 (56)). Here we see Sartre's anti-reductionism at work: any general conflict is necessarily lived on a concrete level of praxis, and the totalising intelligibility of this lived praxis refers to and signifies (through a series of mediations) the general conflict.

Sartre then investigates an internal conflict between the sub-groups of a larger group (CDR II, pp. 51-94, Aronson 1987, pp. 76-113). The divergence of opinions within a group becomes transformed into an open conflict "... at the precise moment when *the same matter* is claimed by each subgroup *against the other*" (CDR II, p. 56 (65)). In the case of a conflict within a group "... each of the epicentres enters into conflict with the other *in the name of unity*" (CDR II, p. 65 (75)). Sartre claims that such an antagonism — within a group or between groups and praxes — necessarily results in a process of *anti-praxis*, where no one of the combatants is able to realise their aims autonomously. That is, *in a history characterised by antagonism, none of the parties are able to realise their aims and to make history by themselves* (CDR II, pp. 95-99). Antagonism implies that each party necessarily internalises the other's praxis, as the one that is *opposed* or *to be combated*. Even in the case when one combatant is fully successful in beating the other — as in the case of the constitution of a dictatorial society which forbids all opposition — the success is never autonomous: the opposition must thereafter be integrated as *what is false*, or *really integrated* as a part of the winning group.

In the theory of conflict, Sartre introduces another dimension of alienation than the practico inert and the synchronic/diachronic alienation of the group (see Chapter 9). The praxis-processual outcome of an antagonism necessarily alienates both of the original projects. In summary, in a world of conflicts it is impossible to understand history as steered by some predefined project. Instead, the 'project' that defines the totalisation at work in history, or *the truth of history*, can only be found out through *an interpretative investigation that transgresses the imaginary praxes of the combatants*. However, Sartre seems to deny us the possibility of such understanding: "...the being-in-itself of praxis-process is the foundation of any possible objectivity of our history for a witness external to the human species. It remains the case that man *cannot*, under any circumstances, make himself into that witness" (CDR II, p. 322 (333)).

Concluding Remarks on Sartre's Social Theory

In summary, Sartre's theory of society fulfils the demands of a structural and historical anthropology by attempting to bring together:

(i) a structural, system-oriented or synchronic view on society as a field of

social formations, their relations and mediations and
(ii) a historical, process-oriented or diachronic view on society as a continuously moving and totalising field of social formations in practical and conflictual relations with each other.

On the basis of this we can see that Sartre's conception belongs to a tradition where society is not mainly treated from the point of view of nation-states, but in terms of the relations between social formations in general. The methodological perspective continuously and characteristically transgresses the unit of nation-states. It is thus potentially useful for the study of the increasing globalisation of social relations in the contemporary world.

According to Sartre's framework, a *society* consists of a number of different serialities on different levels. For example, a population and its geographical borders define the seriality of the nation-state. This collective may in turn be divided into other serialities, which may transgress the borders of the nation. Socio-economic classes (as in classical Marxist theory) in different societies may have a common status and thus common interests (e.g. the collective of employed industrial workers). One of Sartre's main points is that classes are primarily connected serially, that is, through practico-inert mediations, but do not by themselves form groups.

From the point of view of the problem of rationality, Sartre's conception of praxis and his social theory may either be seen as emphasising *struggle* or *communication*. On the one hand, it seems as if the ideal form of social life is not realisable without the previous struggle against scarcity and the antagonistic struggle between different groups. Sartre's way of leaning towards the Marxist Utopian ideal of a free society seems to indicate the problematic view that an ideal situation of non-struggle can only be reached through struggle. On the other hand, if reason implies recognition of our embeddedness in the world and of conflict, does this really lead to the imperative '*continue the fight*' or, perhaps, to some ways of *minimising the negative consequences* of conflict? The latter option would emphasise the importance of *communicative interaction* between different groups and between different cultures, rather than struggle. I shall briefly indicate how this, in my opinion more interesting option and outcome of Sartre's anthropology, could be schematised.

Sartre's investigation in the first volume of CRD concludes with both (i) a standpoint on the conditions and the extent of our understanding of what we do, and (ii) an account of why a full understanding of what we do is impossible. Sartre vacillates between the (classical Marxist) view that a full understanding is possible only if we can be said to make history in common (the translucidity of common praxis, see also Chapter 9), and the view that we are completely unjustified even to imagine the possibility of such a situation (the necessity of both synchronic and diachronic alienation of praxis, see Chapter 9).

The second volume of CRD was to pose the problem of the *rationality of action* on the basis of this conception. It was intended to rethink the problem of rationality in the perspective of the intelligibility of conflicts and antagonisms. Although Sartre never finished this investigation, I think it is possible to reconstruct, at least what appears to be at stake in this. The problem of rationality concerns under what conditions and to what extent alienation and antagonisms are themselves intelligible as internal features of praxis (unreflective level), and what would be a *rational way of acting in such a situation* (reflective level, see Chapter 9).

On this level Sartre's insistence on the participatory nature of his investigation and on the transhistorical possibility of communication becomes most forceful. Thus, a non-struggle option might possibly be the described in the following manner:

(1) by showing the mutually binding conditions between different and antagonistic praxes (sharing a world), and
(2) by emphasising the necessity of understanding ourselves as related to others, and others self-understanding as related to ours (the bond of reciprocity),
(3) Sartre could be claimed to insist on the need for positively reciprocal interaction and communication, as a means both to self-understanding and to limit the possible disastrous consequences of alienation and antagonism (reciprocity of non-common praxes).

This is of course a strongly reconstructive account of the problem of rationality in Sartre. To make it a little less controversial, let me quote a passage where Sartre himself seems to indicate such an imperative of real, communicative reciprocity. In the preface to Frantz Fanon's book *Les damnés de le terre* (on European colonialism) Sartre's describes his task: "[Fanon] often speaks *of* you [Europeans], never *to* you ... As a European, I steal this book from the enemy, and out of it I fashion a remedy for Europe" (Sartre 1965, pp. 9 and 12). That is, our understanding of the other's views of us is both a means to deepen our own self-understanding, and a means to *cure us*. This reconstruction is more a conclusion on how I think the imperatives of Sartre's anthropology might positively be taken today, and not on how Sartre himself actually understood them.

Notes

1 Sartre is often described as a philosopher that overemphasises the dimensions of freedom, intentionality, transcendence and action (Bourdieu, op. cit. Chapter 6). By this is often meant that he emphasises the subjective, experiential and intentional aspects of action as against objectivist models. Although this is true to some extent, we can now clearly see that Sartre primarily intends to defend and make intelligible a position that emphasises the internal bond between subjectivity and objective reality. Existentialism would hardly deserve its name if it did not emphasise existence and reality, sometimes even as against ideas and subjective experience.

2 For a comprehensive introduction to this work, see Aronson 1987.

3 Kari Palonen interestingly takes this idea of *outwitment* as a central feature of Sartre's conception of the political (1992, see also my essay "Kari Palonen ja politiikka ulospelaamisena" (1994)). In my opinion, although this idea may be taken as descriptive of the intelligibility of political praxis as taken on the level of the *unreflective* (see Chapter 9), it does not manage to pose the problem of the political on the *reflective*, normative level (authentic and reflective politics). In that case, the realm of the political would have to be set on the basis of the practical *consequences* of this intelligibility. See also my remarks below on the possibility to reconstruct Sartre's views on the rationality of praxis.

8 The Quest for Understanding: Epistemology and Interpretation Theory

The Epistemological Problem

In this chapter I discuss Sartre's *epistemology*, that is, his views on the *interpretation* of human beings, praxis and socio-historical reality. In the previous chapter I argued that Sartre's concept of 'praxis' differs from the everyday concept of action by (i) covering a wider field of human undertakings and (ii) strongly emphasising concrete relations of materiality and sociality. It is at least in these senses a hermeneutical concept of action.

The standpoint of praxis as key to understanding shall be understood as both *fundamental* and *limited*. The main thrust of Sartre's argumentation is indeed to demonstrate how our understanding of human beings and socio-historical reality is to be based on what human beings do. On the other hand, it does *not* imply that *all aspects* of this reality are to be described in terms of intentional undertakings and activities. Biological, material and other circumstantial conditions circumscribe the action-aspect of behaviour, and these do not as such follow the logic of action. In so far as these domains are seen to be wholly outside the concerns of praxis, they may be called *nature*, in so far as they are studied within the perspective of praxis, they may, if we follow Sartre, be called *practico-inert*.[1] This leads us to the heart of *the epistemological problem*. The epistemology of praxis must account both for the intelligibility of projects and actions and for their bonds of interiority with the world.

In such a perspective, the epistemological problem appears two-folded. First, if the knowledge and truth concerning human beings and human reality differ in kind from the objectivism of natural science, what can *the justification of knowledge claims, objectivity* and *truth* mean in this context? Second, if one agrees with Sartre that avoiding *relativism* is a meaningful task, *how is this to be carried through in a hermeneutical perspective?*

The latter question can be initially clarified by means of a distinction between *subjectivism* and *relativism*. Phenomenology and hermeneutics proceed on the basis of an internal perspective. But by 'an internal perspective', or an outlook that depend on a certain perspective, is not meant something that opens itself only to a single subject. The internal perspective in question may be intelligible to a number of individuals, perhaps even to all (e.g. the universality of the hermeneutical problem). That is, hermeneutics takes as primary concern to develop *an ontology of internal perspectives*. On the basis of this, the epistemological question 'What is the limits, validity and scope of such internal perspectives?' might then be raised. To what extent can such a perspective transgress the borderlines of cultural and historical differences?

Sartre poses the epistemological problem as a problem of *truth* and *meaning*. Sartre is both concerned with *understanding*, or *meaning*, and with the *Truth of Man* and the *Truth of History*. In Chapters 3, 5, 6 and 7 I have indicated some aspects of Sartre's standpoint on these issues. In this chapter I shall mainly focus on three issues. First I give an account of the different *types of knowledge* and knowledge-type notions employed by Sartre. These function as a major scheme for his views on knowledge. I then discuss Sartre's conceptions of *meaning*, *truth* and the problem of what may be understood by epistemological *validity* in this context. Third, I exemplify Sartre's views with a discussion of his *interpretation* of Flaubert.

Types of Knowledge in Sartre's Epistemology

I shall first account for the different *types of knowledge* and *knowledge-type notions* used by Sartre in CRD. Although this typology is not as such systematised anywhere by Sartre, I argue that Sartre quite consistently uses them along the lines of my reconstruction.

Thomas Flynn (1976, 1977) and Steve Hendley (1991), largely following Flynn, have shed some new light on Sartre's views on epistemology. Flynn distinguishes between an (Cartesian-Husserlian) *epistemology of vision* — which dominates Sartre's early philosophy in EN — and an (Hegelian-Marxist) *epistemology of praxis* — which dominates his later thinking (1976, p. 21-22 and 27-34). The epistemology of praxis is not an outright rejection of the earlier conception, but an integration of the phenomenological ideas of intuitive and apodictic certainty with the dialectical idea of historicity and practical transcendence (see also Sartre 1947, p. 132). A phenomenological epistemology of praxis must combine the demand of an immediate ground in experience and an emphasis on the practical surpassing of the known.

Flynn places main emphasis on the totalisation at work in praxis, on the place of knowledge in the agent's own comprehension of what he is doing and on the practical nature of knowledge. According to Flynn "... the methodological tool [the progressive-regressive method] of Sartre's new epistemology of praxis ... requires that we read human actions and products as so many signs pointing back to an original choice of self (the hermeneutic of existential psychoanalysis) and as the unfolding of that self-choice in terms of the agent's own self-understanding..." (1976, p. 30). This places knowledge within the perspective of a hermeneutic of the self. But this interpretation in my opinion places too little emphasis on how meaning and truth is constituted by how praxis intervenes and participates in history. Since Hendley's otherwise highly illuminating discussion of Sartre's views on reason and relativism largely uses a similar, his discussion remains unsatisfactory for much the same reason.

Flynn distinguishes between mainly three types of knowledge at work in Sartre: the comprehension inherent in praxis, conceptual, analytical or reflective knowledge (*connaissance*) and the knowledge provided by existentialist historical materialism (*Savoir*) and intended to 'illuminate and decipher' concrete, historical situations (1976, p. 34). The task of interpretation becomes (i) to describe the experienced objects phenomenologically, (ii) to analyse in a formal manner its different dimensions and conditions of possibility and (iii) to totalise ".... the historical phenomena in its inner necessity" (1976, p. 29).

This characterisation is largely correct, but it suffers from the lack of one the most important dimension of Sartre's epistemology: what Sartre calls *intellection,* and thereby the question of the *real meaning* of what we do as an indicator of *truth.* Although Sartre emphasises the self-centred and practical dimensions of knowledge, he also emphasises the need for socio-historical and non-agent centred interpretations of meaning, as central to the validity of our understanding of ourselves, our own and other's praxes. There is thus, perhaps surprisingly, a strong emphasis on the need of *research.* This is perhaps best exemplified by his own eagerness to study Flaubert in such an extensive manner. In order to illustrate my claim, I shall reconstruct a slightly different typology of knowledge-notions in Sartre.

In French two words are translated into English as 'knowledge': *connaissance* and *savoir.* Sartre does not explicitly comment on their difference, and I shall assume that he uses them in an ordinary sense. By 'connaissance' is usually meant 'knowing in general' or knowledge as it is 'present in a subject', and by 'savoir' usually knowledge as 'true and justified belief' or 'scientific systems of knowledge'.

Sartre's epistemology in CRD is based on a distinction between mainly four different types of knowledge: (1) indirect knowledge (*connaissance indirecte*), (2) comprehension (*compréhension*), (3) intellection (*intellection*) and (4) Knowledge (*Savoir*) with a capital first letter. These notions are not sharply distinguished by Sartre, but they refer to different kinds of knowledge and play different roles in Sartre's discourse:

(1) *Indirect knowledge*, or *ontological knowledge* of the structure of existence.
The kind of knowledge we have of the mode of being of human existence or the human condition, that is, of structural features like transcendence, freedom, being-for-others, etc. (SM, p. 171-74). Indirect knowledge is both, in its unexpressed form, inherent to our self-consciousness, experience and projects, and the kind of philosophical knowledge phenomenological ontology makes manifest (EN).

This knowledge is indirect in three senses. First, it is "... the result of reflection on existence" (SM, 171 (126)). It has its ground in the internal relation between immediate and pre-reflective consciousness, and it is disclosed by what in EN is called pure reflection. Since the reflective attitude itself belongs to consciousness, it is not situated outside the object of study. It thus cannot become a direct, conceptual or external knowledge. By 'indirect' is thus meant a kind of knowledge that falls within hermeneutical circularity. Second, it is indirect by being presupposed by all the different anthropological disciplines, although they do not study it as such (SM, p. 171). The human and social sciences study humans as objects in the world, and they necessarily presuppose certain hypotheses about human beings: consciousness, intentionality, action, freedom, intersubjectivity, etc. Third, it concerns the kind of things we spontaneously presuppose about ourselves and other human beings in everyday life.

(2) *Comprehension*, or *experiential understanding*
The type of knowledge that is inherent to our own undertakings and conscious behaviour, and in our experience of other human beings (SM, pp. 152-53 and 171, CDR p. 76). Comprehension is the first of two concepts of *understanding* in Sartre, intellection being the other. In the following I call it *experiential understanding*.

Whereas indirect knowledge concerns our knowledge of what kind of beings we are (ontology), comprehension concerns our concrete grasp of our undertakings and actions. Thus, the paradigmatic example of a comprehension is the self-understanding of what I am doing inherent in my action.

What is comprehended in action is the *project* in which we are engaged, the *situation* in which this project is set up and our *choices* of means: "I shall ... reserve the term *comprehension* for the totalising knowledge of any *praxis* in so far as it is intentionally produced by its author or authors" (CDR, 76 (190)).[2] Comprehension thus connotes practical understanding and know-how.

'Comprehension' replaces the notion of pre-reflective consciousness on the level of concrete experience and the lived. The notion of comprehension inherits the feature of inherent pre-reflective certainty (my certainty about my own concrete plan), but it may also be reflective (planned action). According to Sartre, however, comprehension does neither necessarily constitute a correct or full understanding of the real meaning of an action nor the kind of knowledge in which the sciences are primarily interested: it connotes the existential kind of understanding inherent in everyday life.

Comprehension is both the epistemological starting point and the goal. The notion is foundational, not in the sense of *validity*, but in the sense of *real ground* (see section 7.1). That is, knowledge is comprehended by subjects, and the knowledge of praxis starts from the agent's own understanding of what they do. Comprehension functions as a kind of real locus of knowledge. This implies that at the heart of the problem of epistemology is the problem how and to what extent we can deepen and develop our comprehension and reach a more justified or full understanding of the object studied. This movement from initial pre-understanding, through interpretation, to a deeper understanding is deeply characteristic of hermeneutics (see Chapter 4).

(3) *Intellection*, or *interpretative understanding.*
The type of knowledge or understanding provided by hermeneutical-scientific investigation, analysis and interpretation. Whereas comprehension concerns the internal and subjective meaning of an action, intellection is concerned with the truth or real meaning of action. Intellection is a type of knowledge that is expressed in a totalising form, by the means of empirical evidence, theoretical notions and schemes and as the result of a progressive-regressive investigation (SM, p. 174, CDR, p. 76, see also FI 1, p. 38). Intellection is thus a second concept of understanding used by Sartre. In the following I call it *interpretative understanding.*

The notion of intellection connotes what is usually meant by an attempt to reach a correct or justified understanding of something: "by intellection I shall mean all the temporalising and dialectical evidences in so far as they are capable of totalising all practical realities" (CDR, 76 (190), modified translation). Whereas 'comprehension' conveys the practical totalisation involved in everyday practice, 'intellection' conveys the systematic use of the principle of totalisation in order to provide justified knowledge (epistemic totalisation). Sartre thus hermeneutically distinguishes between two levels of understanding: the pre-understanding of comprehension and the discursively expressed and developed understanding of intellection.

It may also be clarifying to make a distinction *within* the notion of interpretative understanding itself. Since Sartre's anthropology is both oriented theoretically towards the development of a method and oriented empirically towards the interpretation of reality, one should distinguish between *theoretical principles of intelligibility* and *empirical-interpretative investigation* itself. In both, however, it is an intellection-type of knowledge that is at stake. The theoretical principles, such as the formal categories of seriality, group and institutionalised group, orients the investigation in a formal sense, whereas an empirical-interpretative investigation studies real social formations. By *'Sartre's concept of understanding'* I shall thus mean the totality covered by the three areas of *experiential understanding*, *interpretative understanding* and *theoretical principles of intelligibility*.

(4) *Knowledge*, or *objective and scientific knowledge*.
There is a certain ambiguity in Sartre's use of the notion of 'Savoir'. First, it is used for the type of knowledge that is embodied in theoretical systems, universalising concepts and the objectivistic conception of science (positivism and analytical rationality). For example, by 'Knowledge' Sartre refers to the type of knowledge typical for the natural sciences. Since Sartre is critical of this type of knowledge as adopted within the human sciences, the term is often used in a pejorative sense:

> ... Marxism possesses theoretical bases, it embraces all human activity; but it no longer *knows* [*sait*] anything. Its concepts are *dictates*; its goal is no longer to increase what it knows [*connaissance*] but to be itself constituted *a priori* as an absolute Knowledge [Savoir] ... today social and historical experience falls outside of Knowledge [Savoir]. [Marxism] ... has reabsorbed man into the idea [and] ... dissolves [real men] in a bath of sulphuric acid (SM, 28 and 43-44 (35, 45)).

In other passages, however, Sartre uses 'Knowledge' in a less negative sense, even as a final goal to be achieved: "... the moment which will surpass this opposition [between Marxist *thought* and the *comprehension* of alienated existence] must reintegrate comprehension into Knowledge as its non-theoretical foundation ... from the day that Marxist research will have taken on the human dimension ... as the foundation of anthropological Knowledge [*Savoir*], existentialism will no longer have any reason for being" (SM, 179 and 181 (131-32), slightly modified translation). Sartre thus imagines a future ideal, where the integration of a perspective of understanding with a scientific system of knowledge is completed in such a manner that Knowledge is no longer opposed to understanding.

This vision may, of course, be interpreted in two ways: either that understanding has been integrated within Knowledge, or that Knowledge has been integrated within understanding. Since the main thrust of Sartre's conception is that science ought to enable us to understand, it would be strange to claim that Sartre would hold Knowledge as the ideal into which understanding is to be integrated. Regardless of which interpretation one settles for, Sartre clearly reserves a place for such Savoir-type knowledge within his overall conception.

The basic distinction at work in Sartre's epistemology then is between a knowledge that *negatively do not enable us* to understand, or even leads to *misunderstanding*, and a knowledge which *enables us to understand or make intelligible* the world in which we live. In this sense *understanding* functions as a *normative ideal of knowledge* in Sartre.

The problem of epistemological validity and truth is then not mainly a problem of comprehension, but of the validity and truth of our interpretations (totalising intelligibility). This recognition is important since Sartre's epistemology is sometimes (although not by Flynn and Hendley) identified as a question of individual's subjective understanding of themselves or reduced to our experiential understanding of what we do. The *pre-reflective certainty involved in comprehension*, although an epistemological *starting point, does not and cannot provide us with epistemological validity and truth*. For this one needs interpretation. The point of interpretation, however, is mainly to deepen our understanding, not to develop an external theory of history. The distinction between comprehension and intellection is thus not rigid:

> This perpetual dissolution of intellection in comprehension and, conversely, the perpetual redescent which introduces comprehension into intellection as a dimension of rational non-knowledge [*non-savoir*] at the heart of knowledge [*savoir*] is the very ambiguity of a discipline in which the questioner, the question and the questioned are one (SM, 174 (128)).

Another reason to emphasise the dimension of intellection in Sartre is that neglecting it makes it difficult to understand why Sartre engages in the kind of lengthy interpretative work like IF. Indeed, if one would primarily be interested in experiential understanding, why care about how Flaubert lived, how the circumstances conditioned his life and how his choices actually turned out.

Epistemological Foundations: Meaning and Truth

I characterised the epistemological problem involved in the question of the intelligibility of praxis as a problem of *meaning* and *truth*. It thus integrates the dimensions of *understanding* (meaning) and *validity* (truth). Whereas 'understanding' may be seen to represent the concrete presence of knowledge (theoretical and practical) in a subject, the problem of validity concerns the justification of such knowledge-claims.

As I mentioned in Chapter 7, for Sartre "... the epistemological starting point must always be consciousness as pre-reflective apodictic certainty [*certitude*] (of) itself and as consciousness *of* such and such an object." (CDR, p. 51 (167)). I argued that Sartre in CRD in fact replaces pre-reflective consciousness with the certainty involved in our experiential understanding. Experiential understanding encompasses a grasp of our own project and situation, a grasp that is certain in the sense that the subject cannot be mistaken about how he himself sees them (imaginary praxis). However, I also claimed that according to the new idea of human action proposed by Sartre "the truth of the imaginary *praxis* [comprehension of the concrete project] is in the real *praxis* [the real relations between the project and the socio-material setting], and the real ... includes implicit references to the imaginary *praxis* as to its interpretation" (SM, 45-46 (46-47)). This implies that although *meaning* resides primarily in our experiential understanding (the imaginary construction of a project), this does not, and cannot as such, accomplish *truth*. Truth or validity is always dependent on interpretative understanding or *intellection*.

The situation is complicated by the fact that Sartre constantly emphasises the two-folded nature of this task: it is both oriented towards the *concrete truth of the present* and the *general truth of the human condition of historicity*. Thus: "... it will set out from the immediate ... so as to rediscover, through deeper and deeper conditionings ... the absolute concrete: historical man" (CDR, 52 (168). On the other hand, it is "... not trying to reconstruct the real history of the human race; we are trying to establish the *Truth of History*" (ibid.), and answer the question "*Is there a Truth of*

Man?" (CDR, p. 822 (14), slightly modified translation). How is this co-presence of an orientation towards the *concrete* and towards *general truths* to be understood?

I have already indicated the general form of Sartre's standpoint on this issue in the previous chapters. The general truth of man and history cannot be manifested in the form of a 'human nature' or 'law of history', but in the form of *methodological principles* that functions as *general guidelines for an interpretation of the concrete*. These principles, again, are rooted in *an ontology of the human condition* and *the intelligibility of praxis*. Thus, the truth of man and history must always be *a truth in becoming*: the general principles only provide guidelines, but never as such concrete truths.

By this step Sartre comes close to a hermeneutic conception of truth, although he, in contrast to Gadamer, gives a place for methodological principles that are developed on the basis of an ontology. However, Sartre's discourse on truth is unfortunately not systematic. In CRD he only indicates in passing that his conception of truth is modelled on Heidegger's. Thus, truth is characterised as *the disclosure* or *unveiling of being* (CDR p. 19). Fortunately, however, Sartre earlier studies of truth is now available in the posthumously published manuscript *Vérité et existence* (1992b), which was written in 1948 as a commentary on Heidegger's essay "Vom Wesen der Wahrheit" (1977b). It seems to me that the conception developed there is largely preserved in CRD.

In *Vérité et existence* Sartre distinguishes between two modes of truth. Truth, he says, may be *dead* or *alive* (1992b, p.12). Living truth is a becoming, or a continuous process of unveiling, while dead truths are the result of a process that has come to an end. Thus, eternal truths (mathematics), indubitable truths (Archimede's law) and historically biased theories (Newton's physics) are all true, but they are dead truths that once have been living. In this sense they do no longer participate in the disclosure of the present.

Sartre then defines truth, along with Heidegger, as an unveiling or disclosure of being (nature, human being, history, etc.). By 'an unveiling' is meant a process that makes some part of reality visible, while leaving the rest in the dark. Truth is thus identified with the manifestation of a certain domain of being to a subject:

> Truth is therefore a certain dimension that comes to Being through consciousness", it is a "... progressive disclosure of Being", a temporal process that "... confers on [Being] ... a new dimension of being ... Thus truth is not a logical and universal organisation of abstract 'truths': it is the totality of Being to the extent that it is manifested as a *there is* in the historialisation of

human-reality (Sartre 1992b, pp. 4-5).

The task of a 'scientific' investigation thus becomes to unveil or light up a certain domain of being, in a way that may be claimed to be justified or valid. Thus, truth is revealed in a process of interpretation. And, according to Sartre in CRD, it is possible to develop justified methodological guidelines for such unveiling.

As I mentioned in Chapters 5 and 6, the unveiling of truth is a *totalisation* and a *singularisation*. The interpretative process of totalising the facts at hand should not be understood to imply the hope to capture the whole of a reality (e.g. a human being or history) in it's entirety. Truth is necessarily manifested as a particular and limited unveiling, both structurally (e.g. this part of reality) and historically (e.g. contemporary reality), and, as Sartre says, truth is conditioned by *ignorance* (1992b, p. 59). If truth is a totalisation, it can only be this in a singular and not in an all-encompassing form: it only refers to the whole through a series of significations. In CRD Sartre, in the context of a study of an individual, describes this process as aiming at *the real meaning of the process*. The aim of the progressive moment of investigation is thus:

> ... to rediscover [*retrouver*] the totalising movement of enrichment which engenders each moment in terms of the prior moment, the impulse which starts from live obscurities in order to arrive at the final objectification — in short the *project* ... by [which] a man aims at the production of himself in the world as a certain objective totality ... This project has *a meaning [sens]* ... In truth the problem is to invent a movement, to re-create it, but the hypothesis is immediately verifiable; the only valid one is that which will realise within a creative movement the transverse unity of *all* the heterogeneous structures (SM, 147-48 (111-12)).

That is, validity implies the success of a totalising integration. Sartre does not in fact say very much more about the problem of validity than that, and the crucial problems connected with this issue remain unexplained.

I have thus constructed a distinction between a theoretical investigation of *the intelligibility of praxis* and an empirical-interpretative investigation of *the real meaning of some concrete praxis*, were the first is to function as the guideline (method) for the second. The epistemological starting point of both, however, is *the experiential understanding of the project-centred meaning of praxis*. I shall end this section with an account of Sartre's *concept of meaning*.

The meaning of the concept of meaning is a much-debated issue in contemporary philosophy. It cannot be taken for granted what 'the meaning of action' means. I shall limit myself to a commentary intended to illuminate Sartre's use of meaning-type notions. A conception of the meaning of action is intended to answer questions related to how one is to understand it. 'Meaning', in this broad sense, corresponds to the kind of descriptions, evaluations and assessments contained in the interpretation of an action.

'Meaning' belongs to the family of meaning-type notions, such as sense, signification, significance, etc. Sartre elaborates with mainly two such notions, which can both be translated into English as 'meaning': '*sens*' and '*signification*'. Although Sartre fairly consistently uses the terms for different discursive purposes, they should not be taken as strictly distinct .

The distinction between 'sens' and 'signification' corresponds loosely to that between 'comprehension' and 'intellection' (SM, p. 152, CDR, p. 76, Flynn 1992, pp. 233-34). By 'sens' Sartre means the kind of meaning contained in the experiential, subjective or internal understanding of one's own or some other person's action: it is thus "... lived in interiority" (CDR II, p. 402 (410)). In the following I shall translate 'sens' as 'experiential meaning'. Comprehension is an experiential grasp of a meaning that is internal to what oneself or someone else is doing — in short of one's *project*.

By 'signification' Sartre means kinds of meaning (i) stemming from the contextual relation between praxis and the material and social environment, or "... the ensemble of contextual factors" (CDR II, p. 402 (410)), (ii) stemming from the relation between, for example, a certain praxis and the human condition and (iii) that are revealed by interpretative investigation (SM, pp. 102-3, 146-47, CDR II, p. 402). Signification is thus a meaning-concept relatively independent of an agent's experience of his undertaking. For example, although I may intend only to pick up a certain object that lies on the table and carry it to the next room, my action may in certain circumstances carry the signification of 'theft' independently of my comprehension of it as such.

Significations are characteristically descriptions of an action that are revealed on reflection or interpretation. In line with his emphasis on non-reductionism, Sartre denies that it would be possible to reveal single and all-encompassing significations, instead "... every act, every word, has a hierarchized multiplicity of significations" (SM, 102 (83)). It is of primary importance that the norm of totalisation is not understood as a norm to reduce multiple significations to a single one. The movement of integration in totalisation is to be understood as a relational approach that relates different significations to each other in a coherent but non-reductionist way.

Sartre gives numerous examples of significations. I shall mention a few. Sartre takes the example of a black ground-crew member at an airbase (probably in the 1950's) (SM, p. 95-96). Since he is black, it is, at that particular time and place, socially impossible for him to become a pilot. Thus, the situation carries the signification of 'racism' (a relation between a certain person and the social context). One day he steals an aircraft. According to Sartre, although it was no part of his personal intentions to revolt against the racist context, his action was rooted in his personal wish to fly, the social context by itself signified the act as an 'anti-racist revolt'. The act concretely realised the unconditioned possibility (see Chapter 9) of both being black and flying an aircraft, and this value revolted against the racist context.

Sartre also mentions another kind of signification: *personal obsession*. The act of flying was not planned by the person as a political action, but its motive and concrete condition of possibility was rooted in his personality. The idea of flying had become an obsession, because he both passionately wanted to fly and was practically denied it. This kind of signification may thus be called an *existential signification*. Thus 'racism', 'political revolt' and 'personal obsession' are types of significations which may be revealed by an interpretative investigation, although none of them necessarily belong to the agent's comprehension of the act. The importance to include all these significations is that the real condition of possibility of this concrete action (of its truth) is exactly the co-presence of all significations in a single person (overdetermination): being black in a racist society, and having a personal wish to fly. Significations may thus be both highly abstract and general (the social structure) and concrete and existential (wishes).

In another example Sartre discusses the attitude of greediness in employers (SM, pp. 101ff). Objectivist Marxism describes greediness as rooted in the general socio-economic practice of economic Malthusianism, and in the class-structure. Although this is probably true, it is only a very abstract signification. Sartre emphasises that an attitude is not simply caused by the circumstances, but it depends on the way a certain individual lives his history (childhood) and society: "greed ... is therefore *also* a defiant way of living his body and his own situation in the world" (SM, p. 102 (83)).

Significations are thus descriptions of meanings that are typically revealed by interpretative investigation. It is important to note that an interpretation cannot consist just of a list of significations: this part only constitutes the *regressive* part of an investigation (SM, pp. 140ff). 'Regressive investigation' conveys the idea of an analytical disclosure of sets of contextual significations, but the goal of an interpretation is not regressive analysis as such, but the progressive reintegration of all facts and significations into a totalising narrative.

As the passage quoted above indicates, the final goal of interpretation (progression) is not a signification but a *sens*-type meaning. But in this case, by *sens*-meaning is not initially to be understood an experiential meaning. A *totalisation* must be defined as an *attempt to reintegrate regressively deciphered significations* with the *original experiential meaning* to an *interpretative understanding of real meaning*. A Sartrean investigation should thus start off from the delimitation of a meaning inherent to our everyday comprehension (the immediately concrete). In its second moment, it observes that this experiential meaning can never exhaust the full meaning of an action, and begins to study contextual significations (the regressive disclosure of the concrete setting). In the third moment, these significations are to be reintegrated in a totalising historical interpretation (the progressive disclosure of history in becoming).

Finally, the significations and historical meanings are then no longer (in the ideal case) external to experience, but are to be internalised in this very experience. They may thus be experientially revealed to the agent as the truth of the concrete present (in the case of a study of contemporary reality). Thus, interpretative understanding is integrated within experiential understanding in the form of a norm to continuously pass from one to the other, from immediate comprehension to interpretation and back. This standpoint forms the epistemic part of Sartre's conception of practical reason (see Chapter 9 for its normative dimension).

In conclusion then, although comprehension and pre-reflective consciousness functions as epistemological starting points (as foundations in the sense of real grounds) the problem of epistemological validity cannot be limited to the lived and practical dimension of comprehension. Sartre's critical investigation of reason is intended to demonstrate that this certainty does not constitute knowledge, truth or a valid interpretation. In order for truth to be unveiled, the necessities at the heart of intelligibility must be studied.

CRD is concerned with the problem of intelligibility on a formal and general level: it studies the truth and validity of certain methodological principles. Sartre seems to believe that he by means of such a phenomenological-hermeneutical investigation is able to reach a level of *transhistorical or transcultural validity*, although he simultaneously claims that it is valid only in relation to the kind of society and history he himself lives in.

By reflection on the socio-material bonds of interiority that defines the lived experience of the investigator (first level of historicity), one may reach a theoretical level (the intelligibility of praxis, social formations and conflict) that is not reducible only to the features of that particular kind of society. However, although, for example, the theory of social formations is seen as having (presumably transhistorical) validity, this does not imply that it constitutes the only valid approach to any kind of society (second level of historicity). It might be that the categories of seriality, group and institution are neither sufficient nor valid in a study of societies that are different than ours. Thus, for example, seriality, institutionalisation and antagonism are typical features of modern Western societies, and the importance of conflict is, according to Sartre, dependent on the historical condition of scarcity. In this sense Sartre's theory of social formations raises a claim of transhistorical validity, but this does not exclude the possibility of change, or the need of another perspective. This forms the core of Sartre's combination of validity and historicity.

Sartre's Interpretation Theory at Work: the Neurosis of the Family Idiot

In order to exemplify Sartre's interpretation theory at work, I shall examine an example in greater detail. I shall focus on Sartre's empirical-interpretative study of the physical and mental breakdown of Gustave Flaubert in 1844. According to Barnes' interpretation, this event "... decisively fixed the meaning of [Flaubert's] life ... and [it] did not essentially change thereafter" (1981, p. 11). It settled the stakes of Flaubert's orientation in life, made it possible for him to become a writer and eventually led him to write his masterpiece *Madame Bovary*. Sartre calls this part of his investigation "Elbehnon, or the Last Spiral" and it constitutes the third of his four-part study. It forms a kind of point of culmination in the work.

CRD is concerned with the validity of certain methodological principles, and IF with the validity of a particular case study. As I said above, these levels are naturally connected with each other. Thus, true to the spirit of phenomenology to base theory on the things themselves (and to his modified empirism), Sartre claims that "... the method *is created* through the very work itself in obedience to the requirements of its object" (FI 1, p. x (8). The nominalism defended in CRD demands that "... if some real fact — a historical process, for example — develops dialectically, the law [*loi*] of its appearance and its becoming must be ... the pure ground of its intelligibility" (CDR, p. 44 (160-61)). In this case, then, the starting point and object of study is not the bonds of interiority of the investigator, but his experiential encounter with the facts about Gustave Flaubert. Thus, instead of describing his investigation as an internal, reflexive self-critique, Sartre characterises it as a kind of problem-centred post-mortem examination:

> Now we must begin. How, and by what means? It doesn't much matter: a corpse is open to all comers. The essential thing is to set out with a problem (FI 1, p. x (9)).[3]

In the part I shall discuss Sartre carries out both a regressive and a progressive investigation. It is oriented towards deciphering the *intelligibility* and *real meaning* of Flaubert's nervous breakdown and subsequent neurosis. Sartre describes his biographical interpretation, borrowing from Aron, as a 'true novel' [*un romain vrai*] (Sartre 1978b, p. 112, Flynn 1992), or in my reformulation, a narrative that is rooted in imagination but containing truth claims. An interesting feature of this example is that it both (i) fulfils the demand to make a human being intelligible in a totalising manner and (ii) exemplifies the combination of the idea that (a) a person lacks a complete self-understanding of what is going on in his life (real meaning) with (b) the (hypo)thesis that we in principle have the means to understand it.

After nearly 1800 pages of interpretative work Sartre reaches the point where he is finally able to interpret what was, according to both Flaubert and Sartre, the most important event in Flaubert's adult life: his nervous breakdown at the age of 23 (See also Barnes 1981, pp. 182-244).

One evening in January 1844 Gustave Flaubert, in company with his elder brother (a medical doctor, like his father), was returning, from the family's country house, to Paris in a cabriolet (FI 4, pp. 3-17). Gustave was driving, and quite wildly. Suddenly, at Pont-l'Evéque, another wagon appears in the dark and passes them on the right, and: "Gustave dropped the reins and fell at his brother's feet as if struck by lightning" (FI 4, p. 3). He remained paralysed for a few minutes, but slowly retained consciousness. The attack was soon followed by others, not, however, as dramatic as the first. These attacks had the practical consequence that Flaubert was unable to continue — or rather, even to start — his career as a lawyer: he was now ill, and consequently unable to have a normal (bourgeois) occupation.

The breakdown has been interpreted differently (FI, pp. 18-41). His father diagnoses it as 'cerebral congestion' and a 'nervous illness' of an epileptic kind, in short, a purely *medical* or physical event. Biographers have discussed whether it was not in actual fact *hysteria*, that is, a *psycho-*

somatic illness. Sartre chooses the psychosomatic option, but insists that the important thing "... is not to search for a concept that subsumes Flaubert's attacks but to ask ourselves whether or not they have *meaning* [*sens*]" (FI 4, p. 18). The point is not to find a universal, covering concept by means of which the illness is diagnosed, but to study the illness (hermeneutically) on the level of *the lived*. This implies that to study the meaning and significations of the event, in the light of the unique experiential and active life of the person and his circumstances. The study is thus to be based on "... a notional approach" (FI 4, p. 42).

Sartre interprets Flaubert's illness as a *neurosis*. As such it has the structure of a project with an intentional orientation or meaning, although it was not consciously planned. Sartre thus localises its intentionality on the level of what is usually called the unconscious. While Sartre accepts the existence of the phenomenon we call unconscious, he rejects a rigid distinction between conscious and unconscious. The introduction of the notion of a *lived totalisation* is intended to capture the internal bond between consciousness and the unconscious (pre-reflective awareness and comprehension). The study of Flaubert's neurosis is thus intended to demonstrate the fruitfulness of an approach that does not work on the basis of a rigid distinction between different levels of mental life.

The lived is both a *totalisation* and a *singularisation*. All the different conditions, circumstances, wishes and projects of the person are concretely brought together into *the singularity of decisions*, *solutions* and *a life*. It is impossible for a person to have a complete overview of this process: it is primarily lived and not contemplated. Although it is internally connected to the material, social and cultural circumstances (relations, norms, imperatives, models of interpretation, etc.) of the times, these are (almost) never as such the immediate objects of our choices and concerns. The circumstances are only referentially signified by the lived.

The unifying scheme of such a totalising interpretation is "... to stay constantly on the level at which the internalisation of the external is transformed into the externalisation of the internal" (FI 4, p. 19). The investigation proceeds on the basis of the hypotheses that the reality studied itself constitutes a totalisation (internalisation-externalisation), and that the interpretation must be a totalisation (a comprehensive account). Thus, "... the meaning which we shall bring to light is bound to escape a conceptual determination; it can be grasped in its complexity only as the totalisation and living unity of the contradictory and complementary intentions of the neurosis" (ibid., p. 42). In regard of Flaubert Sartre tries to establish that the illness was "the immediate, negative and tactical response to an emergency", as the subtitle goes.

The first task is to decipher the meaning of the attacks as originating in the concrete, practical surpassing which envelops a certain constellation of intentions and projects in the person. A main topic is to demonstrate that Flaubert's totalisation or solution is intelligible on the basis of the conflictual and contradictory nature of the constellation of intentions. Sartre identifies mainly three such mutually exclusive imperatives at the source of Flaubert's illness.

First, through the strong but submissive links Gustave has with his family, especially his father, (constitution realised during early childhood) he carries the value to please his father and fulfil his expectations and hopes (FI 1, see also Barnes 1981, pp. 17-70). His father expects him do what a normal son of a bourgeois family should do: to have a respectable bourgeois profession. Since his elder son already is a medical doctor like himself, he hopes that Gustave would become a lawyer.

Second, Flaubert has a strong feeling of unease and disgust with these plans. Again, Sartre detects the ground of this emotional constellation in the constitution of Flaubert's personality during childhood. Gustave was the second son of the Flaubert family, and he was not the main heir of the family (which was important in those times). In addition, he was born after the death of a girl child and before the birth of third child of the family. The latter, again, was the daughter their mother had so sincerely hoped for. According to Sartre, Gustave became an in-between child, who neither got sufficient attention from his father nor his mother. Sartre thus characterises Gustave's family situation as 'lack of love', and his childhood as constituted by *a problem in the relation with others*, which most concretely was expressed as *a problem with language* (internalisation, one of the reasons why he later wanted to become a writer) (FI 1, p. 14). As a consequence, Gustave became a dreamer: that is, one who lives in the imagination and is strongly emotional (externalisation). These personality traits leads him into acting and writing, but such interests were not regarded as respectable by the 19th century French bourgeois. The personality traits thus stand in conflict to the expectations of his family background.

These conflictual intentions do not by themselves form a contradiction in Gustave's personality. It would still be possible for him to react actively, for example by open revolt, or to reflectively search for a solution. The important thing is that this option is not available to Flaubert. Thus, a third trait is that he (again through the family relations of his childhood) has constituted himself as *passive* in character (FI 4, pp. 42-44). Passivity implies that direct action, planning and the setting up of reflective goals are not a normal, everyday part of doing things. Although he, like all other human beings, makes himself through his actions and undertakings (praxis as the intelligibility of the person), the explicit task to take his life into his own hands in an active manner does not belong to his actual repertoire (constitution). Of course, he might change, but the problem of changing oneself is that it often presupposes an active attitude to oneself. Flaubert is thus caught in the enclosed cage of passivity: passivity cannot as such carry one out of passivity.

In summary, the three intentions that make up the origin of Gustave's neurotic and psychosomatic solution is the real contradiction in Flaubert between the imperatives 'to please the family expectations', 'to do what he likes most: dream and write' and 'to remain a passive person'. These are the outcome of the regressive investigation: they analytically detect the presence of a series of given significations in Flaubert.

But these imperatives and contradictory orientations are not by themselves sufficient *to cause a neurosis*. What is needed, according to Sartre, is a situation of emergency, where the person is forced to make a concrete decision. The progressive investigation, which is intended to reinvent the concrete temporalising process of Gustave's lived totalisation, must study this, the real moment of Gustave's neurosis.

In the case of Flaubert, the option of active decision is closed. What remains open is *illness*. Illness, however, is not something one might consciously impose on oneself, it is something that happens unexpectedly. By being passive in character it thus satisfies the conditions of a solution for Flaubert (pre-reflective comprehension). Thus:

> ... a fall is etching itself on the horizon. This presentiment is merely the internalisation of the only objective solution to the problem. Since refusal to act is impossible and necessary, he *must* impose passive obedience on himself as a strict impossibility of obeying; Flaubert must *suffer* it ... in spite of his rush to do his father's bidding; he must *discover* it in himself not as a minor handicap ... but as a radical incapacity. It is no longer a question of enduring transitory and reparable failures but of revealing to others and to himself that he is a *man-failure* (FI 4, p. 43).

The event that triggers the actualisation of such a fall is the concrete situation in which Flaubert finds himself in January 1844. The holiday is over, he must return to Paris, take his exams and became a lawyer. But he cannot do it. He is ridden through with emotional turmoil.

The intentions and the situation together make up "... the objective set of conditions that make a solution possible. These conditions are abstract;

from this starting point, the solution is not yet defined in its singularity; yet these conditions constitute the rigorous framework in which it must be found: fall beneath man and let the catastrophe land *unexpectedly* on his shoulders" (ibid.). Thus, the *actual solution* must in the last instance be *a subjective moment of invention* (praxis): "Indeed, while enumerating objective conditions and organising them, our primary aim is to show how these conditions were maintained and surpassed toward objectivity by the subjective moment, that irreducible element" (ibid., p. 19). Thus, Flaubert's solution is radically unique, individual and fully intelligible only as an ongoing, integrating process of totalisation.

In the two chapters that make up part three of Sartre's investigation, he first investigates, regressively, the different significations of the neurosis as a response to situation and then progressively the (interpretative and experiential) meaning of the neurosis as a strategy and concrete solution of Flaubert's dilemmas. However, these together establish only *a first level of intelligibility* of the real meaning and the truth of Flaubert's illness. In the fourth part Sartre returns to the question of the real meaning of Flaubert's illness on the level of the relation between the person and the epoch. I shall return to this issue in Chapter 9.

In the regressive part Sartre discusses a set of significations (FI 4, pp. 42-150): belief as passive resolution, the circumstances as stimulus, the difference between neurosis and necrosis, hysterical commitment, neurosis as a regression and Flaubert's illness as 'murder of the father'. I shall not go into the details of these studies. It suffices to observe that these significations make up a set of descriptions, which are not only grounded in a project, but in the being-in-the-world of a human being, that is, in the condition of being a totalising lived experience that internalises and externalises.

In the progressive part Sartre attempts to reconstruct the real meaning of the process as such. The narrative is ordered around a certain (notional) meaning, which is claimed by Sartre to organise the facts. Thus, Sartre characterises the meaning of the nervous breakdown and subsequent neurotic illness as *a positive strategy or project of "loser wins"* (FI 4, pp. 151-355), an expression that Flaubert himself used. By means of 'the fall' Flaubert has constituted himself as a failure, or loser (from a bourgeois point of view, internalisation). This failure is in fact the solution that enables Flaubert to become a writer, without openly betraying his wishes to please the family. The loser is the winner (externalisation). The evaluation of this as a case of 'winning' Sartre grounds in the statements of Flaubert himself: he has become a writer, he writes the masterpiece *Madame Bovary* (and other works) and for the first time in his life he is quite pleased with himself. The *pessimistic misanthrope has converted to optimism*, as the subtitle to the second book of part three goes.

This example demonstrates how Sartre's conception of method, his thesis about internalisation and externalisation and the problem of validity are closely connected to the interpretation of an empirical and unique material. It also shows something of the limits and extent of the intelligibility of praxis as an action-centred perspective. In addition, one might observe that on the level of interpretation discussed in this example the social significations of seriality and common action are not at all put into play. That is, on the plane of the 'psychological' and 'social-psychological' the interpretation must use other categories than the purely social categories of praxis. But, in summary, the interpretation still works on the basis of the hypothesis that human beings are, in the final analysis, to be understood on the basis of what they do and on the basis of their innerworldly relations. It thus constitutes *a hermeneutics of praxis*.

Notes

1 Although Sartre does not discuss these issues in any detail, he clearly reserves both another intelligibility for organic life, the brain and physical nature and reserves a place for the study of language, cultural artefacts, the institutional structure of society and the economy that falls somewhat outside the action framework. In the latter case, however, Sartre continues to emphasise that these, in the final analysis, are intelligible only on the basis of human praxis. Besides discussing the natural sciences in CRD, in IF we find a particularly revealing passage, which shed light on Sartre's views on the place of neurology: "... when we sleep, torn away from action by neurological disconnections, the dimension of *possibility* disappears with our practical capacity, and everything we conceive during our waking hours ... we find again in sleep *through belief* in the form of suffered realization ... The project as transcendence cannot disappear — since it is existence itself; but it flows back on the present as purely suffered future ... in sleep we have lost the capacity to *make* the future which is made and suffered in the waking state" (FI 4, p. 45).

2 The English translation strangely has 'totalising group or any *praxis*' as a translation of 'la saisie totalisante de chaque *praxis*'.

3 Sartre chooses Flaubert's description of himself in terms of a *deep and hidden innate wound* as a suitable starting point (FI 1, p. x).

9 The Normative Dimension of Sartre's Anthropology

Introduction

So far my investigation has mainly focused on the thematic constellation of understanding, intelligibility and interpretation, taken as knowledge-type concerns with human beings and human reality. As is generally recognised, however, the dimension of *normative commitment* is central to Sartre's concerns. In this chapter I shall thus examine the normative dimension of Sartre's anthropology — that is, the fifth and last of the themes I differentiated in chapter 3.

By 'normative' I mean roughly all kinds of 'judgements of prescription, evaluation, merit, etc.'[1]. In the case of Sartre I take the normative dimension to include both *ethics* and *critical social theory*. In the investigation I neither aim to carry through a full-scale interpretation of the normative dimension of Sartre's philosophy as a whole, nor shall I limit my treatment to Sartre's attempts at reconstructing Marxism in CRD. Instead, I shall focus on the *relation between the idea of an anthropology* — as a hermeneutical 'science of understanding' — *and the imperative of normative commitment* that stands at the basis of Sartre's project. The question how these two dimensions fit together in an overall conception is the main theme of this chapter. It is thereby intended *to deepen the discursive self-understanding* of what Sartrean anthropology is made up off. That is, if the answer to the question 'what is anthropology?' is given in the form of an appeal to commitment, how is this to be understood?

I shall not limit my treatment of this issue to the claim that Sartre's concern with understanding actually is guided by normative issues. I shall rather focus on the task to clarify the parallel claim that the normative dimension of Sartre's conception cannot be fully understood if one neglects the centrality of understanding and intelligibility for these issues. Sartre, in part, *grounds normative issues* by the means of an appeal to *anthropological intelligibility*. How Sartre actually fares with this argumentative step has not in my opinion been sufficiently clarified.

Any attempt at a comprehensive account of the normative dimensions of Sartre's thought faces considerable difficulties. The fact is that both of Sartre's main philosophical works, EN and CRD, explicitly suppresses or postpones almost all treatment of normative issues. And despite a continuous renewal of intention, Sartre never worked out his views on ethics into a systematic treatise. This does not mean that we would lack material on such issues, quite the contrary. But the material available mainly consists of shorter essays and manuscripts, and they do not constitute a fully worked out conception.

In addition to EN, CRD and IF I shall mainly use the following works of Sartre as source material:

- Sartre's works on the task of writing, such as "*Presentation* des *Les Temps Modernes*" (1988b) and "Qu'est-ce que la littérature?" (1988a), originally published in 1945 and 1947,
- his unfinished notebooks for an ethics *Cahiers pour une morale* (CM, written in 1945-47, published posthumously in 1983),
- extracts from and commentaries on Sartre's two manuscripts on a second ethics from the mid 1960's: the so called *Rome Lecture* of 1964 (of which only an extract called "Détermination et liberté" (1970) has been published) and the undelivered and unpublished *Lectures at Cornell University* — scheduled for 1965 but cancelled by Sartre due to the American bombing of Vietnam. I have not studied these manuscripts in original (they are available at the Bibliothéque Nationale, Paris), and I shall mainly have to rely on secondary sources: Bowman and Stone 1991a, Stone and Bowman 1991b, Simont 1992 and Anderson 1993.[2]
- the lecture series from 1965 on the task of intellectuals: "Plaidoyer pour les intellectuels" (1974c).

In my interpretation I shall aim at a sufficiently coherent and systematic overall conception. Since Sartre himself never achieved this, my interpretation will be even more reconstructive than is the case in the previous chapters.

Commitment

From the time of the Second World War and the liberation of France Sartre was deeply involved with the issues of his times. In works like "*Presentation* des *Les Temps Modernes*" and "Qu'est-ce que la littérature?" he appeals to an ideal of *commitment* (*engagement*). For Sartre himself this commitment took many different forms, from an appeal to literature to the concrete association with different political groups and movements (see for example Hayman 1986, pp. 173-75, 244-302 and 405-19). The appeal to commitment thus characteristically encompasses both a *discursive-theoretical* and a *concrete-practical* dimension. I shall restrict myself to Sartre's views on the commitment of philosophy, or rather, intellectual writing in general.

I think one can say that Sartre by 'commitment' generally means 'to engage ones writing (literary, essayist or philosophical) in the issues of the times in order to communicate with the times' (Sartre 1988a, pp. 36-38 and 48-61, see also Goldthorpe 1984 and 1992). But 'commitment' importantly does not, Sartre emphasises, imply the subordination of one's thought to some pre-set goal, political organisation or party. Intellectual commitment must be a free kind of participation, conceived either individually or in co-operation with others, but as neither *pledged* nor *institutionalised*[5] (see Chapter 7). Thus, in "*Presentation* des *Les Temps Modernes*" Sartre sums up his conception in the following manner:

> In summary, our intention is to help effect certain changes in the Society that surround us ... we align ourselves on the side of those who want to change simultaneously the social condition of man and the concept he has of himself ... concerning the political and social events to come, our journal will take a position in each case. It will not do so *politically* — that is in the service of a particular party — but it will attempt to sort out the conception of man that inspires each one of the conflicting theses, and it will give its opinion in conformity with the conception it maintains ... if we succeed in persuading a few readers to share our views, we will not indulge in any exaggerated pride; we will simply congratulate ourselves for having rediscovered a good professional conscience, and for literature's having become again — at least for us — what it should never have stopped being: a social function ... It is not ... simply a question of effecting an advance in the domain of pure knowledge: the more distant goal we are aiming at is a *liberation* (Sartre 1988b, pp. 255 and 261).

In the early phase of 'classical existentialism' (up until the end of the 1940's) Sartre interpreted this to imply the task for philosophy to work out *an ethics* (BN, 628). After roughly two years of work, however, he abandoned the project, and soon became more and more deeply involved in concrete political issues. In CRD, again, two other normative dimensions seems to have replaced ethics: commitment to the socio-political ideals (although not the dogma) of Marxism, or the aims of a *critical social theory*, and a focus on the problem of *reason*. As Sartre himself retrospectively commented, his earlier concerns with morality gave way to an increasing (political) realism (Sartre 1978d, pp. 76-81). He did no longer believe that an ethics, or a critique of society that is based on universal values, was either a possible or sufficient enterprise for a committed thought. Sartre did not for long feel at ease with this position, but soon recognised that he could not fulfil his task without an appeal to a morality. Consequently, in the period after CRD Sartre again returned to the problem of morality.

It is not easy to sort out Sartre's views on the relation between *ethics, historical reality* and *political commitment*. For one thing it is not that clear what Sartre actually means by 'ethics' and 'morality': a philosophical discipline or a feature of concrete life? The principle aim of my investigation is not, however, to try to solve this puzzle, but to investigate Sartre's views on the task and scope of anthropological philosophy and expressed thought in general. This actualises to the issue of *the possibilities, limits and scope of intellectual writing*. What is writing? What can we say? What does what we say actually mean? Sartre mainly deals with this issue in terms of the questions of *the nature of committed writing* and *the task of the intellectual*. In so far as these are taken to concern what and why one writes, their most general object of study is *the discursive self-understanding of the praxis of writing*. In a broader framework it touches on the problems of *existential morality* in general, or the question how I am to live.

In "Qu'est-ce que la littérature?" Sartre outlines his vision of the ideal of commitment on the basis of a certain conception of language and communication. The telos of language in its everyday prosaic use, Sartre argues, is *to communicate*. Communication, again, is a kind of *praxis*. The writer, regardless of whether he writes fiction, philosophical essays or political appeals, is thus a person that engages in a praxis whose final aim is communication.

According to Sartre, the writer engages in "... a certain method of secondary action which we may call action by disclosure" (1988a pp. 36-37). This disclosure may naturally take different forms, dependently if one communicates directly (essay) or indirectly (fiction or theatre). The linguistic communication of the writer reveals and discloses (or hides in the case of ideological writing) features of the real world, and thereby influences and modifies our understanding of the world. For Sartre this ontological claim has the moral implication that *the writer ought to embrace the self-understanding of his being as revelatory, disclosive and change-oriented*. Since writing is praxis, the *authentic writer* ought to recognise this as his own mode of being, and assume responsibility for it. However, as is the case with all communication, writing can naturally never lead to the full realisation of an ideal. All writing is situated in time and place, and, like all praxis, is destined to be surpassed by history. Thus, "since the writer has no way of escaping [his era], we want him to embrace his era — tightly ... Right here in our own lifetime is when and where our cases will be won or lost" (1988a, p. 252 and 254). Here another central dimension of Sartre's ethics is emphasised: the necessity of *historical situatedness* as ground of intelligibility and concrete morality.

The ideal of the praxis of committed writing outlined in these programmatic remarks encompasses what is usually understood by the activity of an *intellectual*. By 'an intellectual' is generally meant a person that, with the help of his academic skills, actively engages in the issues of his times. In the 1965 lectures "Plaidoyer pour les intellectuels" (1974c) Sartre specifies his views on the committed intellectual, this time informed by the standpoint developed in CRD. Sartre proceeds in a characteristic fashion: he first discusses what an intellectual is, then his possible functions and last the intelligibility of his praxis.

According to Sartre, an intellectual is a person with an academic education — a scientist, philosopher, lawyer, medical doctor, etc. — who, for some reason, has come to recognise the need to call into question and/or turn against the dominant ideology of his society (1974c, pp. 231-46). Sartre thus distinguishes between intellectuals and non-intellectual academics. The latter he calls *technicians of practical knowledge* (p. 232 and 244).

Scientists are specialists in a certain domain of knowledge. According to Sartre, knowledge is always connected to practice — either directly (it is actually used, for example, in technology), or indirectly (it is assumed or it may be used, for example, in public debate) — independently of what the scientist himself thinks or wants (p. 242).[4] The person of academic skills may therefore be defined as a technician, who upholds and supports the system of knowledge, although he does not himself apply it directly to social matters. His participation in social life is then not rooted in an intention on his part, but it is due to the specific *bond of interiority* that resides between his work and the circumstances.

Since the work of the technicians of practical knowledge is most often supportive of the dominant system of knowledge, it may be *ideological* in nature. According to Sartre, scientific thought is ideological in so far as its universalisations are not *practically* universalised in social reality *to concern all human beings*, but its power and efficacy is restricted to gain only a limited layer of society (pp. 240-44). The ideological character of knowledge is thus not primarily dependant on individual intentions, but on the historical relation between a knowledge and the society in question.

An intellectual is a person who does not accept the self-understanding of scientific work as politically neutral, and who questions the idea of non-participation. He forces himself to transgress the domain of his specialist concerns, and explicitly posits an intention to engage his academic skills in social matters. That is, he does not only engage in applied science (technology, etc.), but in social life as such. In that case "... the agent of practical knowledge becomes a monster, that is to say an intellectual; *someone who attends to what concerns him* (in exteriority — the principles which guide the conduct of his life; and in interiority — his lived experience in society) and whom others refer to as a man *who interferes in what does not concern him*" (p. 244). According to Sartre, the intellectual ought to make use of what he has learned as a technician of practical knowledge: to "... apply the rigorous methods he uses as a specialist ... freedom of research (and contestation); rigour of inquiry and proof; quest for truth (disclosure of being and its conflicts); universality of results obtained" (p. 247). In other words, he is to use the classical methods and principles of scientific inquiry.

What does the intellectual do? Does he perhaps become a *moralist*, or someone whose sole concern is to criticise social and political life on the basis of an appeal to universal values? Sartre is critical of this alternative. An intellectual that restricts himself to the expression of universal values — for example, criticising all use of violence or promoting the value of freedom as such regardless of the circumstances — is actually a "... *false intellectual*" (p. 252). Thus, "one of the principal traps an intellectual must avoid in his enterprise is to universalise too fast" (p. 249). The *true intellectual* must first carefully study the actual groups in question, and the real grounds of their positions. Sartre criticises those who at the time of the Algerian war reverted to a general condemnation of the use of violence, without considering the differences in real motives between the parties. Sartre defends the rebels use of violence: "what these intellectuals failed to understand was that the Algerian rebellion — an insurrection of the poor, disarmed and hunted by a police regime — could not but choose *guerrilla war and the use of bombs*" (p. 250). The true intellectual must be able to combine an ethical concern with universal values and a socio-historical diagnosis of the situation. This constitutes the basis of what Sartre means by *concrete morality*.

In this context Sartre also puts some of the hermeneutically biased ideas of CRD into action. For instance, the intellectual is himself a person that is conditioned by the historical circumstances in which he lives (pp. 248-50). His work should therefore not be limited to the investigation of a certain object (e.g. an ideology, false idea, injustice, event, etc.), but he must also *scrutinise the relation between himself* and *the society* in question. Thus, in the case of for example the study of racism, he must "... constantly return to himself to liquidate the traces of racism within him left over by his childhood, by a rigorous investigation of the 'incomparable monster' that is his self" (p. 249). This task to make conscious one's own prejudices has obvious parallels with Gadamer's conception. In order to do this; he must study what it in general means for a human being to be both a subject of actions and an object that forms a part of the historical world. In this way, Sartre's conception of the intellectual converges with his anthropology as a study concerned with human beings as both objects (historical intelligibility) and subjects (the being of the human, ontology).

In summary then, the intellectual ought to engage in a twofold task: (i) to study actual praxes, events and situations, or to focus on *historical intelligibility*, and (ii) to ground his evaluations and critique on a conception of human being as both subject and object, or to study *anthropological foundations*. In this sense, Sartre's views on committed writing and the committed intellectual reveal a strong emphasis on approaching normative issues by recourse to the level of the intelligibility of praxis.

The Place and Status of Ethical Reflection

A discourse on the normative justification of action (in writing or concretely) must be able to answer at least two basic questions. First, what grounds or principles can justify (prospectively or retrospectively) an action as right? Second, why should I act on the basis of grounds instead of just doing whatever I feel like? The second concerns the answer to questions like 'why be moral?', 'why commit myself to some good cause?' and 'why act politically?'; the first questions like 'if so, on the basis of what values?'.

Although Sartre's views on these issues are found scattered in different essays and manuscripts, I do think it is possible to perform a relatively coherent reconstruction of them. This, however, seems to demand an initial acceptance of continuity between Sartre's early and later views on morality. This possibility, again, seems to be contradicted by Sartre's own statements. Sartre later denounced his early views on morality in CM as "completely mystified", and refers to the second, non-mystified, ethics as one "which is related to the problem of realism as well as that of morality" (1978d, p. 81). On the other hand, this does not mean that Sartre would have denounced everything that he wrote about morality in the early days, but initially only implies that he considered its general orientation and goal as misconceived.

I shall adopt an interpretative strategy according to which the standpoint of the later Sartre (and his second ethics) functions as the primary perspective, and make use of Sartre's earlier views insofar as they contribute to clarifying that perspective. In addition, since I also aim to criticise Sartre later standpoint on morality on the basis of the alternative of a thought-out hermeneutics of praxis, my interpretative standpoint actually goes beyond that of the later Sartre (if it really manages to go beyond in an evaluative sense is quite another matter). I shall begin by picking out *four guidelines* to the problem of morality in Sartre: (i) the relation between morality and history, (ii) the distinction between the unreflective and the reflective level of existence, (iii) the being of value and (iv) Sartre's explicitly posited ethical-political ideals, and then return to his argumentation on normative issues.

A dominating trait of Sartre's discourses on ethics, both in CM and after CRD, is that he situates *the problem of morality* on the level of the *relation between ethics and history*. In CM Sartre claims that "ethics [*la morale*] must be historical: that is, it must find its universal in History and must grasp it in History" (NE, p. 6 (14). In the *Rome lecture*, again, Sartre searches for "an ethics of history" which would realise "the identification of history with the dramatic development of morality" (quoted by Anderson 1993, p. 128). A first interpretation of these, rather uncommon, formulations is to take them as typically Sartrean reformulations of one of the basic problems of ethics: the relation between values and ideals and their implementation in reality. According to Sartre, ethics should not only deal with abstract questions about values, but must deal with the place, relevance and impact of values in a non-ideal reality. Thus, "... [morality] presupposes man actually involved in a world, and that one sees what happens to freedom in it" (1978d, p. 81 and 77).

In this conception of *concrete morality* as a problem concerning the relation between morality and history, Sartre criticises mainly two options: an *idealism of universal values* and *sociological positivism*. First, Sartre argues that an ethics focused solely on the problem of *universal values* (e.g. freedom, mutual recognition, equality, non-violence) cannot as such form the goal of concrete morality. In concrete life value judgements are always posited in situations, and the understanding of the situation is and should be crucial for concrete decision-making. This implies an *ethics of situations*. A situation-dependant morality does not necessarily imply an arbitrary relativism of values. Sartre believes (i) that situations may be made intelligible in a unified manner (regressive-progressive interpretation), and (ii) that norms and values are already part of the praxis and social relations in question in the situation. Value judgements never take place in a value-vacuum, and the values involved in social relations are never arbitrary to the persons involved.

Second, a concrete morality cannot stop at the point of sociological positivism, which claims that norms can be studied simply as social facts (1974a p. 246-48). Here (in the *Rome lecture* and the *Cornell lectures*) Sartre again comes close to a hermeneutic conception. It is certainly true, Sartre admits, that norms, on one level, appears as given facts of social custom: "... *the imperatives of a present society* appear *at a certain* (normative) *level as an unconditional future and at another level ... as a repetitive past*" (p. 247). Social norms orient action both in the sense of imperatives of 'how one should act' and through imperative guidelines of 'how one has previously acted in situations like this'. The problem of concrete morality, however, cannot stop at this level. It concerns *values as chosen by concrete individuals in their praxis*.

This brings us to *the place and status of ethical reflection*. According to Sartre, whereas EN and CRD are situated on the level of the *unreflective*, ethical discourse must be situated on the level of *reflection* (BN, p. 628, NE, pp. 5f, 12, 411, 470-91, cf. Anderson 1993, pp. 41-42). EN and CRD describe the main features of human being-in-the-world as they are on the level of the unreflectively lived, but do not pose the moral problem. The moral problem concerns our possibilities *to reflectively take the conditions revealed into account in our praxis*.

Normative-ethical commitment is thus characteristically situated on the level of *reflection*. I shall reconstructively call it *reflexive* in two senses: (i) it is based on a *conscious attitude of reflection* towards one's own condition, that is, on an understanding of ones mode of being, situation, etc. (reflective consciousness) and (ii) it is reflexive in the sense that reflective understanding is *made use of* in one's concrete projects and actions (the reflexivity of praxis). Strictly speaking then, only the second of these constitute the level of morality. If we follow Sartre's claim in CM that "ethics is the theory of action" (NE, 17 (24)), reflection cannot be reduced to a level of consciousness, but *reflection must be seen as a part of praxis*.

But how can one claim that EN and CRD are situated on the level of the unreflective? They are philosophical works, and surely philosophy is typically a reflective quest. I think one should here distinguish between *a philosophical kind of reflection* involved, for example, in ontological description, and a *practical-ethical kind of reflection* involved in normative engagement. Whereas ontological-philosophical reflection results, for example, in description of a mode of being, practical-ethical reflection is oriented towards normative judgements and choices of action. It conforms to the idea of a *practical reason*.

In modern philosophy it is commonplace to separate questions of knowledge (facts and their validity) from questions of ethics (values and their justification). Thus, it has been claimed, at least since Hume, that we are not justified in deducing evaluative judgements from facts. In science this distinction has frequently been used in order to defend the integrity and autonomy of science. If one, on the other hand, contraposes knowledge and ethics from the point of view of ethics, the situation appears somewhat differently. Thus, no one would claim that moral decisions and justifications would be independent of knowledge. Quite the contrary, moral claims can be justifiably criticised if they misrepresent facts.

Sartre's ethics and critical social theory are strongly based on his ontology and views on socio-historical intelligibility. A striking thing is the co-appearance of certain ideas as both ontological 'facts' and values in Sartre. In some cases judgements of facts and judgements of value are parallel, in some cases they oppose each other. For example, according to Sartre (i) freedom is both an ontological fact about human beings and a moral and political ideal, whereas (ii) bad faith, alienation and social conflict appear on the factual level and their opposites, authenticity, non-alienation and reciprocity, on the level of morality. What, then, is the actual relation between these realms in Sartre? What is the being of value?

Initially one should observe that norms characteristically appear on two levels: as 'given' features of social custom (in habits, through jurisprudence, etc.) and as subjectively posited by individuals (explicitly or implicitly). Does the problem of a concrete morality, as Sartre sees it, concern the question how I am to live or what kind of morality an ideal society should realise? The answer is both! The idea of normative commitment is constantly informed by the image of an ideal social morality and ideal society. I shall return to this below.

What is the place of values in human life? Why should we conform to moral values? Already in EN Sartre argues that the positing of values is a necessary dimension of the human condition (BN, p. 84-102). The primary sources of value are negativity, freedom, situatedness, future-orientation and imagination as inherent features of the human condition. According to Sartre, consciousness is necessarily directed towards 'what is lacking', or future-oriented goals:

> Thus, *in the human world*, the incomplete being which is released to intuition as lacking is constituted in its being by the lacked — that is, by what it is not. It is the full moon which confers on the crescent moon its being as crescent ... human reality is that by which value arrives in the world ... Thus value taken in its origin ... *is* the beyond and the *for* of consciousness (BN, pp. 87 and 93 (125, 132)).

Values arise on the basis of our understanding of the world, through the experience that something is lacking, as the full moon is lacking in the experience and understanding of the crescent moon as crescent.

Although values arise in the world through the very mode of our existence (pre-reflective consciousness), this does not constitute the level of *moral consciousness*. This must be reflective (and thus intersubjective and linguistically mediated, see chapter 5): "... reflective consciousness can be properly called a moral consciousness since it cannot arise without at the same moment disclosing values" (BN, p. 95 (134)).

In his post-CRD notes on ethics, Sartre engages in the problem of the nature of values in a manner that is closely related to the themes and problems of CRD.[5] According to Bowman and Stone, the work was to be a regressive and progressive investigation of the dialectical relation between morality and history (Stone and Bowman 1991b, p. 57). It was intended to study regressively the place of norms in social reality, and to investigate progressively the actual ethos of practical life: the relation between praxis, ethical values and historical reality. Sartre thus understands the problem of morality as *a problem of praxis*.

In the *Rome lecture* Sartre distinguishes between several types of *norms* (the enveloping category for Sartre) (Sartre 1974a, pp. 241-42, Stone and Bowman 1991b, pp. 61-71): *institutionalised imperatives* (laws, regulations, etc.), *customs* (carry the sanction of social disapproval), *values* (judgements which concern ends of action), *goods* (means for the realisation of imperatives or values), *exemplary behaviour* and, finally, *ideals* ("... the intention of uniting norms in a synthetic movement toward an end which would take them into itself" (Stone and Bowman 1991b, p. 64)). According to Sartre, the primary function of norms in social life is to regulate human relationships.

What is common to all types of norms is that they appear as *unconditionally possible*. By means of this term Sartre distinguishes between the nature of norms and values and that of historically lived reality. By 'unconditionally possible' Sartre means that all norms carry the trait that 'regardless of situation it is always possible to posit them as such'. The value of a certain value, for example sincerity, depends neither on an antecedent cause, nor on the historically conditioned possibility to realise it in practice. Regardless of situation it is always possible to uphold the ethical imperative 'one ought not to lie!'. The point is not to claim that we (in the ethos of practical life) always should follow such norms, only that they are always possible to posit as such. An example found in Sartre that more clearly demonstrates the unconditional nature of ethical imperatives is the value of a resistant activist 'never to talk when tortured'. This is set up exactly as an ideal independent of the horrifying reality of torture. The question whether or not the person holds out does not, according to Sartre, affect the value to keep silent. Sartre concludes: "(1) on condition that one put *ones life at stake*, every moral requirement is capable at the limit of being met *no matter what* the antecedent and external determining conditions may be; and (2) *everybody's* most profound possibility consists in the possibility of staking his life on an imperative" (1974a, pp. 243-44, (737)).

Norms and values by nature constitute unconditional possibilities. In our actions we might realise them or not. The problem of ethical reflection is both to decipher (hermeneutically) the real value of some specific value, for example by studying its impact on and relation to social reality and to decide what values actually are justified in concrete praxis. That is, according to Sartre concrete morality is always *a problem of praxis*, which means both that given norms receive their actual value for us only through *our own practical judgements and decisions*, and that morality is necessarily *inscribed in history*. This also means that the question 'why I am to conform to moral values?' primarily concerns, not conformity with given norms of social custom or pure universal values, but the question of *the intelligibility of what I am* (dealt with by modified philosophical anthropology) *and what I do* (dealt with in terms of regressive-progressive investigation). I shall return to this below.

Main Moral Values and Political Ideals

Sartre is not shy to reveal his own moral values and socio-political ideals. This naturally also makes him vulnerable to criticism. An initial inventory of the values and ideals posited by Sartre at different times provides us with a list of the following kind: *freedom, authenticity, generosity, non-alienation, reciprocity, common praxis, integral humanity* and a *socialist society*. It is much more difficult to determine what these notions actually contain, how and if they fit together in an overall conception, whether Sartre changed his 'value-system' during his lifetime and by means of what arguments he justifies them.

It is an unsettled issue whether Sartre's values and ideals may be claimed to remain the same throughout his life, or to what extent they actually change. What is clear is that his emphasis and the meaning of notions like freedom change somewhat. If we follow Sartre's own retrospective comments we should divide his thought on this issue into three periods: (1) an early ethics focused on *freedom, authenticity and generosity* (up until 1948), (2) a middle period of *political realism* ("... you do it because it works, and you check it out, you evaluate it according to its efficacy rather than some vague notions having to do with morality..." (Sartre 1978d, p. 78)) focused on the struggle against alienation and social oppression (the 1950's and CRD) and (3) a second, dialectical ethics focused on the ideal of *integral humanity* (from 1965 onwards) (Sartre 1978d, pp. 76-81 and Anderson 1993, pp. 1-4). On the other hand, when one study the values actually defended by Sartre at these different periods there appears to be a strong convergence. Thus, I can find no reason to claim that the later Sartre would have rejected the ideals of freedom and authenticity. And the social ideals defended by the later Sartre can also easily be found in works like EH and CM. In the following inventory I shall not try to settle this issue, but stay true to my intention to read Sartre from the point of view of the anthropology of CRD.

First, in EN and CM the emphasis is on an *ethics of authenticity*. 'Authenticity' means 'being true to oneself', in some determined sense of 'true' and 'self'. But contrary to what is often assumed by the critics of Sartre, authenticity does not imply the positing of a genuine inner self to be true to.[6] Instead, Sartre's conception of authenticity is (self-evidently, I would say) modelled on his conception of human being as a being-in-the-world, a being in situation and a being of action. Thus, in *Réflexions sur la Question Juive* (1948c) Sartre characterises authenticity in a way completely opposed to the idea of an inner self:

> Authenticity ... consists in having a true and lucid consciousness of the situation, in assuming the responsibilities and risks that it involves, in accepting it in pride or humiliation, sometimes in horror and hate (p. 90).

This formulation in my opinion implies at least two things about authenticity. First, 'being true to oneself' here means 'accepting the intelligibility of the human condition'. Second, 'to assume responsibility for and act on the basis of situational intelligibility or a diagnosis of the times. Since Sartre's hermeneutic conception of the human condition implies embeddedness in the world (society and history), the two aspects of intelligibility of oneself and of the situation fit together.

Second, the social aspect of an ideal of *reciprocity* or *mutual recognition* is inherent in Sartre's conception of freedom and authenticity. This is already the case with his early ethics. As I said above, in Sartre's writings freedom appears on two levels: as an ontological and an ethical category. On the unreflective level (that is, non-ethical) the relation between individual freedom and sociality initially appear as a relation of conflict (and later in CRD as serial alienation and struggle): the free transcendence of each individual implies that each attempt to transcend and objectify each other. Regardless of the validity or non-validity of this claim, on the reflective level the futility and inauthenticity of continuous conflict is disclosed. Since freedom can only be limited by another freedom, the mutual recognition of freedom becomes part of the ideal of authenticity. The only way I can preserve and develop my freedom is through others recognition, and this implies that I recognise others as free beings. I shall return to this issue below.

In CM this social dimension of freedom is most clearly brought forward in the identification of *generosity* as the highest level of freedom: "Method: Values reveal freedom at the same time that they surrender it. Any ordering of values has to lead to freedom. Classify values in a hierarchy such that freedom increasingly appears in it. *At the top: generosity*" (NE, p. 9 (16), my italics). Sartre thus bases his view on a *hierarchy of values*: values that crush freedom, intermediary values, social values and values of subjectivity. The highest of, "this hierarchy [or values of subjectivity] leads us to see like a light above the plane of generosity, freedom properly speaking" (NE, p. 470 (486)). Generosity, again, is characterised as an act of giving and this "... gift presupposes a reciprocity of recognition" (NE, p. 369 (383)). Finally, Sartre introduces the notion of the *appeal* [*l'appel*] — a type of interhuman relation — as an ideal form of generous intersubjectivity:

> An appeal is a request made by someone to someone in the name of something ... The appeal is the recognition of a personal freedom in a situation by a personal freedom in a situation ... An appeal is first of all the recognition of diversity ... The only authentic form of willing here consists in wanting the end to be realised by the other ... In every appeal there is a gift ... The appeal, in effect, is a promise of reciprocity (NE, pp. 274, 279, 281 and 284 (285, 290, 292 and 295)).

Both in CRD and in Sartre's second, dialectical, ethics the value of the mutual recognition of freedom is preserved, although it is now extended to imply a certain socio-political ideal (socialism). Thus, what Anderson prefers to call *Sartre's ethics of integral humanity* is built up by the positing of a *moral goal of human history*: a society in which all human beings recognise each others freedom and make history in common. Paradoxically, it is exactly the positing of this ideal that leads Sartre to what he calls his realism. In order to achieve the ideal, all means of struggle, even violent ones, are justified. Although Sartre claims that he later returned from political realism to ethics, this initially only means that he has come to realise the ethical structure at the bottom of this political struggle. This I think is one way of interpreting his statement in the *Rome lecture* that "... the historical moment has come for socialism to rediscover its ethical structure, or rather, to unveil it" (quoted from Bowman and Stone 1991a, p. 111).

In addition to these two values, it is important to re-emphasise that Sartre's conception of rationality implies *the norm of totalising intelligibility*: a socially relational, temporal and synthetic understanding of human reality that emphasises our bonds of interiority with the world, including mediated reciprocity. It is thus a norm of the correct interpretation of human reality. In its critical function it criticises as ideological such interpretations that violate the norm of totalisation, and which fulfil the social function of legitimating a certain social order by denying this norm. Since the concrete, social violation of a norm of rationality may be claimed to give rise to pathological side effects in society, it may also be used to diagnose concrete expressions of social pathology. Furthermore, a solution to such social pathologies must base itself on the acceptance of this norm. Thus, in his concrete critical-diagnostic interpretations in CRD and IF, Sartre delimits the socially divisive power of analytical rationality both as an ideological source of legitimacy for the existing order and as a possible source of social.

The existence of the ideal of a moral goal of history is clearly present already in CRD:

> One of the most striking characteristics of our time is the fact that history is made without self-awareness ... In this sense History, which is the proper work of all activity and of all men, appears to men as a foreign force exactly insofar as they do not recognise the meaning of their enterprise (even when locally successful) in the total, objective result ... the plurality of the meanings of History can be discovered and posited for itself only upon the ground of a future totalisation — in terms of the future totalisation and in contradiction with it. It is our theoretical and practical duty to bring this totalisation closer every day. All is still obscure, and yet everything is in full light. To tackle the theoretical aspect, we have the instruments; we can establish the method. *Our*

> *historical task, at the heart of this polyvalent world, is to bring closer the moment when History will have only one meaning, when it will tend to be dissolved in the concrete men who will make it in common* (SM, pp. 29 and 89-90, (35, 75-76), my italics).

And

> As soon as there will exist *for everyone* a margin of *real* freedom beyond the production of life, Marxism will have lived out its span; a philosophy of freedom will take its place. But we have no means, no intellectual instrument, no concrete experience which allows us to conceive of this freedom or of this philosophy (SM, p. 34 (39)).

Sartre here refers to the ideals of 'a unitary meaning of history' and 'a margin of real freedom for everyone', and sees his investigation as oriented by these ideals. Especially the last passage shows that he thinks that we do not even have any intellectual means to understand what a world where these ideals are realised would be like.

I have claimed that Sartre posits the reconciliation of *an investigation of the socio-historical situation* with the positing of a *universal ethical value* (1974c, pp. 248-60). We can now see that Sartre, in trying to resolve this apparent contradiction, makes, what I want to call, an *exit through Marxist Utopianism.* He actually posits that "true intellectuals ... suggest that the human universal is *yet to come*" (p. 253), a universal that is "... a social universality ... where all men will be *truly* free, equal and fraternal" (p. 254), and that they in the meantime ought to practice "*a concrete and unconditioned alignment with the actions of the underprivileged classes*" (p. 261), since these represent the future. This *Utopianism*, or the positing of an ideal society which is beyond the grasp and practical possibilities of the present, is further confirmed by Sartre's appeal to the ideal of '*making the human*' as the ultimate goal of human striving. That is, as is particularly interesting from the point of view of an attempt to answer the question 'what does Sartre mean by 'anthropology'?', Sartre posits *the human* not only as an object of study, but *as a normative-ethical ideal.* By 'the human' he does not only mean something already existing that we should try to understand better, but something not yet existing which we ought to try to realise. This is perhaps nowhere as clear as in Benny Lévy's last interview of Sartre:

> ... as you know, for me there is no a priori essence; and so what a human being is has not yet been established. We are not complete human beings. We

> are beings who are struggling to establish human relations and arrive at a definition of what is human ... we are seeking to live together like human beings, and to be human being. So it's by means of searching for this definition ... that we will be able to consider our effort and our end. In other words, our goal is to arrive at a genuine constituted body in which each person will be a human being and in which collectivities will be not less human (Sartre and Lévy 1996, p. 67).[7]

This exit through Marxist Utopianism is, in my opinion, a highly problematic and disappointing feature of Sartre's ethical thinking, especially in a contemporary perspective. Instead of engaging in the difficult question of discussing the normative grounds of critique, Sartre falls back on a pre-set ideal that orients his views. He thereby manages to avoid many difficult problems. However, it is also possible to find in Sartre a more promising route of argumentation than his exit through Utopianism. I shall now go into this other possibility, inherent in Sartre's anthropology and more in tune with the idea of a hermeneutics of praxis.

A Reconstruction of Sartre's Normative Ethical Argumentation: Ethical Ideals and the Intelligibility of the Human

I have discussed Sartre's conception of the being of value, and delimited which specific values and ideals Sartre himself defends. I have also claimed that, according to Sartre, the ideas of *commitment* and of *concrete morality* implies that a Sartrean ethics cannot be satisfied either with a 'meta-ethical proof' of the necessity of value-positing, or with the 'normative-ethical' positing of certain universal values. Such an ethics must also, self-evidently, fulfil the task to justify these values and, more crucially, to deal with the relation between values (unconditional possibilities) and conditioned, historical reality. Thus, 'why', according to Sartre, 'shall we accept such things as freedom, reciprocity and the unitary meaning of history as ultimate ideals?' and 'how shall we conceive of these values in the concrete morality of a non-ideal reality?'.

The answer to the first question can, I think, be found in Sartre, although only through some reconstructive work. The answer to the second question depends on whether one accepts Utopianism or not. That is, I claim that Sartre makes it too easy for himself by taking recourse to Utopianism in order to deal with the relation between ideals and reality. I also believe that this kind of solution ought to be rejected. The point of my criticism is not that Sartre was wrong. It is quite futile to criticise dead persons for what they have said and done, in times perhaps different than one's own. Instead, my interest lies with the possibilities to develop a 'quasi-Sartrean' position that drops all references to a Utopian end that might justify the means. That is, *on this level* I offer the possibility of a *Sartrean hermeneutics of praxis* as an *alternative* to the route that Sartre actually took in the 1950's and -60's. Hermeneutics is opposed both to metaphysics and Utopian idealism: it constitutes an attempt to think postmetaphysically about the possibilities of understanding and ethical-political matters. That is, on the level of his 'ethics of socialism' Sartre remains an unhermeneutical thinker.

An important reason is that I find Utopianism dangerous. The search for objective and normative moral principles and the positing of Utopian models of the ideal society share the dangers of becoming authoritarian. The history of the 19th and 20th-century has revealed the dangers of unified truths as political weapons (the justification of imperialism as a moral task, national socialism, the social embodiments of Marxism, the global penetration of 'the strong that gain in a liberalism of the free market', etc.). In this sense I agree with Foucault that "... the ethico-political choice we have to make every day is to *determine which is the main danger*" (1997, p. 256, my italics), rather than to find ultimate solutions.

In the following I shall attempt a reconstruction of a possible way Sartre might have argued in defence of the values of 'freedom and reciprocity'. I shall reconstructively interpret Sartre to say that ethical ideals are argumentatively justified by recourse to the *intelligibility of the human*. I argue that the main bridge is the bond between our (reflectively revealed) understanding of ourselves as intersubjective, free beings of praxis and our dependence on reciprocal recognition for the authentic realisation of our projects.

As I said above, the relation between ontology/intelligibility and moral values in Sartre appears to be relation of correspondence. Thus, on the level of intelligibility Sartre claims (i) that human beings are *free beings of action* and (ii) that human relations are reflectively revealed as *mediated reciprocities*. Analogously, on the ethical plane Sartre claims that the primary ethical and socio-political value is the *mutual recognition of freedom*.[8] Thus, if the realised social freedom of A implies or leads to the social unfreedom or oppression of B, this violates the ethical ideal of freedom. The value of freedom implies mutuality or, as Sartre says in CRD, positive reciprocity.

On the other hand, Sartre reaffirms the inner rift between facts and values by positing a radical gulf between values as unconditionally possible and the intelligibility of historical human reality as conditioned. Eager to avoid overtly idealistic and utopian claims, Sartre declares that, in the present state of affairs, the realisation of the ideals of 'a real freedom for everyone' and 'the realisation of a unitary reciprocally common meaning of history' appear both *impossible* and, to make it worse, fully *inconceivable* to us. Thus, Sartre has to image an ideal, where the condition of historicity has changed so radically that we are unable even to imagine what such a life would be like, and denies that it is possible to realise under the present conditions of human historicity: "... we must abandon any idea of humanity historialising itself in the development of a single temporalisation" (CDR, p. 666). These ideals, by appearing both unimaginable and inconceivable, thus seem to constitute a (both frightful and unjustified) jump into the unknown.

Another important example is found in the theory of social formations. Sartre posits the group as both the realisation of an ethically ideal form of sociality, and denies the possibility that group action could remove alienation:

> ... the group is both the most effective *means* of controlling the surrounding materiality in the context of scarcity and *the absolute end* as pure freedom liberating men from alterity (CDR, p. 673 (756)).
> ... group action is always doomed to synchronic alienation except in the hypothetical case when the practical community is identical to all the individuals in the common field; then it is doomed without qualification to diachronic alienation (CDR, p. 668 (750-51)).

The realisation of a positive reciprocity between mediating Thirds (a common project) in the (organised) group, in a situation where there are other groups and collectives in the field, is doomed to immediate alienation and, in a situation where everyone would belong to the same group (humanity historialising itself), it is doomed to historical alienation (the gulf between generations). It appears that the levels of praxis and ethical ideality are mutually exclusive.[9]

It is characteristic of Sartre's (and Heidegger's) existential phenomenology that the truth of the human appears in a twofold manner. First, ontology reveals a certain necessary structure: transcendence, freedom, project, need, praxis, sociality, etc. Second, ontology reveals that all these features, on the level of the concretely lived, belong to a structure of *freedom in situation*. Thus, they appear as *necessary conditions*, but *not causal determinations of the lived*. The concretely lived is always lived in freedom, uniqueness, attitudes and future-oriented projects; a human being is a being that has the ability to and must take up an attitude to his existence. Thus, freedom may attempt to escape from freedom, reciprocity may be negated in refusal or oppression, praxis may be turned into active passivity, group action into seriality, appeal into demand, etc.

A first link between intelligibility and ethics is that all these attitudes, whether of recognition or refusal, must be understood on the basis of the general intelligibility of the human (epistemic normativity). There is a necessity of freedom, of praxis, of practico-inert materiality, of mediated reciprocity, etc. The escape from freedom is an act of freedom; it is a smokescreen or an act of bad faith. The negation of reciprocity is grounded in a primary, positive reciprocity: oppression is recognition but practical negation of fundamental reciprocity. Active passivity is itself an active way of being (see Chapters 5 (freedom), 7 (reciprocity) and 8 (the case of Flaubert's passivity)). Thus, on a first level of normativity, the intelligibility of the human as freedom, mediated reciprocity and praxis appear as unsurpassable and inescapable norms of the understanding of what we are and do.

Norms of intelligibility are still not the same as ethical values. Norms of intelligibility tell us how we are to understand what we do, but not what we ought to be, how we ought to act or what we ought to respect in others. How is one to justify that a human being, on a moral level, ought to be treated and recognised along with his intelligibility? Why are freedom and positive reciprocity moral values?

Although ethical values are posited as unconditionally possible, the moment of morality is still a historically conditioned praxis. Thus, the problem of morality depends on the intelligibility of praxis.

A second link between intelligibility and ethics in Sartre is that norms of intelligibility are norms of how we are to understand the meaning of a human action. Value, according to Sartre, is primarily the positing of an end of action on the basis of the given: "... I posit in principle that every end has a value and that every human activity is haunted by value" (NE, p. 275 (286)). Value is a part of the meaning of an action. The moral dimension of the meaning of an action is connected to the value it has for me or for anyone who is influenced by it. If norms of intelligibility inform me about the real meaning of my action, they also inform me about what values the action may have for others and myself.

A central value for human beings as historical beings is to be able to *realise what ones posits as willed*. The realisation of a goal in praxis, however, is dependent on the meaning of what one does, not only on its physical realisation. Thus, to strive for the realisation of a certain goal means to will a certain meaning to be realised. But the meaning of what we do depends on the presence of others in the field, and on their recognition of this meaning. This implies that to will to realise something means to will that *others recognise the meaning of what I do in a way that conforms to my original intention*. This, again, implies *reciprocal recognition*. What may originally be a demand from my side that the other ought to recognise what I do, at the heart of the intelligibility of implies that I recognise the other as a free being of values, praxis and intersubjectivity. I cannot simultaneously expect and demand that my praxis is recognised by the other, and refuse to recognise that the others positive recognition is an act of freedom or praxis. Thus, in the ideal case, demand must turn into an *appeal*, an appeal to the other to recognise my action, and this appeal implies reciprocity.

'Reciprocity' implies both (i) that one cannot but understand other human beings as free beings of project and action, and (ii) that one cannot but understand oneself as a free being of project and action that is necessarily related to other such beings. Thus, reciprocity is both a condition for the understanding of others and of oneself. In addition, reciprocity is necessarily mediated, which implies (iii) that we understand the world in terms of other human beings, other human beings in terms of the world, ourselves in terms of the sociality of the world and the world in terms of our sociality

These observations imply that the problem of the intelligibility of praxis necessarily includes a moral dimension. This, again, means that although universal values are posited as unconditionally possible but not realisable, the moral dimension is unavoidable. Thus, the relation between ethical ideals and conditioned history is not one of mutual exclusion. Stone and Bowman quotes a revealing passage from the *Cornell lectures*:

> Ethics envisaged as a determination of activity appears at first as an essential but provisional moment of all praxis: indeed praxis tears itself away from the given — that is, from present conditions — by transcending it toward a nonbeing from which praxis returns to the given in order to invent its own conditions of possibility. In this moment of invention, praxis posits its goal as unconditional, that is, as a future nonbeing which creates, from the heart of the future, the means for its realisation (quoted and translated by Stone and Bowman 1991b, p. 71).

Thus, the intelligibility of praxis implies to understand that praxis is ethical in nature, and that it almost never constitutes a complete success. Sartre can claim both that 'a real margin of freedom for everyone', 'positive reciprocity' and the formation of a group constitute ideals, which may, to a certain extent, be realised here and now, and that they equally necessarily (in our history) will neither be complete (synchronic alienation) nor lasting (diachronic alienation).

I have thereby given a (rather sweeping) reconstruction of an answer to the two questions I asked in relation to the normatively ethical argumentation of Sartre. I tried to show how the positing of certain ethical ideals might be seen as connected to the intelligibility of the human in Sartre. I also emphasised that the positing of values is a necessary feature of praxis, although they can never be realised in a complete manner. My answers were not intended to constitute final interpretations, but to shed some further light on Sartre's views on praxis, the human condition and his conception of anthropology.

Elements of a Sartrean Critical Theory

I have thus tried to reconstruct Sartre's ethical argumentation on the question how one of the central ideals of Sartre, the mutual recognition of freedom, is to be justified. Concrete morality and critical social cannot, however, rest with such ethical argumentation, although they must certainly be informed and oriented by it. According to Sartre, concrete morality is a question of praxis: if the perfectly ideal is unrealisable in practice, what am I to do? Likewise, critical social theory is concerned with the diagnosis of the historical present. The positing of values is the positing of the unconditionally possible. But what are their impacts in conditioned, historical reality, and what is their relevance for critical social theory? Although Sartre never clarifies these issues in any systematic manner, I shall try to reconstruct a possible way of interpreting them.

A critical social theory may incorporate at least three thematic orientations: *interpretation*, *diagnosis* and a *therapeutic* dimension. The interpretative dimension links critical theory to the scientific domains of knowledge and understanding, while the diagnostic and therapeutic dimensions are inherently normative. This distinction shall not be seen as definitive: as Habermas argues, within the framework of critical theory the interpretative dimension must also be seen as oriented by normative concerns (Habermas 1978, pp.43-64 and 187-300).

The distinction between *diagnostic* and *therapeutic*, again, communicates a difference between the kind of *hopes* and *criteria of success* associated with this such a participatory intellectual enterprise. By 'diagnosis' may be meant both 'the detection of an illness' and 'a recipe for possible cure'. As Benhabib points out, these expectations may be seen either as mainly *anticipatory*, in an interpretative sense, or as *utopian*, in a more idealistic sense (Benhabib 1986, p. 142). Furthermore, if the utopian dimension more directly addresses practical questions, it may be characterised as *therapeutic*. By 'therapy', again, one may choose to mean anything on the scale from 'local cure' to 'fully revolutionary action'.

In Sartre there are elements of all of these. Besides the interpretative dimension I have discussed in the previous chapters, Sartre attempts to diagnose the present, mainly by the means of a concept of *alienation*, and was keen to express his opinions both on local therapeutic cures[10] and revolutionary-utopian frameworks (see above). I shall neither go into the details of these 'situational analyses', nor discuss Sartre's Utopianism any further. Instead I shall provide an interpretative reconstruction that connects a Sartrean conception of critical social theory with his views on the intelligibility of praxis and socio-historical fields.

Above I indicated how Sartre's views on the presence of a norm of totalisation in his answer to the question of the intelligibility of praxis enables us to reconstruct the connection between the two values of practical freedom and social mediated reciprocity. Our possibilities to realise the meaning intended in our actions depend on the meanings and significations of the action in relation to other persons, and on their recognition of my project and praxis. This again demands that I recognise others as free and social beings of action. This may be described as the *core of Sartrean ethics* as *grounded in a hermeneutics of praxis*.

A critical social theory set up on the basis of such an ethics, again, should at least address the questions of (i) the *social and historical conditions* for *the realisation of freedom and mediated reciprocity*, and (ii) the social and historical sources of negative social states such as *alienation* and *oppression* as societal opposites to these values. Such an attempt should shift ground from a perspective focused on the intelligibility of praxis as such to a perspective *on the intelligibility of social fields and historical processes*. Sartre's theory of social formations, social bonds and social conflict is an attempt to fulfil such demands (although Sartre never expresses himself exactly in that way). Thus, for example, the theory of the group demonstrates both how a limited realisation of the mutual recognition of freedom is possible, and in what sense all such attempts are doomed to alienation in the long run (in our society, Sartre adds). The understanding of these conditions and such historical intelligibility forms the basis of Sartre's critical social theory.

Sartre's hermeneutical conception of the intelligibility of praxis (individual, serial, group or antagonistic) raises the *norm of totalisation* (or a synthetic, dialectical conception of reason) as the foundation of the claim that all praxis is necessarily embedded in a social and historical world of meanings (and significations), and that such meanings are crucial for our understanding of what we do, can do and ought to do. The norm of totalisation thus functions diagnostically both to detect the *sources of alienation* and as a *socio-political ideal*. In the following I shall shortly indicate how it works within the perspective of critical social theory, leaving a full elaboration of this issue to the future.

Sartre's diagnosis of the present is both concerned with such negative features of social reality as *alienation* and *oppression*, and with false interpretations of it, or *ideology*. By 'ideology' Sartre seems to mean an interpretation of social reality that manages to illuminate only a part of it to the exclusion of other, equally central parts. Since ideologies function to legitimate social order, the task to disclose such one-sidedness of interpretation has an important socio-critical function. Sartre's totalising conception of rationality and the intelligibility of the present are thus also critical of ideology.

Sartre investigates discrepancies between concrete social life and interpretations of it, but also the norm of totalising intelligibility as grounded in concrete social praxis itself. He discloses the root of social injustices, pathologies and ideological interpretations as concrete *violations* against the social bond of reciprocity. In a first phase he attempts to make intelligible the sources of such violations, in a second phase to reveal the true intelligibility or real meaning of the events studied.

A violation of the norm of totalising intelligibility may be understood both as present in social reality itself, and in the interpretation of this reality. In case social reality is ordered in such a way that it *practically violates* the principles of intelligibility, we may say that reality itself (as construed by human beings) constitutes a violation against the epistemic norm. For instance, the pre-dominance of serial divisions, institutions and hierarchical organisation (i) diminishes the possibilities for a large part of human beings to influence this reality, and (ii) violates in itself against the value of positive reciprocity. Thus, although a norm of intelligibility (rationality) informs us descriptively what human reality is like, the concrete organisation of this reality may violate against the norm. This does not make the norm invalid, at least not insofar as violation is itself intelligible on the basis of the norm. A real violation itself fulfils the norm if it is intelligible as a praxis and totalisation. According to Sartre, the serial, institutionalised and hierarchical organisation of social reality is a result of praxis, and it totalises the whole by subordinating it to a specific order. In this way, the dimensions of intelligibility and normativity interact.

All praxis contains an understanding of what is done. A praxis that violates against the basic intelligibility of praxis (the social bond of reciprocity) is often supported by an interpretation that either legitimises or covers up this violation, in short, an ideology. The critique of ideology is intended to delegitimise such interpretations by disclosing it's ideological function, and replace it with a correct interpretation.

A crucial example in Sartre of such an ideology is the employment of *analytical rationality*. Analytical rationality turns our attention away from the singular reality of praxis, historicity and the bonds of interiority. It focuses on non-concrete universality and divides reality into its constituent parts. In this sense, the ideal of analytical rationality corresponds to the real division of social reality by serialisation, institutionalisation and the division of labour. Since it thus corresponds to reality, analytical rationality may be claimed to convey a correct way of viewing this reality (a source of misunderstanding). According to Sartre, analytical rationality corresponds to reality in a way that defends status quo (it is thus a structural, but not a historical form of rationality), and covers up the fact that reality is continuously shaped and reshaped by concrete human praxis (individual or social). In short, it replaces the totalising intelligibility of praxis as the source of history, with divisions, structures, static systems and material processes.[11]

I shall not discuss Sartre's views on *alienation* in any greater detail. I have already mentioned three basic levels of alienation: practico-inert materiality, non-group-like relations and conflict. Without commenting too much on the history of the concept, I shall argue that Sartre's concept of alienation is mainly a social concept. At least since Marx, alienation has generally been understood in three possible dimensions: (i) as a feature of the relation between a human being and the objective world (the objective results of action, etc.), (ii) as a feature a persons relation to himself and (iii) as a feature of the relation between human beings.

Sartre first discloses alienation on the basis of the internal relation between human beings and the material world (CDR, p. 227). The necessity of praxis to be inscribed in practico-inert objects is, indeed, a first *condition* of alienation: it constitutes a first level of otherness (alterity). On the other hand, it does not *as such* constitute alienation: "... the freedom of a action which ends in failure is simply freedom which fails..." (CDR, 237 (345)), and not alienation. Alienation requires that the result of an action returns as *another action*, that is, as a meaning that was not intended by the agent. In the case of practico-inert materiality, this happens first "... as soon as man begins to designate himself, not as the mere reproduction of his life, but as the ensemble of products which reproduce life..." (CDR, 227 (336)), that is, in so far as human beings began to understand themselves primarily on the basis of processes. In addition, "certainly men do not grasp the real measure of what they do ... But if History escapes me this is not because I do not make it; it is because the other is making it as well" (SM, 87-88 (74)). The main locus of alienation is thus the domain of, what I have called the social meanings of action.

To sum up, it seems to me that praxis, according to Sartre, may be alienated: by being (i) objectivistically interpreted as a physical process (objectivism), (ii) analytically interpreted as separate from other praxes in the field (analytical interpretation), (iii) socially interpreted differently by some other individual or group in the field (conflict of interpretations), (iv) re-acted against by some other group in the field (conflict of actions) or (v) lead to the opposite of what was intended due to socio-material circumstances (social counter-finality).

I set out to investigate the relation between ethics and critical social theory. In the theoretical moment of this normative investigation, ethical ideals are seen by Sartre as grounded in a norm of intelligibility. In the cases discussed as examples of unconditioned possibilities, all contain the real possibility of being realised in practice. Thus, the ideals 'not to lie' and 'to keep silent despite torture' are both cases where the possibility of their immediate realisation has a concrete form. The same cannot perhaps be said with the social ideals of freedom for everyone, mutual recognition and the unitary meaning of history, because, according to Sartre, we do not seem to have the means even to understand what they could possibly mean.

Or have we? It might be argued that Sartre has in fact given us exactly such an example of an ideal social formation: the (organised) group. Although it is the case that the group is necessarily alienated, it is still realisable in a limited fashion. Thus, the possibility of the limited realisation of an ideal is unconditionally possible, although this ideal is destined in contemporary history to become alienated from it's status as ideal. I do think that this interpretation stands quite close to Sartre's own self-understanding. The problem is then turned into what we are to say about the necessity of alienation. Sartre does not, in fact, say much about this problem: he is safeguarded by his distinction between practical and theoretical tasks. He can thus always claim that intellectual activity, as a limited form of activity, is only able to communicate the intelligibility of this ideal and its alienation. The rest is and must be up to real praxis.

Sartre's critical social theory, if one pushes the Utopian dimension of his Marxism to the background, is thus firmly rooted in the kind of anthropology possible within the framework of a hermeneutics of praxis. Sartre never provided a systematic account of the normative questions involved. My interpretation is thus reconstructive in two senses: it emphasises the hermeneutical dimension at the cost of the metaphysical-utopian, and it attempts to reconstruct a line of argumentation that is actually not found in Sartre's writings. By this I have fulfilled my promise to use the idea of a hermeneutics of praxis as a critical instrument to go beyond Sartre, while preserving many of his central ideas. Before concluding this chapter I shall give an account of how Sartre uses both his interpretative method and normative issues in the biography on Flaubert.

The Relation between Flaubert and his Times: Subjective and Objective Neurosis

There is an interesting example of a diagnosis of society in the third volume of IF. Sartre discusses the relation between Flaubert and the society of the second empire in France (1852-1871) on the basis of the personality of Flaubert, and the reception of *Madame Bovary*. The novel, which by both Flaubert and Sartre is characterised as a 'rejection of the reading public' (the bourgeoisie), is interpreted by his readers as a *realism*. Sartre interprets this as an indication (signification) of the objective neurosis of the society in question.

The interpretation is strengthened by means of a claim that the subjective neurosis of Flaubert (see Chapter 8) corresponds to the objective neurosis of the society (FI 5, pp. 29-32, see also Barnes 1981, pp. 247-309). Sartre describes such a harmonisation of a person with his times by means of the notion of *programmation* (see for example FI 5, pp. 401-13). A person may be said to be programmed if his way of life fits well in with the culture and society in which he lives. Sartre's notion contains more than that, however. Flaubert is programmed in the sense that his life symbolises (totalises) the epoch in a specifically interesting way: "… the finitude of an individual or micro-organic temporalisation *can* incarnate the finitude of a macrocosmic temporalization, that is, the finitude of a *historical period* … What counts for those that are diachronically significant insofar as they are retotalising is that whether short or long, quick or slow, they are the era itself in its entirety, gathered up in a program" (FI 5, p. 402 and 409). The use of the notion of programmation also conveys that the non-alienation of a person does not imply that the society in question is non-alienating: a person may be programmed so that his (false) interpretation of reality corresponds to its organisation.

Madame Bovary is interpreted by the public as a realistic work: Flaubert has often been characterised as 'the father of realism'. This interpretation is actually quite absurd, according to Sartre (FI 5, pp. 25-32). Flaubert understood his own writings as imaginary, as a refusal to communicate, as art for arts sake, etc. Surprisingly, however, the public recognises itself in the work. Sartre asks "... how is it conceivable that a neurotic work, produced by a patient as a means of subjectivization, could disclose to the reader anything other than a singularity that is posed for itself against the universal, and consequently presents itself during reading as the absolute Other, crying out to the public: 'You are not me because I do not want to be you'" (FI 5, p. 26). The public must have misunderstood the book. But misunderstanding, as a serial feature, is not necessarily rooted in bad thinking, but in the *social conditions of understanding*. The book could only have been misunderstood, if the social conditions of the bourgeois public were contradictory and neurotic: a society, in which the public welcome a work directed against them as a realistic description, must be neurotic.

By 'neurosis' Sartre means either a state of mind (subjective) or a feature of a society (objective). "Neurosis..." Sartre writes, is "... an adaptation to illness" (FI 5, p. 3). In the case of an objective neurosis, Sartre claims that a society is neurotic if its internal features (the relation between it's social formations), its actual praxis (the dominating praxis-process) and the interpretation of them (ideology) stand in a conflictual relation to each other (for Sartre's interpretation of the Second Empire, see FI 5, pp. 29, 187-312 and 413-621, see also Barnes 1981, pp. 278-300). The society in this example (the Second Empire) is (i) the outcome of the failed revolution of the underprivileged classes in 1848, (ii) a society where the bourgeois class, for the first time, finds itself in charge of history and (3) a society factually ruled by an emperor (Napoleon III). The neurosis of this bourgeoisie society is, according to Sartre, rooted mainly in a contradiction between the values of this class, and their own defensive reaction against their realisation (universalisation). The bourgeoisie of 19th century France generally supported universal values (freedom, equality and justice). In addition, they are practitioners of a scientific world-view: they believed in science, and in the existence of a universal human nature. But the realisation of universal values would imply that all human beings and social layers would be affected by the ideals. As long as the bourgeoisie is not 'in power', this does not raise any major problems. But suddenly this class finds itself 'in charge of history', but they have just defeated the claims to equality (etc.) by the underprivileged. Thus, their power status stands in open contradiction to their values. According to Sartre, it is in order to cover up for this contradiction that they can accept an emperor as ruler.

According to Sartre's interpretation, of which I can only communicate a small glimpse, the bourgeoisie were led from their belief in a universal human nature (analytical rationality and a scientific world-view), to a double limitation of this universalist claim. First, the universality of human nature is inverted into a hatred of man: there is indeed a human nature, but it is inherently evil. Second, as a consequence of the first, the possibility to realise universal goodness is grounded in a rejection of evil: to realise the good one must raise oneself to a higher level, above nature, and thus also above the lower classes. Goodness, then, becomes accessible only to their class.

A consequence of this kind of thinking is that Flaubert's parallel rejection of the good in man (his rejection of the public), and his turn to the imaginary, can be experienced as realism. Flaubert's rejection of man corresponds with the bourgeois hatred of man, and this is why Flaubert can find himself at ease in the Second Empire. I shall not, however, enter into this issue.

Concluding Remark

I have, by the means of a strongly reconstructive interpretation, tried to reveal the scope and limits of the normative dimension of Sartre's anthropology. I have tried to explicate, as clearly as possibly, the orientation, tensions and problems connected with this discourse. I have tried to illuminate Sartre's real attempts at reconciliation, but also showed that he (naturally) has not removed all problems. I have tried to show how the normative dimension of Sartre's anthropology encompasses the levels of ethics and of critical social theory, as well as a concern with the problem of rationality. I have also claimed that Sartre grounds a great deal of his normative issues on his conception of the intelligibility of human beings and human reality.

These observations enable me to resituate my earlier discourse on rationality in relation to Sartre's anthropology as a whole. Sartre's discourse on rationality should not be interpreted as aiming at the assertion of some normative principle, which would function as a concrete imperative intended to regulate our actions and moral decisions. On the normative level, Sartre's anthropology is an attempt to combine and reconcile issues of rationality, an imperative of understanding and normative-ethical engagement by taking concrete human beings and human reality as its ground. And here can be found one of the dimensions in which Sartre's conception of anthropology remains a challenge to contemporary thought.

Notes

1 Cf. von Wright 1963 and Österman 1995 for the meaning of 'normative' and the classification of value judgements. Besides ethics and critical social theory, the normativity involved in the problems of *rationality* and *epistemological validity* may naturally also be contained within the normative dimension (see Chapters 6 and 8).

2 See Stone and Bowman 1991b and Anderson 1993 for an account of the sources of Sartre's second ethics. "Détermination et liberté" was strangely translated into English as "Determinism and freedom" (1974a). The translation of 'détermination' as 'determinism' and not as 'determination' looses the obvious Kantian dimension of Sartre's discourse. As is well known Kant characterises ethics as rooted in the problem of "... the ground of the determination of the will..." (Kant 1883a, p. 107)). An extract from the Cornell lectures called "Kennedy and West Virginia" has been published in *Sartre Alive* (Aronson and van den Hoven (eds.) 1991).

3 In Sartre's own case, the ideal of commitment was for a short time (during the years 1952-56) interpreted as the need of a close (but still neither pledged not institutionalised) co-operation with the French Communist Party. Cf. Sartre 1968 and Hayman 1986, pp. 276-302.

4 Observe here the implicit connection with the technical and practical interests in Habermas's *Erkenntnis und Interesse* (1978) published at about the same time.

5 In the following I base my interpretation mainly on Sartre 1974a, Bowman and Stone 1991a and Stone and Bowman 1991b. I thus 'fuse' the *Rome lecture* and the *Cornell lectures* into a single discourse. Since I have not studied these manuscripts, I cannot take up any standpoint on the question whether they actually converge.

6 See especially BN, pp. 62ff and 70n, NE, 474-515 and Sartre 1948c, pp. 90-141. Cf. Bell 1989, Gorz, 1990, Anderson 1993 for a discussion of Sartre's conception of authenticity.

7 The status of this interview, conducted shortly before Sartre died, is problematic and much debated (see Aronson 1996). However, as I mentioned above Sartre expresses similar thoughts in his preface to Fanon's book (1965), in "Plaidoyer pour les intellectuels" and, according to both Bowman and Stone (1991a, esp. pp. 117-20) and Anderson (1993, p. 117), in the *Rome lecture* and the *Cornell lectures*.

8 For an investigation of the value of freedom in Sartre, see Detmer 1986, esp.

pp. 62-93. Detmer's investigation, however, is mainly restricted to EN and, more importantly; he does not regard Sartre's ethical concept of freedom as an intersubjective and social concept.

9 See also NE: "All ethics presupposes the end of History (or rather the end of History and the appearance of the realm of ethics)" and "in an alienated society, all behaviour must be alienating, even generosity" (p. 141 and 368).

10 See for example Sartre's interpretation, diagnosis and suggestion for therapeutic cure (free Algeria!) of French colonialism in Algeria in Sartre 1964a, 1964b and CDR, pp. 714-34.

11 Another feature that may be said to represent Sartre's critique of ideology is his constant introduction of new terminology. Sartre has often been criticised for using new and strange terms. I believe one of the reasons for this is the observation that our everyday understanding and language are filled with concepts and terms that are the opposite to a language of praxis and processes. Thus, when Sartre redescribes actions as praxis, objects as practico-inert, moral imperatives as unconditioned possibilities and scientists as technicians of practical knowledge, he communicates an implicit critique of the ideological (analytical) content of the first expressions.

10 Conclusions

Sartre's Anthropology as a Concern with the Present

I have tried to show in what ways Sartre's anthropology, as set up in CRD, is concerned with the *question how we are to understand human beings and human reality*, *how Sartre fares* in dealing with this issue and staked out the principle features of his *paradigm of praxis*. I have also tried to reveal the conditions and limits for characterising this philosophical standpoint as *hermeneutical*, and by means of that indicated my views on in what ways Sartre's philosophy still constitutes *a challenge to contemporary thought*, although a full assessment of this issue would surely require a more genuinely comparative study of Sartre and contemporary thought than what has been carried out in this work.

The construction of the standpoint I have called '*a hermeneutics of praxis*' was intended, amongst other things, to bring forward this latter question. By 'a hermeneutics of praxis' I have, through and through in this work, meant both a certain interpretation of the philosophy of the later Sartre and a philosophical standpoint independent of the writings of Sartre. The challenge I want to pose is whether and to what extent such a position is of substantial importance to contemporary debates in hermeneutics, critical social theory and ethics. The project to work out this challenge in more detail is in my opinion an important future task, which however goes beyond the scope of this work. In this final chapter I shall confine myself to summarising my conclusions and assessment.

Sartre's anthropology, his concern with concrete human beings and their reality, the problem of rationality, social theory, the intelligibility of history and the grounds of concrete morality can be characterised as a comprehensive concern with *the present*. Thus, in QM Sartre explains the principle aim of his idea of dialectical totalisation exactly as the *determination of the meaning of the present*:

> ... dialectical totalisation must include acts, passions, work and need as well as economic categories; it must at once place the agent or the event back into the historical setting, define his or its relation to the orientation of becoming, and determine exactly the meaning of the present [*sens du présent*] as such (SM, 133 (103)).

The orientation of this concern is not however principally philosophical or metaphysical, but must be inserted within a general interest in the self-understanding of ourselves and our epoch, and perhaps most persistently a practical and moral commitment in individual life, the justification and goodness of human actions and the issues of the times: "Since the writer has no way of escaping, we want him to embrace his era – tightly … We are convinced … that one *cannot* remove one's stakes from the board … It is the future of *our* time that must be the object of our concern" (Sartre 1988b, pp. 252-53).

The task to determine the meaning of the present, then, is not a case of speculative philosophy of the Hegelian type, but is concrete, participatory and historically situated. Its starting point is the epistemological conditions that we cannot ever develop a complete overview of who we are and our situation, but that all our decisions will necessarily be informed by the limited understanding we in fact have. In this thesis Sartre is revealed as a philosopher of the Enlightenment (or a Modernist): if we only would understand our condition and our situation better, we would have the opportunity to make better decisions on what is right and wrong.

The modifications in conception that takes place between the early and the later Sartre is most clearly expressed in the move from a philosophy centred on consciousness to a philosophy of praxis. By means of this Sartre manages to remove some (although not all) of the tensions created by his simultaneous emphasis on the freedom of consciousness and existential being-in-the-world. The concept of *praxis* — in addition to being a concept of *action* and *responsibility* — is employed by Sartre in order to illuminate the *contextual and conditioned embeddedness* of our aims, our possibilities and our understanding of the real meaning of what we do:

> "the movement of *praxis* ... consists ... in plunging into a world that closes in around you. The world which is the object lays siege from all sides to the subject who unveils it and returns his image to him" (NE, 356 (370)).

The idea of an anthropology that is both *structural* and *historical* is intended to capture the two dimensions of meaning that stem from this embeddedness: the *social significations* that stem from an interpretation of action towards the background of the field in which one acts, and the *future-orientation of human projects* and *the historical present,* understood as movements of continuous change and innovation. Sartre's philosophy of praxis removes many of the traits of philosophical idealism still present in EN (despite Sartre's intentions on the contrary), but retains the typically Sartrean two-folded interpretative demand: the human condition must be understood in terms of the relation between *praxis* and the *practico-inert*, the continuous movement of *history* and the structures of the social *system*. This two-folded character may either be described in philosophical terms as a *dualism*, which seems to communicate the existence of a problem, or as an imperative to *recognise complexity* and *avoid reductionist* attempts. The latter traits indicates both that Sartre is closer to the demands of postmetaphysical thinking and the interests of the postmodernists than what they seems to accept, and that we may find in Sartre a real attempt to mediate between universalism and particularism (perhaps most visible in Sartre's ethics). I surely find the latter characterisation both more accurate and more interesting.

Dimensions of an Anthropology

My investigation is posed with an interest to assess Sartre's contribution in a contemporary perspective. In the work itself, however, it appears that I have mainly striven to make the totality of Sartre's project (as I construct it) appear *intelligible* and relatively *coherent*. I have emphasised that my interpretation contains strong elements of *reconstruction*: I have tried to build and re-build a totality that actually was never constructed exactly in that manner by Sartre himself.

On this basis, my work may be accused of presenting Sartre's conception in a *too favourable light*, and of reading in *connections* and a *coherence* that actually *cannot be found* in the material itself. What kind of assessment is that? This critique is partly justified. But the main reason why I have overemphasised coherence and thereby neglected many incoherences and problems in my account is not that I would try to defend Sartre's position. If one is primarily interested in the *contribution* (what we may get out of the material) and not the *validity* (internal coherence and relations to the 'truth') of a certain material, the imperative to develop a comprehensive account must precede critical assessment: understanding is a condition of evaluation and critique. The hermeneutical standpoint that I have adopted requires that one is not primarily interested in whether the author has gone astray or not, but in the critical examination of the presuppositions, prejudices and preunderstanding that is embodied in and arises through the encounter with a certain material.

A further motivation is Sartre's philosophical outlook is deeply characterised by the synthetic, relational and non-reductionist imperative to connect different problems and domains: individual *and* history, epistemology *and* ethics, ontology *and* everyday life, historical intelligibility *and* action, etc. An interpretation that attempts to follow Sartre in this self-understanding, as I have tried to do, should then aim at integrating these domains into a unified framework, even if such a unity is not immediately found in the texts themselves.

Thus, I have asked what are the validity, place and relevance of Sartre's contribution in a contemporary perspective. A corpse is open to all comers, as Sartre said in relation to Flaubert. But *how contemporary* and *how dead* is this corpus actually? I shall conclude my assessment by exposing some of my views on this issue.

I have interpreted Sartre's anthropology as an attempt to answer the question how we are to understand and study human beings and human reality, and his standpoint as centred on the paradigm of praxis. I have differentiated five main dimensions of this anthropology. I have claimed that an *ontology* or a synthetic account of *the intelligibility of the human condition* stands at the core of Sartre's conception. I have treated this ontology as something that simultaneously *integrates* the five dimensions in question and *motivates* their *differentiation*.

The co-presence of a denial of a human nature and a refusal to reject all forms of universalisation regarding the being of the human leads Sartre to posit what I have called a *modified kind of philosophical anthropology*. Originally Sartre conceived this in the form of an *ontology*. The recasting of issue, first in QM and then in CRD, leads Sartre (i) to study the *methodological principles* whereby one ascends from concrete reality to it's conditions, and descends from structural intelligibility to the historical concrete, and (ii) to study these issues from the perspective of the problem of *rationality*. If truth is a question of disclosing being — the singular unveiling of a continuously on-going process — rationality must be concerned with the how and why, or the validity and justification, of such a disclosure. In addition, by posing the problem of rationality the project can no longer be seen as only concerned with epistemological issues (theoretical reason), but also with the reasons embodied in what we do (practical reason). One may perhaps claim that this inner connection subsequently led Sartre to reopen the *normative problems of morality*.

The question of contemporary relevance then concerns at least (i) the validity and limits of Sartre's theory of praxis as a conception centred on our material and social bonds of interiority with the world, and (ii) the contemporary place and status of this kind of theoretical outlook.

Beginning with the latter, Sartre's ontology of existence and the bonds of interiority of being-in-the-world is a perspective that falls quite neatly alongside the traditions of fundamental ontology in Heidegger and the hermeneutical turns of phenomenological philosophy in both Heidegger and Gadamer. This also communicates a rather strong belief in *theorisation*: Sartre deepens his investigation (regressively and progressively) by means of an ontology, a typology of social formations and a focus on the general intelligibility of conflict. Simultaneously Sartre emphasises that this theoretical work must not be seen as independent of context and history. It constitutes what he calls 'a notional approach': the value of the concepts and schemes employed depends on if they enable us to make reality more intelligible or not.

On the contemporary scene the value of such an approach seems to depend on whether one believes in the possibilities and value of such theoretical work or not. Foucault and Rorty seem to claim that totalising perspectives of this kind are neither intellectually possible to defend nor as emancipatory and edifying as Sartre assumes. It seems that in the perspective of the postmodern condition, Sartre is seriously on the wrong track. Others, such as Habermas, defend the value of large-scale theorising by claiming that a full-fledged farewell to the idea of comprehensive accounts constitutes both a performative self-contradiction and a way of hiding behind a refusal to justify ones views. I think this latter critique is correct, and have never really understood why a totalising perspective must necessarily constitute a threat.

In my opinion, Sartre succeeds more than well — and perhaps in a more extensive and sophisticated manner than any other contemporary philosopher — in the task to illuminate the inner connections between action, situation and social meaning. This does not imply that I would find all his views on this issue correct. For instance, Sartre does not really manage to reconcile *praxis* (situation, end, and means) as a paradigm of intelligibility with his theory of *mediated reciprocity* (mutual recognition) as the structure of the human relation. In place of the vacillation in EN between dualism and anti-dualism, freedom and situationality, CRD develops a tension and vacillation between the demands of a *unified conception of rationality* as centred on the *totalisation inherent in praxis*, and the imperative to *incorporate intersubjective and social reciprocity* within this rationality.

At the root of this problem stands the co-presence in Sartre of an imperative to ground rationality on the concrete, and the idea of a unified conception on dialectical rationality. Habermas, who insists on the importance to distinguish praxis from social interaction, the strategic rationality of social action from the communicative rationality of social interaction, would surely claim that Sartre on this very point has missed something important. The main intention is not to embrace Habermas's distinction but to point out this important issue: to investigate the relation between practicality and sociality. I have argued that this issue also arises in Gadamer, through his simultaneous emphasis on linguisticality and the practical dimension of application.

The postmodernist critique of our preoccupation with the problem of reason may regard this as illusory. From this point of view, Sartre's concern with rationality and totalisation is an embarrassing outgrowth of what was originally valuable in existentialism. Sartre's emphasis on a combination of a concern with the particular with a totalising perspective cannot but remain ambiguous. The most valuable features of Sartre's philosophy would then be his real attempts to disclose specific social events with the intention to disclose traits of ideology, terror and cruelty. His concern with the lived would be more valuable that his theory of rationality, and praxis and mediated reciprocity need not be reconciled within a unified conception of rationality. Such a critique is surely highly interesting, although it does not in my opinion manage to do much more than formulate a question.

Sartre's discourse on rationality also suffers from the fact that he conceives of rationality as centred on praxis, but does not explicitly raise this as a concern with the unity of or interrelation between theoretical (intelligibility) and practical reason (morality). It remains symptomatic of Sartre's philosophy that he gives precedence to issues of intelligibility and believes that the issues of practical reason can only be treated afterwards. Thus, Sartre's view on ethical reflection is based on his distinction between a primary level concerned with the *descriptive intelligibility of the unreflected level of existence*, and a secondary level concerned with the *reflective examination* of the practical, historical and ethical *consequences* of this study. This leads Sartre to an order of investigation according to which reflective problems of rationality and ethics cannot come forward at a sufficiently early stage of the investigation, if at all.

A further issue is whether and to what extent Sartre's theory of social formations, his emphasis on scarcity, antagonism and conflict as the major motors of history, constitutes valid or valuable approaches. It must be observed, however, that I have hardly even breached, and more less investigated, Sartre's conception history. I have thus not provided any real means to assess it. I do think, however, that Sartre's typology of social formations and his views on the intelligibility of conflict constitute strong interpretative instruments. The question whether they can legitimately form a totalising (in Sartre's sense of comprehensive and singularising) perspective on contemporary society is less clear. That is, Sartre's perspective on society as centred on relations between groups and collectives must be seen as a more limited paradigm for the understanding of the present than what Sartre believes.

Another dimension lacking in Sartre's social theory is a thorough examination of the normative foundations of critical social theory. The gulf remains open between his study of the sources of alienation, his socio-political ideals and the question of the normative justification of this approach. Despite this, many of Sartre's accounts on the alienation of the age (seriality, conflict and our lack of understanding history) are in no way dead truths, to use Sartre's phrase. On the contrary, the contemporary interest in the historical, communicated by Foucault, Lyotard, and the discourse on modernity and postmodernity, etc., has in fact renewed the contemporaneity of Sartre's interest in the intelligibility of history.

The second and fourth dimensions of Sartre's anthropology, *the idea of a heuristic method* that must learn from reality through *empirical-interpretative investigation*, as the inheritor of the rationality of understanding, function to emphasise *historicity*. I have claimed that at the core of Sartre's search for an anti-foundationalist foundation stand an attempt to make concrete human reality its ground. Such a foundation is neither a product of thought, nor a transcendental condition of possibility, but made up of the internal features of concrete reality itself ('ground' in the sense of being 'earthbound'). The unsettled status of Sartre's claims (ahistorical, transhistorical and/or historically relative), however, means that his conception cannot as such (without reconstruction) contribute very much to a clarification of the problem of historicity. On this matter, Sartre's investigation falls short of Gadamer's.

For example, the question of the validity of Sartre's existential-biographical interpretation of Flaubert suffers from the imperative to be both based on the progressive-regressive method, and to deepen and test the method itself. For instance, how could one on the basis of such a perspective situate oneself in a position that would enable one to evaluate *the criteria of totalisation* itself, since validity depends on whether one in fact succeeds in making the empirical material intelligible in a totalising manner? The presupposition of totalisation, and that 'totalisation' necessarily must mean what Sartre means by it (praxis, signification, singularisation, contradiction, etc.), is not itself scrutinised by Sartre.

A Hermeneutics of Praxis

I have argued that the later Sartre's concern with the concrete orients him in a direction that is closely reminiscent of the idea of hermeneutical reflection: philosophical reflection should proceed on the basis of the *concretely lived* and *concrete experience*. This method is not intended to expose a persons state of mind: critical reflection must enable us to move from our *immediate* but *superficial experiential understanding* of who we are, what we aim at, what we do and what our world is like, to a *contextualised, social and interpretative deeper understanding*. This necessarily includes an understanding of the *society* and the *times* in which one lives.

This hermeneutisation of an existential philosophy of action and commitment is a central motive as to why I have interpreted Sartre's philosophical standpoint as *a hermeneutics of praxis*. As I have said, the use of this phrase was partly intended to emphasise those dimensions of Sartre's standpoint that I find particularly valuable. Thus, I have focused on the question of the *understanding* and *interpretation* of what we do, seen as a problem concerned with our *being-in-the-world* (hermeneutical embeddedness) and *historicity*. I have continuously tried to bring forward Sartre as a philosopher of *situations* — rather than of freedom and self-transparency — and thus mainly focused on his concern to make intelligible the *bonds of interiority* of experience, praxis, materiality and sociality — rather than individual self-realisation. In addition I have emphasised that Sartre's views his own investigation as an *internal reflexive self-critique*, and brought forward his hermeneutical conception of *truth* as the disclosure and unveiling of being.

I have distinguished between two orientations in Sartre's concern with historicity: a largely *formal* or *theoretical* investigation of the *conditions and principles of intelligibility*, and a series of *empirical* and *interpretative* investigations of *concrete reality*: the life of an individual, the praxis of colonialism, the task of the intellectual, etc. The presence of both these tasks makes Sartre's contribution quite unique in 20th century thought.

On these matters Sartre's discourse is both *optimistic* — we can understand, we have the means — and *imperative* — we must try to understand! For what is at stake are not only the progress of science, but also our own *self-understanding* and the possibilities of *a good life*. It is thus clear that *a hermeneutics of praxis* must include the realms of the *ethical* and the *political* or *practical reason*. Sartre claims that the full *intelligibility of praxis* resides both (1) in the conditioning necessity that praxis *internalises* the circumstances (understanding), and *externalises* this internalisation in concrete choices, and (2) in that praxis constitutes a *free* and *innovative* movement of surpassing that posits goals as *unconditionally possible values*. The reason inherent in praxis work on the basis of this two-fold nature.

An intriguing and controversial aspect of my characterisation lies with this combination of *hermeneutics* and *praxis*. The phrase 'a hermeneutics of praxis' appears to be a contradiction in terms: 'hermeneutics' is most often used to connote 'our belongingness to the world' and 'our inherent linguisticality and culturality' (culturalism), and 'praxis' to connote 'the surpassing of this belongingness' and 'individual freedom' (existentialism). In defence of my characterisation I have argued that Sartre in CRD situates his investigation exactly on this level of the relation between world and praxis.

Thus, the hermeneutical dimension, or hermeneutisation, of Sartre's philosophical standpoint consists mainly in this focus on the bonds of interiority of freedom and praxis. A genuinely Sartrean hermeneutic could not be confined to the detection of the presence of contemporary culture, effective-historical consciousness and tradition (internalisation) in experience and praxis. Sartre is keen to retain his (partly metaphysical, partly moral) support for the individual, innovative and moral dimensions of freedom and praxis. He thus tries to resolve the dilemma of the *individuality* of innovation and praxis and it's self-understanding as historically and culturally *embedded*.

In conclusion, then, I interpret the essence of a hermeneutics of praxis as an imperative to focus on and study the real and concrete intelligibility of praxis as embedded in socio-historical reality. The Sartrean perspective encourages us both to investigate the social dimensions of meaning — both theoretically and interpretatively — and to unravel the meanings embodied in the historical movement of the present (the interpretation and diagnosis of the times). In my interpretation I have both emphasised the synthetic, relational and systematic aspects of Sartre's anthropology as such, and lifted out issues that I consider important in a contemporary perspective, and which may be discussed apart from their explicit connections with Sartre. My intention has been to communicate *that* we may learn things, and also some aspects of *what* we may learn from Sartre, independently if we follow him or not. My assessment has thus been concretised in my choices of thematic orientation. In the following step one would have to study, in a more genuinely comparative fashion, the relations between these views and conclusions and the more recent developments in philosophy, but this task falls outside the scope of my present investigation.

Bibliography

A. Works by Jean-Paul Sartre

1943 (EN) *L'être et le néant: Essai d'ontologie phénoménologique*. Paris: Gallimard.

1948a (1940) *The Psychology of Imagination*. Translated by Bernard Frechtman. London: Methuen and Co.

1948b (EaH) (1946) *Existentialism and Humanism*. Translation and Introduction by Philip Mairet. London: Methuen and Co.

1948c (1946) *Anti-Semite and Jew*. New York: Schocken Books.

1950 (1947) *Baudelaire*. Translated by Martin Turnell. New York: New Directions Paperbook.

1955 *Literary and Philosophical Essays*. Translated by Annette Michelson. London: Hutchinson.

1955a (1946) "Materialism and Revolution" in Sartre 1955, pp. 185-239.

1957 (1937) *The Transcendence of the Ego*. New York: Noonday Press. Translated by Forrest Williams and Robert Kirkpatrick.

1962 (1939) *Sketch for a Theory of the Emotions*. Translated by Philip Mairet. London: Methuen and Co.

1963 (1952) *Saint Genet, Actor and Martyr*. Translated by Bernard Frechtman. New York: Pantheon Books.

1963 (SM) (1957) *Search for a Method*. Translated by Hazel E Barnes. New York: Vintage Books.

1964 *Situations V: colonialisme et néo-colonialisme*. Paris: Gallimard.

1964a (1956) "Le colonialisme est une système" in Sartre 1964.

1964b (1957) "Portrait du colonisé", précédé du "Portrait de colonisateur" in Sartre 1964.

1965 (1963) "Preface" in Fanon 1965, pp. 7-26. Translated by Constance Farrington.

1966 "Sartre aujourd'hui" in *L'Arc* 30.

1967 (1948) "Consciousness of Self and Knowledge of Self" in Lawrence and O'Connor (eds.) 1967, pp. 113-142. Translated by Mary Ellen and Nathaniel Lawrence.

1968 (1952-54) *The Communists and Peace with A Reply to Claude Lefort*. Translated by Martha Fletcher and Philip R. Berk. New York: George

Braziller.
1969 (1956) *The Spectre of Stalin*. London: Hamish Hamilton.
1971-72 (IF) *L'Idiot de la famille: Gustave Flaubert de 1821 a 1857*, tomes I-III. Paris: Gallimard.
1972 *Situations IX*. Paris: Gallimard.
1972a (1966) "L'anthropologie" in Sartre 1972, pp. 83-98, originally published in *Cahiers de Philosophie* n° 2, 1966.
1974 *Between Existentialism and Marxism*. Translated by John Matthews. London: New Left Books.
1974a (1970) "Determinism and freedom" in Contat and Rybalka 1974 vol. 2, pp. 241-52.
1974b (1970) "The Itinerary of a Thought" in Sartre 1974, pp. 33-66.
1974c (1965) "A Plea for Intellectuals" in Sartre 1974, pp. 228-85.
1978 (1975) *Sartre in the Seventies*. Translated by Paul Auster and Lydia Davis. London: Andre Deutsch.
1978a (1975) "Self-Portrait at Seventy" in Sartre 1978, pp. 3-92.
1978b (1971) "On *The Idiot of the Family*" in Sartre 1978, pp. 109-134.
1978c (1973) "Elections: A Trap for Fools" in Sartre 1978, pp. 198-210.
1978d *Sartre by Himself*. Translated by Richard Seaver. New York: Urizen Books.
1980 "An interview with Jean-Paul Sartre by Leo Fretz" in Silverman and Elliston (eds.) 1980, pp. 221-39. Translated by George Berger.
1981, 1987, 1989, 1991 and 1993 (FI 1-5) (1971-72) *The Family Idiot: Gustave Flaubert 1821-1857, Volumes 1-5*. Translated by Carol Cosman. Chicago: The University of Chicago Press.
1981 "An interview with Jean-Paul Sartre" in Schilpp (ed.) 1981, pp. 5-51.
1983 (CM) *Cahiers pour une morale*. Paris: Gallimard.
1984 (1983) *War Diaries*. Translated by Quintin Hoare. London: Verso.
1985 (CDR, QM) (1960) *Critique de la Raison dialectique, précédé de Questions de méthode: Tome 1: Theorie des ensembles pratiques*. Texte établi et annoté par Arlette Elkaïm-Sartre. Paris: Gallimard.
1985 (CDR II) (1985) *Critique de la Raison dialectique: Tome 2: L'intelligibilité de l'Histoire* (inachevé). Établissement du texte, notes et glossaire par Arlette Elkaïm-Sartre. Paris: Gallimard.
1988 (1948) *"What is Literature?" and Other Essays*. Cambridge, Massachusetts: Harvard University Press.
1988a (1947) "What is Literature?" in Sartre 1988, pp. 21-245.
1988b (1945) "*Introducing* Les Temps Modernes" in Sartre 1988, pp. 247-267.
1988c (1986) *Mallarmé, or the Poet of Nothingness*. Translated by E.

Sturm. University Park: Pennsylvania University Press.
1989 (BN) (1958) *Being and Nothingness: A Phenomenological Essay on Ontology*. Translated by Hazel E. Barnes and with an introduction by Mary Warnock. London: Routledge.
1991 (CDR, a corrected translation of the original edition of 1976) (1960) *Critique of Dialectical Reason, Volume 1: Theory of Practical Ensembles*. Translated by Alan Sheridan-Smith. London: Verso.
1991 (CDR II) (1985) *Critique of Dialectical Reason, Volume 2: The Intelligibility of History* (unfinished). Translated by Quintin Hoare. London: Verso.
1991a "Kennedy and West Virginia" in Aronson and van den Hoven (eds.) 1991, pp. 37-52.
1991b "I am no longer a realist. An interview with Jean-Paul Sartre" in Aronson and van den Hoven (eds.) 1991, pp. 83-102.
1992a (NE) (1983). *Notebooks for an Ethics*. Translated by David Pellauer. Chicago: The University of Chicago Press.
1992b (1989) *Truth and Existence*. Translated by Adrian van den Hoven. Chicago: The University of Chicago Press.
Sartre, Jean-Paul and Lévy, Benny 1996 (1980) *Hope Now, The 1980 Interview*. Translated by Adrian van den Hoven. Chicago: The University of Chicago Press.

B. Other Works

Anderson, Thomas C. 1993. *Sartre's Two Ethics: From Authenticity to Integral Humanity*. Chicago: Open Court.
Apel, Karl-Otto 1979. *Erklären und Verstehen - Kontroverse in transzendentalpragmatischer Sicht*. Frankfurt: Suhrkamp.
— 1980 (1973). *Towards a Transformation of Philosophy*. Translated by Glyn Adey and David Frisby. London: Routledge and Kegan, Paul.
Apel, Karl-Otto et al. 1971. *Hermeneutik und Ideologiekritik*. Frankfurt: Suhrkamp.
Aron, Raymond 1961 (1938). *Introduction to the Philosophy of History*. Translated by George J. Irwin. Liverpool: Weidenfeld and Nicholson.
— 1975 (1973). *History and the Dialectic of Violence: An Analysis of Sartre's Critique de la Raison Dialectique*. Translated by Barry Cooper. Oxford: Basil Blackwell.
Aronson, Ronald 1980. *Jean-Paul Sartre - Philosophy in the World*. London: New Left Books.

— 1987. *Sartre's Second Critique*. Chicago: Chicago University Press.
— 1996. "Sartre's Last Words" in Sartre and Levy 1996, pp. 3-40.
Aronson, Ronald and van der Hoven Adrian (eds.) 1991. *Sartre Alive*. Detroit: Wayne State University Press.
Barnes, Hazel E. 1981. *Sartre and Flaubert*. Chicago: The University of Chigaco Press.
Bell, Linda A. 1989. *Sartre's Ethics of Authenticity*. Tuscaloosa: University of Alabama Press.
Benhabib, Seyla 1986. *Critique, Norm and Utopia*. New York: Columbia University Press.
Berenson, F. M. 1981. *Understanding Persons*. New York: St. Martin's Press.
Bernstein, Richard J. 1971. *Praxis and Action*. Philadelphia: The University of Philadelphia Press.
— 1983. *Beyond Objectivism and Relativism*. University of Pennsylvania Press.
— 1985. "From Hermeneutics to Praxis" in Hollinger (ed.) 1985, pp. 272-96.
Boschetti , Anna 1988 (1985). *The Intellectual Enterprise. Sartre and 'Les Temps Modernes'*. Translated by Richard C. McCleary. Evanston: Northwestern University Press.
Bourdieu, Pierre and Wacquant, Loïc J. D. 1992. *An Invitation to Reflexive Sociology*. Cambridge: Polity Press.
Bourdieu, Pierre 1990 (1980). *The Logic of Practice*. Translated by Richard Nice. Cambridge: Polity Press.
Bowman, Elizabeth A. and Stone, Robert V. 1991a. "'Making the Human' in Sartre's Unpublished Dialectical Ethics" in Silverman (eds.) 1991, pp. 111-122.
Bubner, Rüdiger 1988. *Essays in Hermeneutics and Critical Theory*. Translated by Eric Matthews. New York: Columbia University Press.
— 1988a. "Logic and Capital: On the Method of a 'Critique of Political Economy'" in Bubner 1988, pp. 63-96.
Burnier, Michel-Antoine 1966. *Les existentialistes et la politique*. Paris: Gallimard.
Busch, Thomas W. 1980. "Sartre's Use of the Reduction" in Silverman and Elliston (eds.) 1980, pp. 17-29.
— 1990. *The Power of Consciousness and the Force of Circumstances in Sartre's Philosophy*. Bloomington: Indiana University Press.
Butler, Judith 1990. *Gender Trouble: Feminism and the Subversion of Identity*. London: Routledge.

Caputo, John 1987. *Radical Hermeneutics: Repetition, Deconstruction and the Hermeneutic Project*. Bloomington: Indiana University Press.

Caws, Peter 1979. *Sartre*. London: Routledge and Kegan Paul Ltd.

— 1992. "Sartrean Structuralism?" in Howells (ed.) 1992, pp. 293-317.

Chiodi, Pietro 1976 (1965). *Sartre and Marxism*. Translated from the Italian by Kate Soper. London: Harvester Press.

Cohen-Solal, Annie 1987 (1985). *Sartre, a Life*. London: Heinemann.

Colombel, Jeanette 1986-87. *Textes et débates/Jean-Paul Sartre: 1: Un homme en situations* and *2: Une œuvre aux mille têtes*. Librairie Générale Française.

Contat, Michel and Rybalka, Michel (eds.) 1970. *Les Écrits de Sartre*. Paris: Gallimard.

— 1974 (1970). *The Writings of Jean-Paul Sartre*, vol. 2. Evanston: Northwestern University Press.

Cooper, David 1990. *Existentialism. A Reconstruction*. Oxford: Basil Blackwell.

Craib, Ian 1976. *Existentialism and Sociology*. Cambridge: Cambridge University Press.

Davidson, Donald 1984, *Inquiries into Truth and Interpretation*. Oxford: Clarendon Press.

Davies, Howard 1987. *Sartre and 'Les Temps Modernes'*. Cambridge: Cambridge University Press.

de Beauvoir, Simone 1953 (1949). *The Second Sex*. Translated and Edited by H. M. Parshley. London: Picador.

Derrida, Jacques 1982. *Margins of Philosophy*. Translated by Alan Bass. Chicago: University of Chicago Press.

— 1982a. "The Ends of Man" in Derrida 1982, pp. 109-136.

Detmer, David 1986. *Freedom as a Value. A Critique of the Ethical Theory of Jean-Paul Sartre*. La Salle, Illinois: Open Court.

Dews, Peter 1987. *Logics of Disintegration*. London: Verso.

Dilthey, Wilhelm 1976. *Selected Writings*. Edited by H. P. Rickman. Cambridge: Cambridge University Press.

— 1976a, "The Construction of the Historical World in the Human Studies" in Dilthey 1976, pp. 170-207.

— 1976b. "Drafts for a critique of historical reason" in Dilthey 1976, pp. 207-45.

— 1976c. "The Development of Hermeneutics" in Dilthey 1976, pp. 247-63.

Docherty, Thomas (ed.) 1993. *Postmodernism: A Reader*. London: Harvester Wheatsheaf.

Douglas, Jack D. and Johnson, John M. (eds.) 1977. *Existential Sociology*. Cambridge: Cambridge University Press.

Dreyfus, Hubert L. 1980. "Holism and Hermeneutics" in *Review of Metaphysics* 34:3, pp. 3-23.

Dreyfus, Hubert L. and Hoffman, Piotr 1981, "Sartre's Changed Conception of Consciousness" in Schilpp (ed.) 1981, pp. 229-245.

Dreyfus, Hubert L. and Rabinow Paul 1982. *Michel Foucault: Beyond Structuralism and Hermeneutics*. Chicago: The University of Chicago Press.

Dummett, Michael 1993. *Origins of Analytical Philosophy*. London: Duckworth.

Elkaïm-Sartre, Arlette 1992 (1983). "Foreword" in Sartre 1992a, pp. xxiii-iv.

Encyclopaedia of Philosophy, Volume Six, 1967. New York: The Macmillan Company and The Free Press.

Etudes sartriennes II-III 1986. Cahiers de Sémiotique Textuelle. Université Paris X.

Fanon, Frantz 1965 (1961). *The Wretched of the Earth*. Translated by Constance Farrington. MacGibbon and Kee.

Fehér, Istvan 1994. "Sartre and Hermeneutics" in *Man and World* 28:1, pp. 65-82.

Flynn, Thomas R. 1976. "Praxis and Vision: Elements of a Sartrean Epistemology" in *The Philosophical Forum*, VIII:1, pp. 21-43.

— 1977. "An End to Authority: Epistemology and Politics in the Later Sartre" in *Man and World*, 10:4, pp. 448-465.

— 1981. "Mediated Reciprocity and the Genius of the Third" in Schilpp (ed.) 1981, pp. 345-370.

— 1984. *Sartre and Marxist Existentialism*. Chicago: The University of Chicago Press.

— 1992. "Sartre and the Poetics of History" in Howells (ed.) 1992.

— 1997. *Sartre, Foucault and Historical Reason*. Volume One: Toward an Existentialist Theory of History. Chicago: The University of Chicago Press.

Foucault, Michel 1970 (1966). *The Order of Things: An Archaeology of the Human Sciences*. London: Tavistock Publications.

— 1972 (1969). *The Archaeology of Knowledge*. Translated by A.M. Sheridan Smith. London: Tavistock Publications.

— 1978 (1976). *The History of Sexuality: An Introduction*. Translated by Robert Hurley. New York: Random House.

— 1979 (1974). *Discipline and Punish: The Birth of the Prison*. Trans-

lated by Alan Sheridan. New York: Random House.
— 1982. "Afterword: The Subject and Power" in Dreyfus and Rabinow 1982, pp. 208-226. Partly translated by Leslie Sawyer.
— 1984. Translated by Alan Sheridan and others. London: Routledge.
— 1988a (1983). "Critical Theory/Intellectual History" in Foucault 1988, pp. 17-46.
— 1989. *Foucault Live*. Translated by John Johnston. Edited by Sylvére Lotringer. New York: Semiotext(e).
— 1989a (1967). "Foucault responds to Sartre" in Foucault 1989, pp. 35-44.
— 1997 (1994). *Michel Foucault. Ethics, Subjectivity and Truth*. The Essential Works of Michel Foucault 1954-1984, Volume One. New York: The New Press.
Frank Manfred 1977. *Das Individuelle Allgemeine*. Frankfurt: Suhrkamp.
— 1980. "Das Individuum in der Rolle des Idioten, Die Hermeneutische Konzeption des *Flaubert*" in König (ed.) 1980, pp. 84-108.
Franklin, R. L. 1995. *The Search for Understanding*. New York: Peter Lang.
Gadamer, Hans-Georg 1971. "Rhetorik, Hermeneutik und Ideologiekritik" in Apel et al. 1971, pp. 57-82.
— 1975 (1960). *Truth and Method*. London: Sheed and Ward.
— 1975a. "Hermeneutics and Social Science" in *Cultural Hermeneutics* 2, Dordrecht: D. Reidel, pp. 307-316.
— 1976. *Philosophical Hermeneutics*. Translated and edited by David E. Linge. Berkeley: University of California Press.
— 1976a (1966). "The Universality of the Hermeneutical Problem" in Gadamer 1976, pp. 3-17.
— 1976b (1967). "On the Scope and Function of Hermeneutical Reflection" in Gadamer 1976, pp. 18-43.
— 1988. "Das Sein und das Nichts" in König (ed.) 1988, pp. 37-54.
— 1994a. "Truth in the Human Sciences" in Wachterhauser (ed.) 1994, pp. 25-32. Translated by Brice R. Wachterhauser.
— 1994b. "What is Truth?" in Wachterhauser (ed.) 1994, pp. 33-46. Translated by Brice R. Wachterhauser.
Goldthorpe, Rhiannon 1984. *Sartre: Literature and Theory*. Cambridge: Cambridge University Press.
— 1992. "Understanding the committed writer" in Howells (ed.) 1992, pp. 140-177.
Gorz, André 1968. *Le socialisme difficile*. Paris: Editions du Seuil.
— 1989 (1988). *Critique of Economic Reason*. Translated by Gillian

Handyside and Chris Turner. London, Verso.

— 1990. “Fragments sur authenticité et valeur dans la premiére philosophie de Sartre” in *Les Temps Modernes* 1990 vol. 1, pp. 504-550.

Haar, Michel 1980. “Sartre and Heidegger” in Silverman and Elliston (eds.) 1980, pp. 168-187.

Habermas, Jürgen 1975 (1973). *Legitimation Crisis*. Translated by Thomas McCarthy. Boston: Beacon Press.

— 1978 (1968). *Knowledge and Human Interests*. Translated by Jeremy J. Shapiro. London: Heinemann.

— 1978a (1965). “Knowledge and Human Interests: A *General Perspective*” in Habermas 1978, pp. 301-17.

— 1979. *Communication and the Evolution of Society*. Translated and with an introduction by Thomas McCarthy. London: Heinemann.

— 1979a (1976). “Historical Materialism and the Development of Normative Structures” in Habermas 1979, pp. 95-129.

— 1984 (1981). *The Theory of Communicative Action: Volume One*. Translated by Thomas McCarthy. London: Heinemann.

— 1987a (1981). *The Theory of Communicative Action: Volume Two*. Translated by Thomas McCarthy. Cambridge: Polity Press.

— 1987b (1985). *The Philosophical Discourse of Modernity*. Translated by Frederick Lawrence. Cambridge, Massachusetts: MIT Press.

— 1988 (1967). *On the Logic of the Social Sciences*. Translated by Shierry Weber Nicholsen and Jerry A. Stark. Cambridge: Polity Press.

— 1992 (1988). *Postmetaphysical Thinking*. Translated by William Mark Hohengarten. Cambridge: Polity Press.

— 1992a. “Metaphysics after Kant” in Habermas 1992, pp. 10-27.

— 1992b. “Themes in Postmetaphysical Thinking” in Habermas 1992, pp. 28-55.

— 1992c. “The Unity of Reason in the Diversity of its Voices” in Habermas 1992, pp. 115-148.

Hartmann, Klaus 1966. *Sartres Sozialphilosophie* Berlin: Walter de Gruyter.

— 1981. “Sartre’s Theory of Ensembles” in Schilpp (ed.) 1981, pp. 631-60.

— 1988. *Studies in Foundational Philosophy*. Amsterdam: Rodopi.

— 1988a. “Praxis: A Ground for Social Theory?” in Hartmann 1988, pp. 341-364.

Harvey, David 1989. *The Condition of Postmodernity*. Oxford: Basil Blackwell.

Hayman, Ronald 1986. *Writing Against: A Biography of Sartre*. London:

Weidenfeld and Nicolson.

Hegel, G. W. F. 1991 (1821). *Elements of the Philosophy of Right*. Translated by H. B. Nisbet. Cambridge: Cambridge University Press.

Heidegger, Martin 1962 (1927). *Being and Time*. Translated by John Macquarrie and Edward Robinson. Oxford: Basil Blackwell.

— 1977. *Basic Writings*. Edited by David Farrell Krell.. London: Routledge.

— 1977a (1947). "Letter on Humanism" in Heidegger 1977, pp. 213-66. Translated by Frank A. Capuzzi.

— 1977b. "On the Essence of Truth" in Heidegger 1977, pp. 111-138. Translated by John Sallis.

Hendley, Steve 1988. "Power, knowledge and praxis: A Sartrean approach to a Foucauldian position" in *Man and World*, 21, pp. 171-89.

— 1992. *Reason and Relativism*. Albany: State University of New York Press.

Hirsh, Arthur 1981. *The French New Left: An Intellectual History from Sartre to Gorz*. Boston: South End Press.

Historisches Wörterbuch der Philosophie, Band 1, 1971. Basel/Stuttgart: Schwabe and Co.

Hollinger, Robert (ed.) 1985. *Hermeneutics and Praxis*. Notre Dame, Indiana: University of Notre Dame Press.

Howells, Christina 1988. *The Necessity of Freedom*. Cambridge: Cambridge University Press.

— 1992a. "Sartre and the deconstruction of the subject" in Howells (ed.) 1992, pp. 318-52.

— (ed.) 1992. *The Cambridge Companion to Sartre*. Cambridge: Cambridge University Press.

Husserl, Edmund 1962 (1913). *Ideas. General introduction to phenomenology*. Translated by W. R. Boyce Gibson. New York: Collier Books.

— 1970 (1954). *The Crisis of European Sciences and Transcendental Phenomenology: An Introduction to Phenomenological Philosophy*. Translated by David Carr. Evanston: Northwestern University Press.

— 1977 (1950). *Cartesian Meditations: An Introduction to Phenomenology*. Translated by Dorion Cairns. The Hague: Martinus Nijhoff.

Jameson, Fredric (ed.) 1985. *Sartre after Sartre*: Yale French Studies 68. New Haven: Yale University Press.

Kant, Immanuel 1883. *Kant's Critique of Practical Reason and other works on the Theory of Ethics*. Translated by Thomas Kingsmill Abbott. London: Longmans, Green and Co.

— 1883a (1788). "Critical Examination of Practical Reason" in Kant

1883, pp. 85-262.

— 1934 (1787). *Critique of Pure Reason*. Translated by J. M. D. Meiklejohn. London: Everyman's Library.

— 1953 (1783). *Prolegomena to any Future Metaphysics that Will be Able to Present Itself as a Science*. Translated by P. Gray Lucas. Manchester: Manchester University Press.

— 1991 (1790). *The Critique of Judgement*. Translated by James Creed Meredith. Oxford: Clarendon Press.

Klockars, Kristian 1994. "Kari Palonen ja politiikka ulospelaamisena" (Kari Palonen on politics as outwitment) in Politiikka XXXVI:3, pp. 200-4.

Kruks, Sonia 1990. *Situation and Human Existence: Freedom, subjectivity and society*. London: Unwin Hyman.

König, Traugott (ed.) 1980. *Sartres Flaubert lesen*. Hamburg: Rowohlt.

— (ed.) 1988. *Sartre, ein Kongreß*. Hamburg: Rowohlt.

Lawrence, Nathaniel and O'Connor, Daniel (eds.) 1967. *Readings in Existential Phenomenology*. New Jersey: Prentice-Hall.

Le Dœuff, Michèle 1991 (1989). *Hipparchia's Choice: an essay concerning women, philosophy, etc.* Translated by Trista Selous. Oxford: Blackwell.

Lévi-Strauss, Claude 1966 (1962). *The Savage Mind*. London: Weidenfeld and Nicholson.

Les Temps Modernes 1990, nos. 531-533 (special number on Sartre). Paris: Gallimard.

Lyotard, Jean-François 1984 (1979). *The Postmodern Condition: A Report on Knowledge*. Translated by Geoff Bennington and Brian Massumi. Manchester: Manchester University Press.

— 1984a "Answering the Question: What is Postmodernism?" in Lyotard 1984, pp. 71-82.

Maler, Eduard 1986. *Sartre's Individualhermeneutik*. München: Wilhelm Fink Verlag.

Marquard, Otto 1971. "Anthropologie" in *Historisches Wörterbuch der Philosophie*, Band 1, pp. 362-74.

Marx, Karl 1978. *The 18th Brumaire of Louis Bonaparte*. Peking: Foreign Languages Press.

— 1986 (1845). "Theses on Feuerbach" in Elster (ed.) 1986, pp. 22-23.

McBride, William Leon 1981. "Sartre and Marxism" in Schilpp (ed.) 1981, pp. 605-30.

— 1991. *Sartre's Political Theory*. Bloomington: Indiana University Press.

Merleau-Ponty, Maurice 1962 (1945). *Phenomenology of Perception*. Translated by C. Smith. London: Routledge and Kegan Paul.
— 1973 (1955). *Adventures of the Dialectic*. Translated by Joseph Bien. Evanston: Northwestern University Press.
Morot-Sir Eduard 1986. "La théorie des significations et du langage dans *Critique de la Raison dialectique*" in *Etudes sartriennes* II-III, pp. 173-186.
Morris, Phyllis Sutton 1976. *Sartre's Concept of a Person*. Amherst: University of Massachusetts Press.
— 1985. "Sartre on the Transcendence of the Ego" in *Philosophy and Phenomenological Research* 1985, pp. 179-98.
Mulhall, Stephen and Swift, Adam 1992. *Liberals and Communitarians*. Oxford: Blackwell.
Olafson, Frederick A. 1967. *Principles and Persons*. Baltimore, Maryland: The John Hopkins Press.
Palonen, Kari 1992. *Politik als Vereitelung. Die Politikkonzeption in Jean-Paul Sartres "Critique de la Raison dialectique"*. Münster: Westfälisches Dampfboot.
Palonen, Kari and Subra, Leena 1990. *Jean-Paul Sartre — un philosophe du politique*. Jyväskylä: University of Jyväskylä.
Pappé, H. O. 1967. "Philosophical Anthropology" in *Encyclopaedia of Philosophy*, Volume Six, pp. 159-66.
Parsons, Talcott 1951. *The Social System*. Glencoe, Illinois: The Free Press.
Ricoeur, Paul 1981. *Hermeneutics and the Human Sciences*. Edited, translated and introduced by John B. Thompson. Cambridge: Cambridge University Press.
— 1981a. "The model of the text: meaningful action considered as a text" in Ricoeur 1981, pp. 197-221.
Rorty, Richard 1980. *Philosophy and the Mirror of Nature*. Oxford: Basil Blackwell.
Saarinen, Esa 1983. *Sartre: Pelon, inhon ja valinnan filosofia*. Tampere: Kymppilehdet Oy.
Said, Edward W. 1993. *Culture and Imperialism*. London: Vintage.
Schilpp, Paul A. (ed.) 1981. *The Philosophy of Jean-Paul Sartre*. The Library of Living Philosophers. La Salle: Open Court Publishers.
Schmidt, Lawrence K. (ed.) 1995. *The Specter of Relativism: Truth, Dialogue and Phronesis in Philosophical Hermeneutics*. Evanston, Illinois: Northwestern University Press.
— 1995a. "Introduction: Between Certainty and Relativism" in Schmidt (ed.) 1995, pp. 1-22.

Schroeder, William Ralph 1984. *Sartre and His Predecessors: The Self and the Other*. London: Routledge and Kegan Paul.

Scott, Charles E. 1981. "The Role of Ontology in Sartre and Heidegger" in Schilpp (ed.) 1981, pp. 277-99.

Silverman, Hugh J. (ed.) 1991. *Writing the Politics of Difference*. Albany: State University of New York Press.

Silverman, Hugh J. and Elliston, Frederick A. (eds.) 1980. *Jean- Paul Sartre: Contemporary Approaches to His Philosophy*. Pittsburgh: Duquesne University Press.

Simont, Juliette 1992. "Sartrean Ethics" in Howells (ed.) 1992, pp. 178-212.

Stack, George J. 1977. *Sartre's Philosophy of Social Existence*. St. Louis, Missouri: Warren H. Green.

Stevenson, Leslie 1974. *Seven Theories of Human Nature*. Oxford: Oxford University Press.

Stone, Robert V and Bowman, Elizabeth A. 1991b. "Sartre's *Morality and History*" in Aronson and van den Hoven (eds.) 1991, pp. 53-82.

Subra, Leena 1990. "Facticité et alterite" in Palonen and Subra 1990, pp. 33-59.

Taylor, Charles 1971. "Interpretation and the sciences of man" in *Review of Metaphysics*, 25:1, pp. 3-51.

— 1975. *Hegel*. Cambridge: Cambridge University Press.

— 1989. *Sources of the Self*. Cambridge: Cambridge University Press.

Theunissen, Michael 1984 (1964). *The Other: Studies in the Social Ontology of Husserl, Heidegger, Sartre and Buber*. Translated by Christopher Macann. Cambridge: MIT Press.

Védrine, Hélène 1990. "Fondement et totalisation chez Sartre" in *Les Temps Modernes* 531-533, pp. 234-51.

Vattimo, Gianni 1997. *Beyond Interpretation. The meaning of hermeneutics for philosophy*. Cambridge: Polity Press.

Wachterhauser, Brice R. 1986a. "Introduction: History and Language in Understanding" in Wachterhauser (ed.) 1986.

— 1994a. "Introduction: Is there Truth after Interpretation" in Wachterhauser (ed.) 1994.

— (ed.) 1986. *Hermeneutics and Modern Philosophy* Albany: State University of New York Press.

— (ed.) 1994. *Hermeneutics and Truth*. Evanston, Illinois: Northwestern University Press.

Wacquant, Loïc J. D. 1992. "Toward a Social Praxeology: The Structure and Logic of Bourdieu's Sociology" in Bourdieu and Wacquant 1992,

pp. 1-60.
Wallgren, Thomas 1988. "Modernitet och postmodernitet i filosofisk belysning" (Modernity and postmodernity in a philosophical perspective) in *Ajatus 45*. Suomen Filosofinen Yhdistys, pp. 3-41.
Warnock, Mary 1965. *The Philosophy of Sartre*. London: Hutchinson.
— 1969. "Introduction" in Sartre 1958, pp. viii-xviii.
Weber, Max 1947. *The Theory of Social and Economic Organization*. Translated by A. M. Henderson and Talcott Parsons. Edited by Talcott Parsons. New York: The Free Press.
Wittgenstein, Ludwig 1953. *Philosophical Investigations*. Translated by G. E. M. Anscombe. Oxford: Basil Blackwell.
von Wright, Georg Henrik 1963. *Norm and Action*. London: Routledge and Kegan Paul.
— 1971. *Explanation and Understanding*. London: Routledge and Kegan, Paul.
— 1986. *Vetenskapen och förnuftet*. (Science and Reason). Stockholm: Bonniers.
Østerberg, Dag 1988. *Metasociology*. Oslo: Norwegian University Press.
— 1993. *Jean-Paul Sartre*. Filosofi, kunst, politikk, privatliv. Oslo: Gyldendal Norsk Forlag.
Österman, Bernt 1995. *Value and Requirements. An enquiry concerning the origin of value*. Aldershot: Avebury.

Index